IN THE HANDS OF GOD

BOOKS PREVIOUSLY PUBLISHED BY THE AUTHOR

THE CHURCH OF POWER: The Invincible Movement Of The Christian Church Through An Upside Down World - Four Lectures And A Sermon On The Acts of The Apostles

PAUL'S MESSAGE OF FREEDOM: What Does It Mean To The Black Church?

A MANUAL FOR LEADERSHIP EDUCATION AND CURRICULUM GUIDE

A MANUAL FOR NURTURE FOR BAPTIST CHURCHES: The Church Training Guide For The National Baptist Convention, U.S.A., Inc.

GOING OUT FULL RETURNING HOME EMPTY: The Basic Need For Comprehensive Training For The Black Christian Educator

THE STANDING FOR CHRIST PROGRAM PART I: From Conception To Five Years Old

I HAVE ALWAYS BEEN

IN THE HANDS OF GOD

The Life Story Of

J. ROBERT BRADLEY

An Autobiography

As Told To

Amos Jones, Jr.

TOWNSEND PRESS
330 Charlotte Avenue
Nashville, Tennessee
37201

1993

Copyright © 1993

TOWNSEND PRESS

Sunday School Publishing Board

National Baptist Convention, U.S.A., Inc.
330 Charlotte Avenue
Nashville, Tennessee 37201

National Baptist Great Personalities Series I

ALL   RIGHTS   RESERVED

Manufactured In The United States Of America

International Standard Book Number: 0-910683-19-0

Library Of Congress Cataloging-in-Publication Data
Bradley, J. Robert (John Robert), 1920-
   I have always been in the hands of God: the life story of J. Robert Bradley., an autobiography/as told to Amos Jones, Jr. p. cm.
   Includes bibliographical references.
   ISBN 0-910683-19-0
   1. Bradley, J. Robert (John Robert), 1920-   . 2. Singers—United States—Biography. 3. Afro-American singers—Biography. I. Jones, Amos. II. Title. III. Title: In the hands of God.
ML420.B765A3   1993
782' .0092—dc20   93-8760
(B)   CIP
                                  MN

Cover design: *Ms. Ruth Epps*

Affectionately dedicated to.........

DR. CECELIA NABRIT ADKINS

Executive Director
Sunday School Publishing Board
National Baptist Convention, U.S.A., Inc.

. . . . . . J. Robert Bradley

Mrs. Lela Ellis Bradley,
Mother of J. Robert Bradley

"The Lawd is gonna give me a manchild, and he is gonna be a servant of the Lawd."

Contents

Editor's Preface		ix
I.	Introduction	1
II.	From Little Rock To Memphis	3
III.	A Marriage Made In Heaven	5
IV.	The Birth Of John Robert Lee Bradley In Pinch	7
V.	Childhood Experiences	11
VI.	The Church In The Early Life Of J. Robert Lee Bradley	17
VII.	Exploring Life Beyond Pinch	23
VIII.	Education In The Early Life Of John Robert Lee Bradley	27
IX.	The Thomas Shelby Factor In The Life Of J. Robert Bradley	35
X.	The Great Discovery: J. Robert Bradley At The National Baptist Convention	41
XI.	Memphis And Beyond: Discovering What's Beyond The Riverbend	45
XII.	The Goodwill Tours	47
XIII.	Transitions	49
XIV.	What's Around The Bend Of The River And Where Do The Clouds Go?	53
XV.	Charles F. Bryan And J. Robert Bradley	55
XVI.	Back To Nashville And Preparation For Service To The World	61
XVII.	The Romance With Nashville	65
XVIII.	A Venture To The North	75
XIX.	On To New York City And Life-Changing Experiences	83
XX.	Training Under The Incomparable Edyth Walker	87
XXI.	The Death Of Edyth Walker	97
XXII.	The World Becomes A Stage: Preparation For London And Beyond	101
XXIII.	The Crucible Of London: Training For Greater Things	111
XXIV.	Doors Which Open Into Europe And South America	123
XXV.	Bradley And The Bryans In London	125
XXVI.	Preparation For The Festival Hall Debut	129
XXVII.	The Recital At The Royal Festival Hall	135
XXVIII.	Return To The U. S. A. And National Baptists	147
XXIX.	To Serve Is To Sacrifice, Sacrificing Is To Serve	151
XXX.	A Return To Where It All Began	157
XXXI.	Flirting Momentarily With Disaster	165
XXXII.	Knighted: Sir J. Robert Bradley	167
XXXIII.	J. Robert Bradley And Race Relations	173
XXXIV.	Showering The Earth With Blessings	179
XXXV.	A Man Of Sorrow And Acquainted With Grief	185
XXXVI.	His Living Shall Not Be In Vain	197

Editor's Preface

This has been one of the most fantastic and exhilarating writing experiences in which I have ever been engaged. To share with J. Robert Bradley as he relived his life's experiences, experiences which wafted him to the plateau of greatness, has truly been unforgettable.

In 1988, three of us from the Sunday School Publishing Board began the arduous task of talking with Dr. J. Robert Bradley and mapping out the journalistic and editorial trajectory which ultimately would result in this publication. The Reverend Enoch Lee Jones, Ms. Brenda J. Holland, and I launched into this journalistic orbit. Reverend Jones' departure from the Sunday School Publishing Board left the difficult task to Ms. Holland and me. We spent long tedious hours probing his thoughts, jogging his memory, dislodging from inactive craters of his mind the precious nuggets of memory which are recorded in this book. Ms. Holland's role evolved into that of researcher of historic data on the life of Dr. Bradley. This project came to be the result of two disciplines, research and writing, both of which played a very important role.

The life story of J. Robert Bradley is a classic example of Divine Predestination. It is unilaterally a case of an individual being pre-ordained to be one of the world's premiere singers. It is amazing, however, when such a life is seen unfolding before your eyes. Those of us who attend the sessions of the National Baptist Convention, U.S.A., Inc., know J. Robert Bradley and know him well. Almost everyone knows him as a great singer, but not too many know of his tremendous struggle and seeming insurmountable obstacles to achieve the prominence he enjoys today. The average worker at the Sunday School Publishing Board in Nashville hardly knows the story which waits to be read in the pages that follow. Once the story is read, you will agree with the conclusion that J. Robert Bradley is truly a great man, a man who is what he is, because he has been in the hands of God.

One of the tremendously impressive things observed of Dr. Bradley in discussions held with him is his deep spirituality. One thing for sure, J. Robert Bradley knows God in his heart and has accepted Jesus Christ as his Redeemer, Lord, and Master. This has been the case since the days of his youth in Memphis. Reliving the days he spent on the banks of the Mississippi and Wolf Rivers were emotional experiences for him. Especially moving in the depths of human emotions was his recapitulation of his new birth experience at his home and old Mt. Olive Baptist Church under Pastor B. R. Bell. On occasions, the interviews were drawn to an abrupt conclusion because of our inability to navigate the swift emotional currents which rushed upon us as a result of the unfolding story of the early religious experiences of J. Robert.

A religious mystic could best describe J. Robert Bradley. His treks to the Mississippi and Wolf Rivers were to sate the hunger and thirst for a mystical union with God as he looked into the great eternal abyss of the heavens. He could dismiss himself from the ordinary and experience the extraordinary. He could excuse himself from his temporal house and experience the Tabernacle Not Made With Hands, an house from God, eternal in the heavens. It is little wonder that he was sent to sing the songs of Miss Lucy Campbell, herself a mystic, all of which were religiously mystical in nature.

Precocity or precocious is a term you will find in the body of the text as we struggle to describe the phenomenon of J. Robert Bradley. This is my way of trying to describe his seeming nonchalance concerning education in his early life. On the surface, it appears that he simply was not interested in education as the so-called "normal" child would be. On the contrary, it was discovered that J. Robert Bradley had a sagacity about himself which discerned God's will for his life in the world of music. This was discovered early in life when he found he could learn music almost at will when other youngsters were struggling with all that was in them. Early in his life, he demonstrated that he could grasp that which was didactically difficult, especially when it came to music. This great ability became more obvious later in life when he demonstrated his mastery of foreign languages, even though he had no formal training in the same. The more this was looked at the more it was concluded that J. Robert sensed the Divine Will for his life early on and sagaciously went about pursuing that will. This sagacity, having the strong sense of God's will in his life, and proceeding to make life-altering choices because of it, was the propelling power which followed him all the days of his life.

Tenacity is another term which could effectively describe the life of J. Robert Bradley. Few people with the disabilities and intellectual handicaps he had could achieve what he did. It takes a special kind of person, one who can hue the line, stay the course, continue the pursuit, and hang in there to reach the goal as he did. The slightest discouragement would deter many persons, especially those who had some seeming weakness in the human fabric. But, not J. Robert Bradley. He hung tough in Memphis during his youth; in Nashville when he only received a pittance for his services; in McMinnville when training was tough and racial bigotry began to vaunt itself; in Chicago, when he was faced with rejection at the Olivet Church; in New York City when the tragic death of his mentor, Madame Edyth Walker, almost brought his career to a halt before it began; and in London, England when he knew not where he would find a financial sponsor for his dream-fulfilling debut at Royal Festival Hall. He was tenacious, he stayed on the journey every step of the way and it paid great dividends.

The saga of J. Robert Bradley is a classic example of how God can take a willing human spirit, one who is pliable and respondent to the Will and Way of Divine Design, and lead him through the labyrinthine paths of life to the victor's circle. If this book does nothing else, it should elicit from all who read it, gargantuan quantities of faith in God to make them what He wills them to be. It should call forth from all of us a willingness to surrender to the Divine Design of Almighty God, believing He is able to lead us into all truth, keep us from falling, and make of us whatever He wants us to be. In the life of J. Robert Bradley, we encounter God as The One who is well able to take one from the deep pits of squalor and poverty and lift him to the pinnacle of prominence. This story convinces us that it is truly exciting to be "In The Hands Of God."

Many thanks go to the Executive Director of the Sunday School Publishing Board and my friend, Dr. Cecelia Nabrit Adkins, for entrusting this great assignment to my heart, head, and hands. Her vision for the Sunday School Publishing Board is one which envelops the great history of the convention and her sainted souls, of which J. Robert Bradley is one of the foremost. She provided every resource we needed to see to it that this work could be brought to closure. She granted every privilege of time and space to write the manuscript which constitutes this publication. Truly she was a great partner and executive in this project.

Many thanks and much appreciation are due to Ms. Brenda J. Holland who provided enthusiasm and pensive questions in the initial interview sessions with Mr. Bradley. She was indispensably instrumental in dislodging the great door of memory which, once it was opened, flooded us with incredibly new information about a man we thought we knew. Ms. Holland's role in this project evolved into that of research specialist. Much credit is due to her for confirming dates, times, names of important personalities and places and the like.

Thanks are due to Mr. Leonard Mitchell of Memphis, Tennessee who gave valuable insight into the early life of Mr. Bradley. The two were childhood playmates. His memory of their boyhood days was as clear as crystal. In jocular moments and in a sharing attitude, he gave all he had so the picture could be as clear as possible. To the staff of the Memphis Public Library at McLean and Peabody Streets, Memphis, Tennessee, we are indebted. They provided invaluable assistance in researching historic materials on J. Robert Bradley which are housed in the archives of the library there.

Thanks are due to Dr. Mary O. Ross, President of the Women's Auxiliary of the National Baptist Convention, USA, Inc. She provided valuable assistance pertaining to Dr. Bradley's Goodwill Trip to Seattle, Washington.

All deference is given to Mrs. Edith Bryan of McMinnville, Tennessee. She was so gracious to give an entire day of her life to talk to us about J. Robert Bradley. It was indeed refreshing and rewarding to hear her open up anew the story of how her husband trained the child prodigy we have come to know as J. Robert Bradley. Her story confirmed all we had heard from the beginning, but it also gave us entrance into new areas which had previously been unexplored. Many thanks are due to her and to her deceased and famous husband, Charles Faulkner Bryan.

Many thanks are due to the staff of the Christian Education Department of the Sunday School Publishing Board for the tremendous knowledge they have of their various jobs and deep devotion and dedication in carrying out their work. They faithfully performed their tasks although I was away from them a great deal while preparing this manuscript. Mr. Richard Yorke is due special words of thanks for meticulously reading the manuscript in its final form and culling out its editorial miscues.

Mrs. Brenda A. Thompson, lead secretary of the Christian Education Department and my administrative assistant, must be placed in the category of "the exceptional." She does her job exceptionally well. Her assistance with this manuscript ranged from working with me as we went through the various stages of its growth and development to coordinating the assembling of documents, pictures, and letters to make up the appendices for the book. For her, there must a bright crown in this life as well as the life to come.

This book could not become reality without the hard work and keen expertise of the Production Department. Mr. John Bandy, Mr. F. A. Adkins, Mrs. Evelyn Campbell, Ms. Ruth Epps of the Pre-Press Department, the men of the press room and the workers of the bindery are all to be commended for their excellent work in bringing together this project. I am delighted to work with these wonderful persons and am grateful for their contribution.

The life story of Dr. J. Robert Bradley as is told in this book will in all probability last a long time. It is hoped that this publication will spawn more perspectives on the life of this great man. Maybe scholars will want to look at his life in more of an analytical sense. As this story stands, however, it is in no way complete. There are many personalities, places and incidents which were not covered. The part which many tremendously outstanding personalities played in the life of J. Robert Bradley simply could not be covered. In some cases where we made an attempt, the coverage was superficial and inadequate. We did not give elaborate treatment to the experiences and relations Dr. Bradley established in South America; e.g., Brazil and the Far East; e.g., China, Japan, and Korea. We could not give thorough treatment of his participation in the Baptist World Alliance, appearing before that august body at least five times, more than anyone else in the history of the organization. We could only give peripheral treatment to his intense engagement with Baptists in the Scandinavian countries of Finland, Norway, and Denmark. None of this was possible because we simply did not have the time or space. Mr. Bradley's life is of such magnitude and multi-faceted that were there an attempt to write it all, one would be constrained to say as John said of the life of Jesus:

> *And there are also many other things which Jesus did, the which, if they should be written every one, I suppose that even the world itself could not contain the books that should be written. Amen.*
>
> **John 21:25**

As for what appears herein, it must be concluded that I am totally responsible for the contents. Understandably, I am proud of the work; however, although every conceivable effort was set forth to ascertain the veracity of every incident and assure the accuracy of information, dates, times, places, names, etc., it could be that there are some inaccuracies which may be found and things which are not quite as history knew them. I am responsible, however, for these omissions, oversights, misstatement of fact and/or misspelling of names, etc., if there be any. I apologize for the same.

In all that we have done, it has been for the glory of God. It is without a doubt and indubitably true that Dr. J. Robert Bradley is a great, great man. I have tried to let the record speak to reflect this greatness in all its many-faceted, refracted prisms of brilliance so that God might be glorified in the life of my friend and the friend of National Baptists, and Christians the world over. I am sure his mother, in her grave, and the others who sleep in the peaceful arms of death, Dr. A. M. Townsend, Professor Charles Faulkner Bryan, and Miss Lucy Eddie Campbell-Williams, are all proud of him. To God Be The Glory! Hallelujah! Amen!

      Amos Jones, Jr., Director
      Christian Education Department
      SUNDAY SCHOOL PUBLISHING BOARD
      NATIONAL BAPTIST CONVENTION,
        USA., INC.
      330 Charlotte Avenue
      Nashville, Tennessee 37201

I HAVE ALWAYS BEEN IN THE HANDS OF GOD
THE LIFE STORY OF J. ROBERT BRADLEY
An Autobiography as told to Amos Jones, Jr.

I.
Introduction

His eye was electric and exploded with a reverent kind of glee. His voice thundered and the room of his apartment shook, as though the earth were quaking, as he roared with great dignity and diction, "I have never had anything, but I have always been able to sing. I have always been in the hands of God!" This was Dr. J. Robert Bradley's assessment of his life as he sat in his finely arrayed apartment on the tenth floor of Capitol Park Towers in downtown Nashville, Tennessee. It was on a crisp Spring evening in April of 1988 when he began to spin the amazing tale of his life. As he took an imaginary journey down the distant road of memory, he unfolded his life's story amid giant bursts of laughter, moments of reflective instruction, and periods of somber tears and impassioned sadness.

Surrounded by memorabilia, such as a special letter from the great theologian, musician, and missionary, Albert Schweitzer, a citation from President William Tolbert of Liberia, knighting him as Sir. J. Robert, trophies, and plaques of every kind, J. Robert Bradley talked endlessly about himself. His life could best be described by his momma, Mrs. Lela Ellis Bradley. On her death-bed, her parting words to him summed up in totality the life of her famous son.

Peering at him through eyes partially blinded by cataracts, Lela Ellis Bradley looked at her son. Her ninety-five year old frame (she was born in 1889) lay leaden and motionless on the hospital bed at Baptist Hospital in Nashville. She knew her time was drawing near. Robert sat faithfully by his mother's bedside, with a devotion rivaled by neither man nor beast. His mother called out to him, with a voice enfeebled by what had now become a hard, losing battle against sickness and a long, protracted journey toward a rendezvous with The Inevitable. "Robert, come here!" "Here I am Momma!" he said, hastily lunging toward the bed, making himself available for whatever need there might be. "Is there anything you need, momma?" he said, with words forced through lips and tongue thickened by sadness and inner sobbing. "No son, I don't need nothing. I have something I want to say to you." J. Robert Bradley leaned over his mother's hospital bedside with ears listening for the heartbeat of the spirit and body which bore him into the world. His mother, with strength drawn from the deep wells of her eternal being, almost sat up in her bed and said, "Robert, I don't have much time left with you. I don't have much to leave you. But, I am going to leave you in good hands. I am going to leave you in the hands of God."

J. Robert Bradley sat helplessly looking at his mother as she lay sinking into the yawning chasm of death. There was a comfort that came over him from the words she had just spoken. The words of his momma were the only things that assuaged his troubled spirit over the thought of losing her to the cold clutching fingers of the hands of death. The nurse came to the bedside of J. Robert's mother. She looked in pity at her and looked in concern for him. She said to J. Robert, "You can go on home, Mr. Bradley. Your mother will be alright. We will take good care of her. If anything happens, we will get in touch with you." For a moment, J. Robert resisted the nurse's suggestions. He looked at his mother while she labored for her breath, making strained efforts to apprehend her breath as each one escaped from her toothless mouth. But then, surrendering to his body's pleadings of weariness, he went on to his apartment and slipped into a sleep checkered with thoughts of his mother. Careening about in his mind, as he sank down into the vast warm chamber of sleep, were the words of his mother, "Robert, I am going to leave you in the hands of God."

In the middle of the night of January 10, 1985, about three o'clock in the morning, the telephone rang out, fracturing the blissful silence which covered the night in Dr. Bradley's apartment. On the other end was J. Robert's friend, Cecelia Nabrit Adkins. Dr. Adkins' friendly, firm, loving and caring voice answered on the other end, as though cuddling him in a great cradle of compassion to absorb the shocking news, it was hers to deliver saying, "Bob, your mother has left us! Now, don't you worry about anything. She is alright now. You don't have to worry about anything, we are going now to the hospital to get her. You go on back to sleep. We will take care of everything." J. Robert Bradley said, "Yes Ma'am, Mrs. Adkins." He surrendered to God's will to take his momma from him. He succumbed to the magnetic magic of sleep and sank into its warm and dark embrace with the words of his mother echoing in the chambers of his mind, "Robert, I am going to leave you in the hands of God." After ninety-five years in the world, Lela Ellis Bradley left her son in the hands of God.

II.

From Little Rock To Memphis

The J. Robert Bradley Saga really begins in the vicinity of the city of Little Rock, Arkansas. It was in the little village of Lonoke, Arkansas, not far from Little Rock, that Lela Ellis was born in 1889. It was there that she lived and grew up into puberty and teenage years. Her family background lies in a bit of obscurity. She often talked of family ties in South Carolina, although that past lay in the dark abyss of ambiguity. Her father and mother are lost in the swift current of history's almost irretrievable stream. Only a sister emerged in the latter years of her life.

The father of J. Robert was also from Arkansas. Recollection has it that John Bradley was raised on a rice plantation owned by the Patterson Transfer Moving Company in Little Rock. He came to Memphis and worked as a stevedore on the riverfront, unloading boats. He spent a great deal of his leisure visiting the drinking places along the riverfront in Memphis. But he was unusual. He played the piano, sang with a deep, rich, resonant voice, and did the cake walk dance. Lela Ellis had worked for white folk in Lonoke, Arkansas. The white lady by whom she was employed died. Lela did not want to go back to the country. Her most viable alternative was to go to Memphis, Tennessee. She had never been taught to read or write, nor would she ever learn, but she felt a great opportunity awaited her to the east. She had little money, surely not enough to book passage to Memphis on a train. However, she was driven by determination to journey to the big city to the east which sat on the river bluff, just above the mighty Mississippi River. The foreboding distance was no match for her deep-seated determination. Her choice was to set out on foot for the one hundred twenty-six mile journey from Little Rock to Memphis.

It was a bright, sunshiny day when petite little Lela ventured out on a rather daring jaunt to the city in the east. At the turn of the century, it was not unusual for travellers to make their journey on foot, even for long distances. The route from Little Rock to Memphis was frequently travelled by horse and buggy and people riding on horseback. There was a train route which carried passengers from one city to the other. But, Lela had not enough money to cover a ticket. So, she set out on foot.

Her youth was in her favor. She was young. She was strong. She had sturdy legs to carry her body and all her earthly possessions. Catching sleep when and where she could, she made her journey. She passed through the little villages of Brinkley and Forrest City. After a long and grueling ten days to two weeks of incessant walking, seeking shelter from the searing sun by day and unseen predators by night, Lela Ellis drew near to her new world, Memphis, Tennessee.

With body tired and legs weary and wobbly, Lela climbed onto the Harrahan Bridge which led into Memphis' south side. She arrived with only fifty cents to her name, and that tied to her neck in an old Bull Durham Tobacco Sack. Approaching the smokey bluff city of Memphis, Lela's eyes laid siege to a small building with a sign which read, "Rooms For Rent." She went in to the lady who owned and operated the rooming house and asked for a room. The lady saw how tired the woman was and quickly agreed to offer a room with her only having to pay for food if she helped out. However, she talked of the number of men she had to cook for and wait on the next morning. Bone weary and blurry-eyed, Lela went to bed. But when morning came, she was up at the crack of dawn. When the lady who owned the rooming house arose, Lela had made the fire in the two pot-bellied stoves and had put on the pots of water for coffee. The owner was so shocked at what had been done that she said to her, "You don't have to pay anything for food. This is wonderful!" The next day, Lela had done the dishes, cooked the food, and so many other things that amazed the owner. The dazzled lady concluded that Lela need not worry about paying rent either. In fact, she offered Lela seventy-five cent per week, including room and board, for helping her out. So, at about twenty-five years of age, Lela began a life in the bluff city of Memphis, Tennessee, a life which would give to the world one of the greatest bass baritones ever.

At this same rooming house was a strong Black man named John Bradley. He was of a beautiful ebony hue. His body bore rippling muscles, developed from daily chores of handling large bales of cotton and enormous crates of goods and merchandise. He loaded and unloaded boats which sailed into the harbor at Memphis. John Bradley was a handsome Black man. He was a natural attraction for Black women who pleasingly flittered about on Saturdays and Sundays in their hoop-type dresses, with starch which stood them at military attention. Women all but swept John Bradley off his feet. Moreover, his stentorian voice was rich and resonant, it thundered bass notes likened to that heard when the heavens are disturbed and thunder claps its giant hands and stomps its prodigious feet and shakes the earth. John Bradley owned a voice which would be bequeathed to a son to come who would bear it to all the world.

III.

A Marriage Made In Heaven

Inevitably, John Bradley encountered this beautifully petite girl who had just wandered in afoot from Lonoke. When he first saw her, he was stunned by her beauty. She was so small, but so beautiful. She had beautiful bodily features. It was really love at first sight. John Bradley did not allow time or opportunities to pass, he told Lela abruptly, "Little ole gal, I'm gonna marry you." Her rejoinder was, "No you're not, not if I know it." One morning while preparing breakfast, John wandered into the kitchen area with humor but unshaken seriousness, "I told you Li'l' ole gal, I'm gonna marry you." Lela's response once again was, "I ain't marrying you. I don't know a thing 'bout you."

Lela's resistance was as effective as holding back raging flood waters with a broom straw. She attended dances at a local music hall with Mary, who came to be known as Aunt Mary although she was no kin. John Bradley saw Lela and brushed up to her with confidence and persistent allurement and said, "I told you Li'l' ole gal, I am gonna marry you." On one occasion, John invited Lela to a movie. Lela had never been to anything like that. She had never been to a movie. John came in from work that day, took a bath and put on his street clothes and they went to a movie.

It goes without saying that dances and movies coupled with a persistent young virile Black man were too much to be resisted by a young woman fresh in from Lonoke. In the course of time, Lela Ellis conceded to marriage to this tall, dark, and handsome man, John Bradley. Theirs was not a marriage of great pomp and circumstance. In fact, there is not a great deal known about it at all. It is known that these two hearts met in the union of holy matrimony and they became one flesh.

Lela's erstwhile resistance to her husband-to-be gave way to marriage and deep-seated love. She really loved John Bradley. Her love was demonstrated in her care for him. She bought him silk shirts for his attire. She had his suits tailor made. He sported Stacy Adams shoes. He wore kid gloves. He carried a walking cane and twirled it when he walked. Lela was proud to be the wife of John Bradley and John was proud to have Lela as his wife.

John Bradley's marriage to Lela Ellis did not bring to a climax the amorous adventures he had with women and encounters with drinking and gambling which often sent him home broke. The stories are myriad of John's episodes with gambling and women. On one occasion, Lela Ellis Bradley was sitting on the porch of the modest Bradley home. John was sitting with her. A young woman approached the porch and asked "Mrs. Bradley, may I talk with your husband for a minute, please?" Agreeing to the young lady's request, Lela saw John Bradley excuse himself to go to the side of the yard to talk with the young lady. After talking with the young damsel for a moment, John nonchalantly strolled back to the porch and whispered to Lela, "I'm going to the corner to get me a pack of cigarettes. I will be back after awhile." Lela said, "Okay!" John was not seen that weekend until Monday morning when he returned to get his clothes to go to work.

Aside from women, John Bradley had a serious penchant for drinking and gambling. On a particular weekend, he failed to come home at all. He had stopped off at one of his favorite drinking spots, which happened to be in Pinch. He got detained with gambling. He got drunk and at the same time lost all of his money. Lela went to Pinch to get him. When she got him home, she took a favorite skillet and began to hit him. As she tried to beat out her frustration over her husband's drunkenness and having no money to pay bills and buy food, she would say to him, "You just got the devil in you." Although John was six feet tall and extremely strong and muscular, whenever Lela beat him with the skillet, he would not retaliate. He would pick her up as though he were a giant picking up a toothpick. He'd say to her as she'd wallop him with the skillet, "Baby, oh baby, don't do this." Kicking and screaming while John virtually with one hand held her suspended in mid-air, Lela continued to wallop her husband about the head and shoulders with her skillet screaming as she did, "We don't have no food. We overdrawn on the rosey," **awhooomph!**

This was John Bradley and Lela Ellis Bradley.

IV.

The Birth Of John Robert Lee Bradley In Pinch

On September 10, 1920, John Robert Lee Bradley was born to John and Lela Bradley in the poverty-ridden section of Memphis called "Pinch." Little would it be known that such a noteworthy personality was being brought into the world in a place known for its squalor and putridity.

John Bradley and Lela Ellis met at the rooming house just off the Harrahan Bridge spanning the Mississippi River. They met and married in a section of Memphis called "Sodom." Tradition had it that everything "diseased" and "decrepid" went on in "Sodom." When John and Lela married, they moved from that part of town to "Pinch." At least this seemed to be a step up from the seething cauldron of wretchedness they had known in "Sodom."

Pinch really was Memphis in its earliest days. Its geographical boundaries were marked by the Mississippi River. Really, Pinch began near Auction and Main streets where there was a large body of water named Gayoso Bayou. This was an inlet of still water which collected in a gulch, away from the swift current of the larger Mississippi River and the smaller Wolf River. Memory has it that Gayoso Bayou was filled with catfish, both living and dead, as well as debris of all sort. The geographical boundaries of Pinch took in Auction Street, North Main Street, Front, Jackson, and as far east as Second Street. At one point in time, the Gayoso Bayou came as far inland as to where St. Joseph's Hospital is today. As time went on, the Pinch District grew, going as far south as Poplar, to Fourth Street. It came to the point where everything to the north in Memphis was referred to as "Pinch."

Pinch became populated by immigrants who came down the Mississippi River and stopped at Memphis. They drifted into Gayoso Bayou on wooden flatboats. Once docked, they dismantled their wooden flatboats and used the wood to construct shanty houses. Ultimately, the shanty house community that emerged came to be known as "Pinch." In the late 1810's, there were five buildings in Memphis, two of these were bars. One was The Tavern and the other was the historic Bell Tavern. It was at the Bell Tavern where many drinking binges happened. One of these involved the legendary icon of American folklore and one-time Tennessee Congressman, Davy Crockett. In the 1830's, after losing a re-election bid to Congress, Davy Crockett set out for The Alamo in Texas. The route he took inevitably led through Memphis. He stopped off at the historic Bell Tavern. It was in Pinch, at the historic Bell Tavern, where Crockett uttered his famous words that became standard in political circles, "My constituents can go to hell. I am going to Texas."

The meaning of the name "Pinch" bore the depraved condition of the people who lived there. They appeared to have been "pinched" by poverty, hunger, and need. Their bodies bore the sign of impoverished conditions; their stomachs were drawn, hence, "Pinchgut." Poverty and pitiful living conditions brought with it frustration. Living on top of one another created tension. In 1861, the newspapers carried this little tidbit:

> *June 28, 1861*
> *Fighting---There was a "shindig" in Pinch yesterday, two*
> *or three pistols were fired but nobody hurt. Several arrests*
> *were made.*

Interestingly enough, the first ethnic group to inhabit Pinch were African slaves. African slaves were brought there, long before the Civil War. They were auctioned in Pinch. To this day, there is an auction block located at Auction Street and Main Street, marking the spot where African slaves were auctioned. An English social reformer, Frances Wright, had an interest in educating the African slaves. She established a plantation called Nashoba in order to accomplish this. The location of the plantation was in the vicinity where Germantown is today. However, her office was located in the Pinch District. These slaves were eventually freed and left the country. They settled in the free Black nation of Haiti.

The first permanent settlers in Pinch were Irish, who came to America to escape the "Potato Famine" in their homeland. The second settlers were Italian. Then, at about the turn of the twentieth century, Jews came from Eastern Europe to settle in this area. Pinch became a veritable "melting pot." Eventually, it took on a peculiar Jewishness for Yiddish, the mother tongue for Jews, was freely heard in the streets. Even the Italians who came as settlers in Pinch acquired the ability to speak Yiddish as fluently as Jews themselves.

Inasmuch as necessity is the mother of invention, the residents of the Pinch District met necessity with the institution of businesses and industries to provide needs. There were shoe shops where cobblers made and remade shoes, and shops of all sorts, some dealing in merchandise brought in on flatboats and river traffic. There was a terrific spirit of determination in Pinch. Even the devastating flood of 1912 could not stave off the determination that marked the people who lived in the area of Memphis called Pinch.

It was here, in The Pinch District, where the newly wed couple of John and Lela Bradley sought refuge from the depravity of "Sodom" in South Memphis. The young couple found a little place in an alley off of Fourth and Poplar where they could call home. The little home place was located immediately behind the Swiss Dry Cleaners and the Bluff City Laundry.

The humble abode was located a short distance from the neighborhood saloon. It was owned by a white man, John Daugherty. It was commonly known that he had a Black mistress named Aunt Sally. However, nothing was ever made of this because it was simply the way of life. It was like a little family in the row of houses which were stacked atop each other in the alley. Aunt Lizzie and Uncle Mike lived just down the alley a piece. Hazel Hearns and her mother, Aunt Mag, lived next door. Everyone knew each other. They shared moments of intimacies together. Whenever there was a need for food or some household item, one shared with the other. It was like the one water hydrant in the back of the row of houses; it was the only one in the neighborhood, but it served everyone. Whatever one had, it was at the disposal of all. Oftentimes while gathering water at the one hydrant, they often exchanged lively gibberish and idle chatter. The goings on of the day could be clearly and graphically heard all over the neighborhood.

Upon moving to their new home, John Bradley continued to take care of his wife by using that wonderfully strong body of his. He drove a six mule freight wagon for Patterson Transfer Company, his old employee back in Little Rock. He was a proud, strong man. With alacrity, he lifted large bales of cotton upon his back and loaded them from the mule-drawn wagon to the boats that were docked at the river's edge. He took pride in his strength, that he could hurl cotton bales as though they were chicken feathers. It was this rugged work, loading heavy cotton bales upon his back, that ultimately ruined his spinal cord, straining his back so that he could work no longer.

Lela busied herself working also. She was an excellent cook. In fact, she was known for her pies, cakes, and cookies. She cooked for white people to bring in some money to assist with the home. Because she was such a good cook, she acquired the nickname "Cookie." It was this name which identified her among all those who knew her.

Shortly after relocating in Pinch, Lela conceived and became pregnant with the first of her two children. She was very proud of her pregnancy. She walked about her yard talking aloud, saying, "The Lawd's gonna give me a manchild. Oh yes, I'm gonna have a manchild. The Lawd is gonna give me a manchild, and he is gonna be a servant of the Lawd." Everyone thought she was crazy talking like that. They said, "Miss Cookie is goin' crazy!"

Miss Cookie was not crazy, indeed. Somehow she had firm communication connections with The Eternal Spirit, God. It was God who assured her that she would have a manchild who would be a servant of the Lord. She did! On September 10, 1920 a midwife by the name of Grandma Burns, assisted by Doctor Craig, helped Miss Cookie give birth to a fat bouncing boy. Both she and her husband, John, gave the new baby the name, **JOHN ROBERT LEE BRADLEY**. He ultimately became a child prodigy and musical virtuoso of the first magnitude.

V.

Childhood Experiences

Pinch became the world of young John Robert Lee Bradley. As he grew up, he learned what it meant to live in what he came to know as "Pinchgut." Living was hard but he enjoyed every minute of it. It was here that he found mountaintop joys and valley deep sorrows. He found an abundance of both. It was here where his life was shaped and directed in a very special and unusual way.

His father gave J. Robert his voice. John Bradley had a deep booming, resonating voice. There is no evidence that John sang, but he gave his son that ability through genetic transmission. He gave J. Robert his compassion and love for people. John Bradley shared with people anything he had. He loved people and he loved his family.

One of the deep valleys of sorrow J. Robert had to traverse early in his life was the death of his father. J. Robert remembered the last years and days of his father's life. His father loved his son. In the latter days of his life, John Bradley's physical stamina gave way. His back had been ruined by the enormous weight of cotton bales and barrels of merchandise he carried daily to earn a meager wage of pennies a week. At times, John Bradley could not walk. Sometimes he called on his young son to walk on his back, to try to gain some measure of comfort and relief from the piercing pain.

The whole maze of problems which plagued John Bradley, his problem with women, drinking, and gambling compounded by increasing physical problems due to his work, caused even more serious problems. He separated from his wife, Lela, leaving his young son with his mother. He moved across the alley from where J. Robert was born. He visited his wife from time to time. In doing so, the two conceived again and Lela bore to John a second son, Van. However, something disturbed John Bradley badly. He was unable to work. He found himself separated from the little beautiful girl who swept him away and melted his heart. He could not take care of the woman he loved and the two sons she had given him. He tried to assuage a surging feeling of colossal failure by going to the house each Saturday giving a small piece of money, maybe two or three dollars. When he could do that, he would say to Lela, "Babe, take care of that boy, take care of that boy," referring to J. Robert. The frustration was too much. The mental pressure of not being able to work and take care of his wife and two sons caused something within John Bradley's mind to go wrong. Deterioration of his mind set in. He completely lost control. He was placed in an insane asylum. John Bradley was never able to make a comeback. His wife never carried his young sons to see him. She did not want young J. Robert or Van to see their father in that condition.

Before J. Robert had reached his seventh or eighth year in the world, he was told that his father had died. He died in an insane asylum. There was no funeral; thus, young J. Robert never said "goodbye" to his dad. But he could never forget him---he had given him a gift that would carry him to the top of the world, his voice.

Without a husband, Lela Bradley had to work all the time in white folks' kitchens to feed her two little sons. But it was in this condition that she had the opportunity to teach her sons the lesson of The Providence of God. Some time after her husband had died, she encountered a time when she had nothing in the house to feed her sons. No food! No money to buy food! There was nothing! As little J. Robert and Van sat before a fireplace in one of the two rooms in the small house in which they lived in the alley off Poplar Street, there was no coal for the fire, but the fireplace was ablaze. A house had been torn down in the neighborhood and little Robert had brought into the house some of the tarpaper and stacked it in the corner of the room. It was with the tarpaper that the fire burned and provided heat. They sat close to the fire to keep warm. Their backs were shivering with cold but their faces and chests were singed with the heat of the blaze. Miss Lela walked about with a bit of nervousness. As she walked about the room, she looked as though she were peering through the ceiling into heaven. As little J. Robert and Van fidgeted and squirmed in their chair before the fire, they both cried to their mother, "Momma, We're hongry!" They went on like this for some time. Hunger pangs tore through their little bodies. The pain was excruciating, indescribable. The metabolic furnaces had burned up all traces of food they had thrown down into their bellies earlier in the day. Their complaints and outcries became more intense and urgent, "Momma, we are hongry!!!"

Lela tried to calm them by entertaining them with the little stories which she was skilled at telling. She often entertained her sons with stories of Brother Fox and Sister Goose. This kind of entertainment kept them fascinated; and, it worked most of the time. But, this time the hunger pain had ripped through their little bellies so that story-telling was not enough.

Robert continued insistently for himself and his little brother, Van, "Momma, we are hongry, Van and me!!!" His mother said, "Well, boys, The Lord is gonna send some bread. So you all go on to bed. He's gonna send some bread...." Her voice trailed off in silent strength that sounded of a faith in a God

Who Would Provide. Robert shouted out incredibly, "Ah Momma, He ain't studn' us!!!! He don't care nothin' 'bout us!!!!" His mother whirled around with a stunned, stern look, her face rendered rigid from the thoughts that her son would rail against God. With her eyes aflame she said, "You see this fist?" Cowing into a dark corner as a little puppy, Robert said, "Yas'sam!" "If you ever talk about Him again, I'll stick this fist all the way down your throat. You hear me? Now, get yourselves in the bed and go on to sleep." Whimpering and hungry, Robert and his little brother pulled themselves into a cold and unfriendly bed, with hunger pains still tearing through their stomachs.

About six o'clock the next morning, someone knocked on the door. It was Miss Fontella who lived downstairs underneath Miss Lela and her boys. When she opened the door, Miss Fontella was standing there. She said, "Cookie (everyone called Lela Bradley Cookie because she cooked in the white folk's kitchen), I cooked a pot of turnip greens, with plenty of ham bones and skins in them. Can you use them?" Miss Lela said, with a deep sense of humility, and a face etched with pleadings, "Yes, Ma'am." Then she said, "I cooked a great big skillet of cornbread with cracklin in it. Can you use that?" "I sho' can use them," was Miss Lela's reply. Miss Fontella continued, "I baked a pan of sweet potatoes...." All the while Miss Fontella was talking, Robert and Van had their ears perked and antennae raised so they could hear everything she said. When Miss Fontella said she had the pan of sweet potatoes, their feet hit the cold forbidden floor at the same time, "Ploppp!." The cold floor was no match for the anticipation that was fueled by hunger.

Miss Lela was busying herself trying to thank Miss Fontella, but Robert and his brother Van were busy pulling at the pots she had deposited with their momma. She hastily cautioned them, however, threatening them with her famed backhand lick. She said, "Wait a minute, wait a minute, ya'll go on in the kitchen and sit down at the table like decent people do. We got to thank God for this food." Sulking and pouting, J. Robert and Van waddled on to the table. Their momma turned around and began to pray. She said, "Now Lord, I want to thank you. You know I didn't have no bread to give these chillun'. But, You told me in Your Word that You would feed me when I was hungry. And here it is. I really want to thank you. These chillun' can go to school with a full stomach. Couldn't nobody do nothing like this but You. I want to thank You, Sir." When she finished praying, she was crying. She reached down and pulled up her apron and wiped her face, reverently and proudly wiping away her tears of joy. She slowly and deliberately moved toward the stove to put on the food. When she heated it, she filled the boys' plates. There was never such laughing and talking between Miss Cookie and her two boys. The Lord had sent them some bread.

This experience was to live with J. Robert for the remainder of his life. His faith in God was to grow to enormous proportions because of how his mother believed God would provide bread for them. He grew up in life believing his life and that of his momma and brother were in the hands of God, who would provide for them. J. Robert made Pinch his world. His bow legs and fat bare feet carried him up and down the cobblestone alleys in his neighborhood. He ran all over Pinch, with all of its dangers. He became a wanderer, exploring his new world. He found himself wandering down to the Wolf River and becoming fascinated with the ebb and flow of the water. He even found himself wandering down to the banks of the mighty Mississippi River. As a little fellow, he became enamored with water, the river, where it came from and where it was going. He found a precious spot on the banks of the Mississippi River where he visited every day. He got up each morning as a man going to his place of employment to visit his favorite spot on the river bank. Actually, this rendezvous spot on the banks of the Mississippi River became the springboard for the life career of J. Robert Bradley. When he reached his favorite spot, he carefully prepared a place on which he could lie flat on his back. He spent hour after hour peering into the heavens, fascinated by its vastness. The fluffy white clouds caught a special interest in his mind. He wished he could be atop them. They could become his chariot wafting him to the far flung parts of a vast world he knew nothing about. His little mind played games of wander and wonder, wondering where the clouds had come from and where they were going and wanting to accompany them in their flight.

J. Robert made a startling discovery while lying on the banks of the Mississippi River, disengaged from the cares of this world. He discovered he could sing. There was something about his bass-like voice which his father had given him that was completely fascinating. He began to experience its rhythmic reverberation. There was something akin to the rhythm of eternity and divine rapture, as he had known it before he was born. This exhilaration was so marvelously, mysteriously, and mystically new but so intimately familiar. There was something about lying on his back on the banks of the river, feeling the surge of its rhythm. There was a strong feeling that he was in tune with the universe, in touch with The Power of The Universe, in harmony and at one with God. Nothing short of his conversion experience would be akin to this feeling. He began to acquaint himself with the rich tremulous sound which came from deep within. Before he knew it, he realized he could sing! He could sing like the singing he had begun to hear in the new world unfolding about him in Pinch, but his singing was as though he had been doing it for aeons and aeons.

Church music, classical music had found a place in his soul and with the virtuosity of the instrument his father had given him through genetic transmission---he suddenly discovered himself singing. He was ecstatic, completely overwhelmed at this discovery. On the banks of the Mississippi River, there was none to attend his concert. He was alone, it seemed. But, ah, the clouds which had captured his little mind, wondering where they had come from and where they were going, became his audience. They could listen to his song. Moreover, they could carry the music and his message wherever they would go. He looked at the river; the waves could join the clouds as his congregation. The waves could clap their hands and provide the staccato rhythm for his songs. There were the reeds jutting up from the river's edge, bobbing and weaving to the rhythm of J. Robert's newly discovered *djin*. So, on the banks of the Mississippi River, J. Robert discovered that he could entertain himself and even have church with the clouds and waves of the river and solicit shouts from the bobbing, weaving reeds whose heads popped up above the river's edge to say,"Amen." He learned the joy of worship---to be at one with God.

    J. Robert had a similar fascination with the river. As he lay on his back, he looked at the distant bend of the river. He noticed how the boats rounded the bend and were never seen again. He wondered where they went. What was around that river bend? This held captive his little mind. He was puzzled and gripped with passionate inquiry, wanting someday to discover what was beyond the bend of that Old Man River. On his back, looking at the elements, captive to the spirit of wonderment, J. Robert discovered another characteristic about his personality---a venturesome spirit. He soon was to discover that the world would become his home.

    He was not very many years in the world before he discovered quite early how to busy himself for long periods of time. He had no need for anyone to keep him company. He knew how to entertain himself with activity uncharacteristic of a youngster his age. He had an unusual manner of entertaining himself by fishing for crawfish. He had no money to buy bait to catch the crawfish. He devised his own technique. He sat on the river bank and simply placed his hand into the water. Whenever a crawfish clamped onto one of his fingers, he quickly jerked him out of the water onto the bank. He became very skilled at this. He got to the place where he could catch crawfish time and again.

    One day he skipped and hopped down from his alley home just off Fourth and Poplar down to the river. He had not a care in the world. He swung his pail gleefully as he went. His little mind was chocked full of dazzling thoughts of catching lots and lots of crawfish. When he got to his favorite spot, he began his ritual. He stuck his hand into the water. A crawfish grabbed hold. He jerked it out and slung it onto the bank. He did this again. And again. And again. By days end, he had a bucket full of crawfish. Just as gleefully as he had gone down to the Wolf River, he started back home the same. He thought over and over of how happy his mother would be that he had caught so many crawfish. They could have some good eating that night because when he left, his mother did not have any food and had no money to buy any for dinner. His mother would be proud of him.

Pinch made an indelible impression on J. Robert's early years. But there was none who made a more indelible impression than his mother, Lela. Although Lela had no formal education, she could neither read nor write, she was a classic actor. She had a style about herself. She had a dignity, an air, a mannerism which demanded attention. Early on in his little life, J. Robert found himself emulating his mother's classic actions, airs, dignified behavior and mannerisms.

Lela was a poised young woman. When she posed for a photo on one occasion, she sat with great dignity and poise. She had a way of holding her hands as she posed for a photograph. She had a way of positioning her legs that reflected culture and class. Normally, she had a handkerchief as a part of her dress. This added dignity and flavor to her dress and public appearance. Lela was a great conversationalist. She apparently came from a background of people who loved to talk. She really could talk.

It was from his mother that J. Robert acquired many of his characteristics, characteristics which would follow him into adulthood and throughout his life. But it was Pearl, however, who influenced his manner of speech more than anyone in the days of his youth. Pearl lived behind the home place of J. Robert, his brother and his mother. She was a high yellow girl and attended St. Anthony School. He often heard her talk while walking or skipping through the neighborhood or playing around about the house. Pearl had diction in her speech. She had voice intonation that was to be emulated. J. Robert Bradley's manner of speech came from Pearl. He often thought to himself, "I really want to speak like Pearl." He did not spend much time with Pearl, if any at all. He really did not know her that well. She only lived behind the home place in the alley just off Fourth and Poplar in Pinch. One thing for sure, she had a profound impact on his life and he wanted to speak like her.

So, Pinch placed its indelible impression on the life of J. Robert Bradley. The swift currents of time, like that of the Mississippi River, all but swept away every vestige of Pinch. Only in recent years has it established a comeback. But the son of Pinch, J. Robert Bradley, flourished as a beautiful lily blooming out of a stagnant pond filled with decaying roots and rotting debris.

VI.

The Church In The Early Life Of J. Robert Lee Bradley

John Robert Lee Bradley's life was influenced by the church from the very beginning. He was blessed with a God-fearing mother who really loved the Lord. When the family moved to Pinch, Lela Bradley became a member of the Jackson Avenue Baptist Church located at Auction Street and Jackson Avenue, just up the street from the J. C. Oates and Sons Funeral Home. The Reverend Bush R. Bell was pastor. From the time her two sons were born, Lela took them to church. Thus, from early in his life, J. Robert heard the strains of church music in the church house, the prayers of the saints, and the preaching of the Word of God. Religion in all its power and fervor swept over his soul and seeped into every fibre of his little being and literally took control.

B. R. Bell was not an educated man, but he could tell the Bible story. He could talk about hell so that J. Robert could not sleep at night. Because of B. R. Bell, young J. Robert believed the devil from hell was in perpetual pursuit of him every night. He would run from him every night when his mother took him to church for the revival meeting. Reverend Bell preached from the pulpit as though he were talking to him, "The Lord told me to tell you, that you is goin' to hell."

Reverend B. R. Bell was a hell-fire and brimstone preacher. He could make you feel the blistering heat of hell's inferno. At one worship service, J. Robert heard Pastor Bell say, "De Lawd is gonna change 'dis ting." This was the way he preached. He said, "Dem Niggas had better wake up." Bell preached like this because Black people lived such despicable lives. During the week they drank hard, fought, and cut one another with knives. But on Sunday, they would go to church. The women arrayed themselves in dresses starched so their ruffles stood out by themselves. When they went to church, after spending a week in suspect living, living lower than the level of righteousness, B. R. Bell told them about hell. He talked about hell so that they could not sleep at night.

Early in J. Robert's life, he demonstrated that he had religion. When his mother took him to church at Jackson Avenue Baptist Church and Mt. Olive Baptist Church, he disturbed the preacher and choir by thumping and patting his big thick feet. They did not bother him, however. They simply said, "Leave him alone. He's going to be alright."

J. Robert had an unusual way of demonstrating his religion---he shouted. He was a shouting child. At Mt. Olive Baptist Church, as a little fellow, he shouted so that Mr. Strawter, an usher of longtime service, had to hold him. Robert shouted so hard that it became a common occurrence that when he began to shout, Usher Strawter rushed to hold him. He would take little Robert up in his big strong arms while he kicked and shouted, praising The Lord. Robert's mother prepared him for his conversion experience. She took him and Van, his brother, to Sunday school and church all the time. When Pastor B. R. Bell left Jackson Avenue Baptist Church and organized Mt. Olive, she was cook for the workers who were constructing the new church building. Mt. Olive Church was to be located now at Auction and Winchester Streets. She worked hard at all she did; preparing food for the workers was no exception. In fact, there were times she worked so hard that she was unable to take Robert and Van to church. She simply was too tired. In her place, however, she solicited the help of Aunt Mollie Bell. Aunt Mollie Bell was an old lady. She had one leg which was shorter than the other. Anyone could tell when she was approaching, she would go up and down from the short leg to the longer leg. When Miss Cookie could not take Robert and Van to Sunday school and church, Aunt Mollie Bell did.

Miss Lela said to Robert one day, "Robert, you are a big boy now. It is time for you to think about your soul." Robert was without words at first. He then, after thinking about what his mother had said to him, for a period of what seemed to be hours and hours, said, "Yas'sum!" She said, "Now, what I mean about your soul, you want to know Jesus Christ as your personal Savior in the pardon of your sins." He obediently said, "Yas'sum," as he leaned harder in his mother's direction, clutching to her every word. "Now, we are going into our revival. I am coming as much as I can, but when I sit on that mangle all day long, from six to five, I'm tired when night comes. But, I am going out there with ya'll one or two nights." This talk with his momma sparked a fire in his little soul that would not be quenched except by the water from the deep well of Eternal Life given only by Jesus the Blessed Savior. Mt. Olive was a tremendous church, known for its great singing as well as the hell-fire preaching of Pastor Bush R. Bell. Singing of the sort heard at Mt. Olive could not be heard this side of heaven. Janie Matthews Bell was the president of the choir and the daughter of Pastor Bell. Grace Taylor was another maker of music at Mt. Olive. She played the piano for the choir. She was the sister of the Reverend L. O. Taylor of Memphis. Reverend Taylor was pastor of the Olivet Baptist Church and a photographer of note. Robert sang in the choir with the playing of Grace

Taylor. Along with him were his other little playmates, Leonard Mitchell, and Tommie Guy. They all sang in the choir, even prior to being converted and baptized.

With the pleadings of his mother and the passionate hell-fire preaching of Pastor B. R. Bell, the fallow ground of Robert's little soul was broken up. "De debil is gonna gitcha," he would say in his unlettered manner of proclaiming The Word. "An' Hell is hot!" he warned. "Yo soul will burn fo eturnity's eturnity.... But there is a Savior! Jesus is His Name. He can save yo soul if you believe in Him." B. R. Bell would make Hell so hot that J. Robert could not sleep at night. This burning message was probably the compelling force the day J. Robert really felt conversion's fire. He was at home in his momma's upstairs apartment, which was one of the five which were located in "The Ark" where they lived on Alabama Street in Pinch. This was just a short distance from their Poplar Street home place where he had been born. While washing dishes that day, Robert was humming to himself one of the songs of the church. Something began to happen to him. There was a warm, satisfying feeling within, akin to that he had felt on the banks of the Mississippi River. It was like a fire within that burned but did not consume. He found himself crying, and not knowing why. Before he knew it, he had gotten happy. He began to shout, "Hallelujah, thank you Jesus!" He got so happy that unbeknownst to him, he picked up the pan of dishes and threw them out the second floor window, dish water, dishes and all, into the hot summer air. Where they landed below and on whose head they landed, he did not know. All he knew, he had gotten religion. It was a happy day for him.

On the occasion when the big revival was held in the summertime of his ninth year, J. Robert professed hope in Jesus Christ as his Savior. The saints of Old Mt. Olive had prayed that The Lord would send down a revival. They prayed down the revival. They prayed that God would send The Holy Spirit and save the souls of the little children. The choir sang every night until the human soul could look over into the realm of heaven. The evangelist for the week was Reverend B. R. Bell himself. As always, he made Hell hot and heaven happy. He preached so that on Thursday night of the revival, J. Robert, at nine years of age, got happy and shouted all over the church. The hallelujah fire was burning in his soul. The light of heaven brightened the whole place in the church house. Robert began to shout, his soul was happy. He had gotten religion. The Lord came into his heart and brought peace to his soul. He suddenly became aware of a splendor and a wonderful peace in his soul that he had not known before. He was suddenly aware that he had been saved from sin. There was a satisfaction in his little soul that one day when he died, he would go to heaven to be with The Lord. As always, Bro. Strawter, the sentinel usher at Mt. Olive, was there to take up Little Robert in his big strong arms while he was yet shouting and kicking. Robert's shout was one of rejoicing, "Thank you!" "Thank you!" "Thank you!" was his exultant cry. He thanked God with tears which he flung up to heaven, tears of joy and happiness. When all his energy was spent with body limp, and nothing but a stream of tears left, Bro. Strawter took J. Robert, as he always did, to the outside of the church house and wiped the tears from his little eyes and assured him that everything was going to be alright. The security he got from that conversion experience, was that which was to sustain Robert all the days of his life. The fire he felt that night in the revival at Mt. Olive Baptist Church in Pinch he would feel for the rest of his life.

It was at church, Jackson Avenue Baptist Church and Mt. Olive Baptist Church, that J. Robert met his life-long friend, Leonard Mitchell. Leonard met J. Robert when he was about four years old and Robert was about seven. Three years separated them. J. Robert's father had separated from his mother. Leonard and J. Robert developed a relationship that was to last throughout a life-time. They were playmates in every sense of the word. They went to church together. They were baptized "in the same Gayoso Bayou." They went to school together. They played together, fought together, had good times and bad times together. Some of the most memorable experiences in J. Robert's youth happened when he was with his friend Leonard.

J. Robert learned that Leonard could sing---probably the reason the two gravitated to one another. They began to sing together. J. Robert liked to imitate playing the piano while Leonard would do the bass. The two of them would sit on the steps of Mt. Olive Church, which Reverend B. R. Bell had built at the corner of Marshmallow and Chestnut Streets, and make music. The summer sun would be blistering hot, but they would make music like crazy and have church.

Oftentimes their music-making gave way to antics and fun which sometimes resulted in monetary contributions from their beneficiaries. One day while making music on the church steps at the Mt. Olive Church, a lady came along dressed in black with a black veil covering her face. She paused to listen to the music J. Robert and Leonard were making on the church steps. As she listened intently, she began to cry and say, "Sing boys!" Her sobbing became more desperate and she began to say, "Sing boys, my poor husband. . . ." Her voice tailed off and was drowned out because J. Robert and Leonard more forcefully got into their act. J. Robert learned early that he was a real showman and at times he executed that characteristic to the utmost. When the woman sobbed, "My poor husband. . . ," J. Robert rushed in with the rest, "...he's gone!" This was done to the rhythm of the make-believe instruments they were playing and the music they were making with their voices. The song they were singing, of course, was made up. Apparently, it carried a great deal of effective weight because the woman sobbed and cried as though she were in a real church service. The lady was so moved at the boys' performance that she reached into her pocketbook and gave them a quarter apiece. They kept on singing as though they had rehearsed for that very moment. When they saw she had plumped down a quarter apiece for their music, they really got busy. As they made their music, J. Robert and Leonard responded to the woman's quarter with another installment, all in rhythm and perfect tune and religious fervor, "...gonna meet him in the morning!" they said. The woman broke down with greater sobs, heaving and weeping deeply as though she were in a church sanctuary filled with sympathetic mourners. She was so moved that she shelled out another fifty cent apiece to the two boys. The boys kept singing and the woman kept sobbing and giving money until she gave out of money. When she gave out of money, she looked into her pocketbook and saw that she had some peppermint candy and said "Boys, ya'll take this." When they saw the poor woman was broke, they quit singing and the woman went away.

Church life, though sometimes humorous but most of the time serious, was an inextricable component of the early formation of the life of John Robert Lee Bradley. His introduction to the church by his mother led him to accept Christ in the pardon of his sins. He was baptized as a boy at First Baptist Church-Chelsea in the year 1929. He was baptized at this church because Pastor B. R. Bell and the congregation at Mt. Olive were in the process of moving. The impact of the church was as a signature placed upon the life of J. Robert, a signature which would last throughout his life. In fact, he ultimately found himself giving his entire life to the church.

VII.

Exploring Life Beyond Pinch

The world of the early life of young John Robert Lee Bradley was Pinch. But those episodes on the bank of the Mississippi River brought to this young man haunting desires to see the rest of the world. In a few, brief years, he had learned every nook and cranny of Pinch. He knew Pinch so well that blindfolded he could take the jaunt from his home at Fourth and Poplar down to the Mississippi River and his rendezvous spot. The little path he had cut was amid a myriad sea of broken glass, bottles, potsherds, rusty tin and dangerous litter of all sort; however, he could run through all the maze of inanimate predators and not get one cut on his bare feet. He had explored every inch of Pinch; so, Pinch held no more challenge to this potential world traveller.

Oddly enough, Pinch did not have the unusually negative effect on John Robert Lee Bradley as such a neighborhood often has on young Black boys. Pinch had always been a tough place to live and raise children. It was a place where hard times manifested themselves in a unique way. This was always true. It became truer as more ethnic groups made this section of town their home. The griddle of life which can be burned unbearingly by the heat of poverty always causes those caught in the throes of misfortune to turn upon each other out of their frustration. Pinch or Pinchgut, as it was known, was a place where poverty took its toll in many ways. One of the ways was that of fighting among the residents. To live in Pinch meant that the police were quick to arrest you because of your penchant to fight. Pinch was the place where prostitution became a way of life for many women. It was a place where gambling and policy, "numbers," were as natural as taking a breath of air. Adults used children to run the policy for them; i.e., they used children to communicate the number that had fallen that day.

While J. Robert was not fatally infected by such a lifestyle, he did not escape its influence. From the time of his birth, living oppressively close to his neighbors, he could hardly help hearing profanity ooze from the puffed and pained lips of those trapped in the gripping jaws of poverty. He saw the liquor traffic and those whose puffed, reddened faces reflected the result of long hours of drinking this poisonous potion. Numbers runners and policy players were commonplace in Pinch. Police and prostitutes, gambling and scrambling from fights and the whole gamut of stench peculiar to Pinch was ever so familiar to J. Robert Bradley. He did not escape all the effects of such a life; but whatever effects there were, they did not follow him wholesale from Pinch.

Such a story of survival and success must be attributed to his father and mother, but especially his mother who began early taking him to church and exposing him to God, His Word, and the power of the Holy Spirit. But it also must be attributed to God's powerful hand to lead this young man through the labyrinthine entrapments of Pinch to rise above its evil clutches. It was no small development in the life of J. Robert when he rose up each day, as a man rises up to go to a job, to go to the banks of the Mississippi River to play all alone. There were no public parks to entertain young children and occupy their time. There were few movies and television had not made its advent. Those were days when children often invented games to occupy their time. So, the banks of the Mississippi River became his park. He could always manage to get a nickel from somewhere. With that nickel, he stopped at Snider's Bakery on the way to the river and bought six large sweet rolls. He'd get a jug of water and race down to the riverbank. At the Mississippi River, J. Robert settled back into the comforting grass and looked into the heavens. He watched the fluffy clouds pass o'erhead, wondering where they went, what was up above them, and what was beyond the bend of the river. He went on to hold a worship service with the waves of the river. When he got a little hungry, he'd reach for a great big sweet roll and eat it. Then, after taking a long, deep drink of water from his jug---he'd let out a big burp! He'd repeat this until he'd eaten all the sweet rolls and drank all the water and was full as a tick. He would then relax, recline, and go to sleep.

The one obvious scar which accompanied him as he emerged from Pinch was the absence of an eye. During the course of his sojourn, he lost his right eye. One day he ventured into nearby Dago Bottom in Pinch. While playing with a young boy there, the young playmate threw coal cinders in J. Robert's face. The cinders got into his right eye so that it became infected. When he went home, he told his mother about his mishap. She did what she could to treat the eye, but the infection grew more serious. Miss Cookie did not have money to take her son to the doctor or a medical clinic. In time, the eye was so infected that it lost its power of vision, endangered his other eye, and had to be removed. Thus, this became the only physical blemish which tarnished his otherwise perfect physique. Beyond this, with no health care protection and a full and intimate acquaintance with abject poverty, J. Robert emerged from Pinch virtually unscathed. His mind and spirit were unusually healthy and robust, prone to flight beyond the restrictive borders and the stench of Pinch.

Incredibly, in all of Pinch's ensnarements and temptations, J. Robert was never ever in any trouble. He was never accused of stealing. He was never engaged in fights, like boys often are. He never carried a knife or weapon of any sort. He never had a run-in with the police. There was something strangely protective of this young man---maybe, the protective hands of God?

With a strong sense of having divine protection as it were, J. Robert ventured out from Pinch to experience the larger world. It started at quite an early age. His journey really started on the banks of the Mississippi River. There, he allowed his mind to wander all over the world. He took imaginary journeys to places he had never seen and to cities and countries about which he had never heard.

When J. Robert began his sorties into outer sections of Memphis, away from Pinch, it was as though he had known the places and people all along. There was not a place where he seemed to be a stranger. He was never among strangers. As a young fellow, he was an excellent conversationalist, he could hold his own on almost any subject with adult or youth. Downtown, South Memphis, East Memphis, North Memphis, he went everywhere and was known everywhere. In a day's time, he covered a great deal of ground, but always found his way back home.

One of his venturesome treks took him to South Memphis and to the home of some of his playmates. On this occasion, J. Robert paddled his ever-present car tire to South Memphis. This was his imaginary Cadillac. When J. Robert ventured out, he was always exercising his imagination. On this occasion, he imagined he was driving his own Cadillac. Brrrrrraaaah, he began as he pumped his hands in an underhand paddle wheel fashion. His bowed legs and bare feet carried him effortlessly behind his car tire, his imaginary Cadillac. Whhhhhaaaaah, he went as in his imagination he opened up the throttle on his imaginary Cadillac. He paddled his car tire and ran at breakneck speed all the way to South Memphis until he arrived at the home of his playmates. As though he had driven his Cadillac up to the house, J. Robert parked his car tire at the side of the steps at the front porch. He stayed and played with his playmates until evening, when it was time for him to go home. On the return trip home, J. Robert repeated the same imaginary trip in his Cadillac. Whhhhhaaaaaah, he went as he imagined himself opening up the throttle on his car and paddled his tire to the north and home in Pinch. His legs churned and his hands whirled like a windmill as he paddled his car tire. He feared no evil. He feared no man. The wind was in his face. The world was his. He was in the hands of God.

Such excursions into the far-flung regions of Memphis were the prelude to journeys that were sure to come later in life. That wonder of what lay around the bend of the river, where the clouds of the sky were going, what was up in the heavens, would ultimately lead J. Robert to venture out into the world, to the north, to the south, the east, and to the west.

VIII.

Education In The Early Life Of John Robert Lee Bradley

JRobert Bradley was educationally precocious. He was so brilliant early in life that he could never bring himself to be interested in school as it is ordinarily known. School did not present a challenge to him. His school was the Pinch Experience. He learned to speak in Pinch. He told his mother, "Momma, I want to speak like Pearl." Pearl, the big Yellow Girl behind his house, whom he only knew at a distance but heard her speak often, was his speech therapist, his tutor to teach him the skills of the tongue, his mentor to instruct him in the marvels of the use of the mouth. His mother, Miss Cookie, gave him instruction in matters of mannerisms. She taught him to appreciate the finer things in life. The crystals she brought from the white folk's house, the lace she bought with the precious pennies she earned cooking and cleaning, washing and ironing were all reflective of her love for the finer things of life. To appreciate the finer things of life, he learned from his momma. The laughing language of the waves of the river and the soft speech of the fluffy clouds gave him a wealth of instruction about the universe. So, school for him did not present so great a challenge. It was boring. The teachers seemed not to know what he already knew, to be in touch with God and His world. He was satisfied with God as his Teacher.

Like most children, J. Robert began school at six years old. His first school was Grant Elementary in North Memphis. It was during this time that he met little Leonard Mitchell, a young fellow who became for him like a brother with whom he established a relationship which was to last for the rest of his life. Leonard was three years younger than Robert. The two struck a chord of similar interests, both could sing and loved to do it.

Although Leonard was three years younger, born in 1923, the two wound up in the same grade in school. They found each other in the third grade. They played together. They had fun together. They sang together. And oh, it was something when they could blend together, singing and playing the piano in an imaginary way. They really could have some fun.

But quite often, J. Robert used his age and size to overwhelm Leonard. For example, the time when the two sang on the church steps at the old Mt. Olive Baptist Church at Marshmallow and Winchester Streets, they really had some fun. But this was a time when he used his age and size to overwhelm his little playmate. When they had sung for the bereaved lady whose husband had died, she was so moved at the singing of these two fine young boys that she gave them a total of six dollars. Apparently Leonard was the treasurer for he held the money securely clutched in his hand. J. Robert's inquisitiveness drove him crazy. He couldn't stand the thought of Leonard having all that money and could not have it for himself. So, he asked Leonard to see the money. When Leonard opened his hand, J. Robert hit it with a great big lick. Whhhoppp! The money flew out of Leonard's hand and J. Robert grabbed it with the skill and strength of vacuum suction and ran like crazy. He cut down through his little trail that led down to the river. He leaped over ditches, hopped over broken glass, and skipped over rusted buckets whose jagged edges reached out to snare him and infect him with deadly tetanus germs. But J. Robert's familiarity with his charted path to the river paid dividends that day and his bowed legs and fat bare feet carried him without a scratch safely to the river's edge to count the bounty of cash he had taken from his friend. Leonard had long since given up on catching J. Robert, although he did give pursuit. It was several days before he saw his friend to ask him to give an account for the money.

When J. Robert discovered that he could sing while on the banks of the Wolf and Mississippi Rivers, this fascination became his only and all-consuming interest. When he went to Grant Elementary School, all he wanted to do was sing. At Grant, he did not like to go to class. When he went to class, he only sat and twiddled his thumbs, looked out the window, and waited for the next opportunity to sing. There were times when J. Robert slipped off from class and hid in one of his favorite places in the school building. Professor E. L. Honesty was principal of Grant Elementary School. He knew J. Robert and knew him well. He always knew where to find him whenever he came up missing. When he found him in his hiding place, Professor Honesty would whip him. J. Robert was such a character, however, that even while Professor Honesty was whipping him he would begin to sing.

During his second year in school, although he was still in the first grade, J. Robert demonstrated the most phenomenal musical ability. Each day, the music teacher was putting one of the students through the paces of preparation for a musical presentation that was to be presented at the Main Street Theater in North Memphis. While the young student was practicing, J. Robert found himself a comfortable place under the steps of the school building and listened to what was going on. The school building was one of those one room facilities with two sets of steps which led into it. While the young student was being taught his part by the teacher, J. Robert was learning as well. The young man practiced so hard each day that he became hoarse. When the time came for the concert, the young fellow was unable to perform. However, J. Robert had sat under the school steps and learned the song so well that he knew it verbatim. The song was "Sweet Little Alice Blue Gown." It was an operetta.

J. Robert approached the music teacher, Mrs. Lucille Rhine Woods, and insisted that he could sing the song and should be given a chance inasmuch as the other student was suffering from laryngitis. Mrs. Woods said, "Go on John, you ain't got good sense, go on. You li'l old nasty rascal." There seemed to be some resentment in her voice, as she responded to little Robert's passionate request. It may have been that she knew the little fellow really could sing. Harry Cash, the assistant principal at Grant School, was standing there when J. Robert was making his appeal to sing. He said, "Mrs. Rhine Woods, why don't you let him try it." She shot back, "Well, I don't want to fool with this child. Get somebody else, I don't want to fool with him." Mr. Cash, with pleading in his voice, said, "Well, let's see." With Mr. Cash being the assistant principal, Mrs. Rhine Woods could resist no more.

When Mrs. Rhine Woods began to play, J. Robert began to sing. When he did this, Mr. Cash just stood there with a look of amazement. Mrs. Rhine Woods hit the piano angrily and hard, because she was so mad that J. Robert had demonstrated such excellent musical ability. J. Robert simply was not her boy.

The time came for the operetta. It was held at the Main Street Theater in North Memphis. A deacon at Mt. Olive Baptist Church had to borrow the money to buy the outfit for J. Robert to wear. He had to be dressed in white pants, a blue coat, and black and white shoes with white socks. The deacon begged the store owner to let him have the clothes so little J. Robert could look nice. He said to the man, "I will see to it that you get your money." That night, J. Robert put on the shoes early. He was so afraid that they would not let him have the shoes that he put them on and would not take them off. The shoes, being new, were very tight and caused his feet to swell. The shoes had to be pulled off his feet. When he did this, his feet blew up like balloons. He walked onto the stage in the white socks and began to sing his song. When he sang his song, the folk began to throw money onto the stage. The stage was literally covered with money, fifty cent pieces, quarters, dimes, and nickels. The audience applauded him time and time again. The money was used to pay off the bill for the clothes the deacon bought for J. Robert.

J. Robert's lack of interest in school was of such that he was never promoted from one grade to another. He remained in the first grade for a long time before being promoted. Even when he got promoted to the third grade, he stayed there for what seemed to be a lifetime. In fact, his friend Leonard, although three years younger, was promoted to the next grade, leaving J. Robert behind in the third grade. And, there J. Robert stayed, twiddling his thumbs, looking into space as though he were laying on his back on the

Mississippi or Wolf Rivers, disappearing into some cloistered place to engage himself in singing.

Robert's seeming insincerity about school and what seemed to be a disdain for education was really a reflection of his precocity. In addition to this, he was preoccupied with thoughts of his obligation at home. Early in his life, when his father separated from his mother and later died, he felt it incumbent upon himself to do something to help take care of his mother and his brother, Van. His mother worked hard day and night. She did all kinds of work for white people, cooking, ironing, washing and the like. She often had to spend long hours on the white folk's place. Beyond all that, she took in ironing and washing. She took in curtains, washing them, starching and stretching them on a rack until they stood up like a man.

When J. Robert was big enough to realize his mother's plight, he felt compelled to do something to help her. He began to make a little money by watching a man's truck filled with fruit and vegetables so other little children would not steal from it. The man paid him $.75 for that chore. He made a dollar for shelling a bushel of peas. Along with that dollar and seventy-five cent, J. Robert raked all of the peas he could off the ground into a gunny sack and included some tomatoes, string beans, cabbage, peaches and the like and went on home. Sometimes he was fortunate enough to come upon a great big juicy watermelon. He placed all this in his gunny sack and made his way home. It was a sight to see, a little fellow like Robert scuffling along the street with a gunny sack bulging with food. He did not want to raise people's suspicion about what he was carrying, lest they try to take it from him---this was Pinch, after all---so he always took the alley route. He took the alley off of Front Street and followed the alley network until he got home. When he got home, his momma, Lela, took out what she wanted and then notice would go out to the others in the neighborhood to come to get the rest. In effect, young Robert was feeding the whole neighborhood. It was in the heart of The Depression, 1929, and thereabout.

J. Robert began to sell groceries on the streets of Pinch, vegetables, fruit, and the like. As he sold his commodities, he would sing. The songs he sang were those his mother had taught him at the Mt. Olive Baptist Church and Jackson Avenue Baptist Church. He walked the streets selling his wares. He sang as he went. As he sold his fruit and vegetables, people sometimes had change coming back. Maybe it was only a few pennies, or a nickel, and every now and then a dime. Inevitably they would say, "Oh, you go on and keep the change." So, Robert went home some evenings with three dollars, or three dollars and a half, and maybe on a good day, he'd have four dollars. He was like the man of the house, although he was hardly ten years old. It was something, however, he felt compelled to do. This was The Depression! Grown men were taking their lives because times were so hard. Some men were jumping in front of cars. Others were blowing out their brains with guns.

Times were hard. But little J. Robert was earning enough money to help his mother and his little brother, Van, to have food, pay rent, and buy some insurance. He slept when he could. He went to school when he could. When people thought he really was not interested in school, J. Robert was really trying to help take care of his momma and little brother.

When J. Robert did go to school, the only class which struck a nerve of interest was the one in music. Mrs. Lucille Rhine Woods was the teacher for that class. It was she who taught the fundamentals of music to both Leonard Mitchell and J. Robert Bradley. She was the teacher of another young boy who subsequently became like a big brother to both Leonard and J. Robert, Thomas Shelby. Professor Harry Cash counseled Leonard and J. Robert on many occasions to guide them in the path of right. Sometimes he wondered if that was doing them any good.

Apparently, the teachers at Grant Elementary School got weary of seeing J. Robert stuck in the third grade. They eventually moved him to the fourth grade. He stayed there for a while until Professor J. Ashton Hayes, principal of Manassas High School, moved him from the fourth grade to the ninth grade in high school. His friend, Leonard, always kidded him saying, "He was the only person who ever went from the fourth grade to the ninth grade." When someone asked Professor J. Ashton Hayes what grade would J. Robert be in at Manassas and what would he do (that is when he was moved from the fourth grade to the ninth grade), he said, "Just let him sing."

Because J. Robert was in the hands of God, Divine providence was always evident in his life. This Providence manifested itself in Robert's school life. Mr. Joe Brenner was the president of the Memphis Power and Light Company. Each Christmas, he sponsored a special program at the city auditorium. The program was for the poor children of Memphis. One day, when Miss Cookie was chopping wood for the fire in the house so she could cook supper, J. Robert walked out into the yard. The day was cold and dreary. The sky was leaking and weeping her cold moist tears. Robert's mother told him to go back into the house. "Ya'll stay in the house," she said, "We don't have nothing." But when he got a chance, he walked up town. He was a walker. He loved to walk through the alleys, barefoot. He never had shoes, but never caught a cold. By the time he ended his walk, he had come to the city auditorium downtown. He heard singing coming from the auditorium. The song they were singing at the time was "Silent Night, Holy Night." As they sang inside, J. Robert began to sing outside on the sidewalk. This singing began to annoy the policeman who was standing guard outside. The policeman could not contain the little one-eyed boy and prevent him from singing, so he went inside to get someone to come outside and get him. His thinking was that the little fellow was singing so that he should be inside singing. When the policeman went inside, he got the attention of Miss Lucy Campbell, who happened to be leading the choir in singing the Christmas songs. He told her that if she did not go get the little one-eyed boy outside and bring him inside so he could sing, they were going to arrest her. Miss Lucy had heard of the little fellow before; in fact, she had heard him sing before although she was not personally acquainted with him. So, excitedly she responded to the policeman that if he did not help her get the little fellow inside so he could sing, she was going to petition her cousin, who was the judge of the town, and have him fired. They both got together on the matter and hastily rushed little J. Robert into the auditorium. He began to sing. All the while, they were giving clothes and Christmas bags filled with goodies to poor children. But while they passed out the Christmas bags, J. Robert was leading the singing. And, Mr. Joe Brenner, president of the Memphis Power and Light Company sat in his seat and wept as a result of the young boy's singing.

Mr. Brenner inquired of who J. Robert was. They told him of his living conditions, his pitiful situation. The man was so moved that he gave J. Robert not just one stocking but two or three. In addition, he gave him a pair of overalls for Van, two pair for himself and sweaters and socks. Mr. Brenner fell in love with J. Robert. He bought an overcoat for himself and his brother, Van, and sent three tons of coal to his mother with some money to boot so they could have a good Christmas.

Mr. Brenner followed up on J. Robert and notified the principal of Manassas High School to take him in school and whatever the expenses were, he would take care of them. He did not like school, but because of such a gracious act by Mr. Brenner, he conceded.

By now, everybody knew little J. Robert Bradley could sing. So, when he went to Manassas High School, they appointed him to lead a group of children to sing. J. Robert got the children so worked up in The Spirit that they often got to shouting as though they were in church. One of the teachers, Mrs. Georgia Quinn, said, "We can't have this at this school!" But the principal, Professor J. Ashton Hayes, a man who quite often spoke his mind in ways unusual, said, "What the hell you mean we can't have it? That little Black Nigger's singing is setting these childrens' hearts on fire and you can't do it with your choir. So, leave him alone!"

It was singing like this that kept him in school. He walked fourteen to fifteen blocks each way to and from school each day. He did not learn much of anything, but he walked anyhow. When he got to school, he sat in class and looked out the window until he got a chance to sing. There was one thing he learned in the seventh grade, however, that would go with him the rest of his life. That was a poem, "The Home Song," by Henry Vandyke. He loved it and memorized it so that if awakened at 3:30 A. M. in the morning, he could recite it from memory.

I read within a poet's book
A word starts the page,
Stone walls do not a prisoner make

Nor iron bars the cage.
But every house where love abides
And friendship is adjust
Assure the home and home sweet home
For there the soul can rest.

In Shakespearean logic and wisdom, there was a divinity which shaped the end of J. Robert Bradley in his school experience. Divine destiny had designed that J. Robert would come to meet one of the greatest personalities the world would ever know and one who would impact his life in a profoundly irrevocable way for good. That person was Miss Lucy Eddy Campbell.

In the field of music, there would be no more powerful personalities than Miss Lucy Eddy Campbell and J. Robert Bradley. Destiny would have them meet through their relations with the church. As a young fellow, J. Robert, accompanied by Leonard Mitchell, and his big brother, Thomas Shelby made their circuit through the churches of Memphis. They sang at Memphis Association Meetings. They sang everywhere. In the course of it all, his path once again crossed that of Miss Lucy Campbell. Miss Campbell was a school teacher at the famous Booker T. Washington High School in Memphis. When she first met J. Robert Bradley, he was about eleven or twelve years old. By now, he was singing in and around Memphis, in churches and at Association meetings. Like a magnet drawing slithers of steel, these two dynamic personalities were drawn to each other.

Destiny would have it that when J. Robert played hooky from Manassas High School, he inevitably went to Booker T. Washington High School. It was there where Miss Lucy taught school. J. Robert found her classroom and sat in the back. He drew no attention to himself, however, Miss Lucy did. She directed her comments to the class and said of him, "This young man has one of the greatest voices of all time. He is going to go on to be great."

In all his days of attending her class, Miss Lucy never took the opportunity to correct J. Robert about his English or speaking habits. He never really accomplished anything academically in Miss Lucy's class. He just sat in her class! She was his friend.

As it turned out, J. Robert Bradley never really completed any school. He never completed elementary school. He was moved from the third grade to the ninth in one fell swoop. He does not take credit for ever completing high school. He never went to college.

IX.

The Thomas Shelby Factor In The Life Of J. Robert Bradley

Often when J. Robert played hooky from school, he was not at home with his little brother, Van nor was he working to get some money to help his mother pay bills and get food for the house. He was with Thomas Shelby, who was busy teaching him classic songs and the finer points of vocal music.

Miss Lucy Campbell had discovered J. Robert. It was she who would introduce him to National Baptists. But, it was Thomas Shelby who was the one personality who played the most prominent role in the formation of the musical life of J. Robert Bradley as a vocalist. He was eight years Robert's senior. He lived in the same neighborhood and was like a big brother to both Robert and Leonard. He took care of them. Especially did he watch out for the two younger boys as they crossed the streets of Memphis. He was concerned that they were not hit by a car. On one occasion, he literally whipped J. Robert for running out into a street. He was fearful that a car would hit the young fellow. So, he sought to teach him the lesson of not running out into a street.

Mrs. Lucille Rhine Woods was Shelby's music teacher, just as she was for J. Robert and Leonard Mitchell. Shelby had a beautiful tenor voice, but he was also instrumentally inclined. He played the piano. He graduated from Grant Elementary School and went on to Booker T. Washington High School. He studied under Miss Lucy Campbell. All the while, he served as pianist at the Pilgrim Baptist Church where Dr. W. Herbert Brewster served as pastor. This was one of Pastor Brewster's two churches. Pilgrim Baptist was on the north side of Memphis, on North Second Street. The other was East Trigg Baptist Church on the south side. Leaving his two little playmates, J. Robert and Leonard, far back in the pack, Shelby went on to enlarge his education at LeMoyne College.

Thomas Shelby loved music. In fact, music was his life. He sought opportunities on every hand to learn more about his craft. As a young boy, he went to church at Pilgrim Baptist and practiced daily on the piano. Even when the weather was cold and there was no heat in the church building, Shelby could be heard inside practicing on the piano. Some of the members of the church complained that the church's piano should not be used for the purposes of practice. That meant that Thomas Shelby would not be able to practice on the church's piano. In that light, the people concerned with the use of the church's piano for practice saw to it that the church building was locked and Shelby could not get in. On one occasion, Shelby found the church building locked and no one around to let him in to practice on the piano. He proceeded to break one of the windows to gain entrance into the church sanctuary where the piano was located. There he was, with hands freezing cold, inside the church building practicing on the piano, having gained entrance through the broken window. When it was discovered that Shelby had been breaking into the church to use the piano to practice, nothing was done about it. Pastor W. Herbert Brewster refused to let the members prevail. He was, in fact, raising Shelby as his own child. He lived in his home, along with his wife, Julia, and daughter, Juanita and W. T., the son. But it was the dedication and determination demonstrated by Thomas Shelby that made him one of the great musicians of his time.

Like the confluence of the Wolf River emptying into the Mississippi River and the two becoming one in destiny, the lives of Thomas Shelby and J. Robert Bradley became one --- destined to be two great luminaries in the field of music. The two complemented each other. It was Thomas Shelby who gave J. Robert Bradley firm guidance on the road to becoming a great virtuoso.

The relationship of the two seriously began when J. Robert was about eight to nine years old. He was driving his cadillac one day, or rather, paddling his rubber tire, through the streets of Memphis. When Shelby saw him, he murmured, "There goes that crazy boy." One day, when he saw J. Robert paddling his rubber tire, he went out and grabbed him and said, "Come here, little old boy!" It so happened that Robert's hair was knotty and knappy as unkempt lamb's wool, just as it was most of the time before he became close friends with Shelby. Shelby snatched him and said "Look at your hair!" He took him inside and began combing his hair. J. Robert began to cry and holler and Shelby shouted back, "Shut up, boy!" He took a whole stick of pomade and put it on J. Robert's head and slicked it back until it became so smooth that a fly would break his neck walking on it. When Shelby finished, he said to Robert, "Now look at you, don't you look different?" J. Robert, with a loud sigh of enthusiastic excitement, eye bucked and electric, wanting to touch his hair with his hands but afraid to disturb its newfound beauty, said, "Oh yeah!"

From that point, Shelby began to take J. Robert to church with him at Pilgrim. He started him to sing for Reverend W. Herbert Brewster. Dr. Brewster was a great preacher, a great pastor, and a great writer. He wrote songs made famous by many artists such as the Clara Ward Singers, Mahalia

Jackson, and Mrs. Queen C. Anderson. He also wrote outstanding plays. One of which was entitled "Heaven Bound." With instruction from Thomas Shelby, J. Robert sang the music for that play. He closed it out with a song, "I Can't Feel At Home In This World Anymore." There was shouting and rejoicing in the church when the little boy with the big voice sang.

In the process of these activities, J. Robert joined Pilgrim Baptist Church as a result of Thomas Shelby's influence. This move reflected the impact Shelby had on his life. Mt. Olive Church had meant everything to the life of Robert. His mother was there and his roots were there. But Shelby seemed to hold out some kind of promise to J. Robert; so, he cast his lot with him at this new church location.

Shelby had completed his high school work, but he did not have the money to go on to college at LeMoyne. J. Robert was simply playing hooky from school. School was not interesting to him. Intuitively, he had the feeling God had something else for him to do. There was this strong feeling that Thomas Shelby was a part of that "something else" that God had for him to do. Thus, he cast his lot with him at this juncture in his life. So, J. Robert met Shelby each morning at 8:00 A. M., just as though they were two men going to work. They went to the church, Pilgrim, where they went to work, that is, to work on songs. Shelby said, "I am going to teach you this song." He had a way of thumping Robert up side the head when he did not sing the song correctly. So when he got tired of being thumped up side the head, Robert sang the song correctly. Shelby also challenged him to "Stand straight up!" He chastised him and said, "Stick that chest out; throw that head back; and, spit those words out, spit them out!!!" Shelby taught J. Robert how to memorize his songs. This discipline brought to him the power to commit to memory volumes of material, no matter how difficult or foreign. It was through this laborious process, this day-to-day grueling routine, that Thomas Shelby taught J. Robert his first classical music.

It was training such as this that eventually went with J. Robert to the far flung corners of the world, training that awakened all the latent musical talents he had in his personality. This training led him to places and palaces of nobility around the world. Among the kinds of songs J. Robert began to add to his repertoire through the tutoring of Thomas Shelby was the famous, "My Task." Another classical song, Georg Frederick Handel's Where E'er You Walk, was taught. It was years down the road, while looking upon the dignitaries of the world, Queens and Presidents of nations, before J. Robert knew the significance of this song. The daily routine of practice and refinement brought to J. Robert Bradley a very impressive repertoire of classical music; and that, at a very early age.

This diligence bore fruit. Preparation was met with great expectations. The more people heard J. Robert sing, with his poise, diction, knowledge of the material, and spiritual sincerity, the more people everywhere wanted to hear him. Preachers began to carry J. Robert with them to revivals in Arkansas, Mississippi, Alabama, and Tennessee. Reverend Peterson took him over to Arkansas to help with the singing in revival services.

Dr. Gayton, Chairman of the Home Mission Board of the National Baptist Convention, USA, Inc., invited him to serve as soloist for his revival at his church in Mississippi. But one of the most outstanding pastors and pulpiteers to employ the services of J. Robert was the Reverend B. J. Perkins. The Reverend Perkins was by all means one of the most renowned preachers known among men during his time. Often he had J. Robert to accompany him as guest soloist at his Mississippi church. Pastor Perkins was a tall man of large physical stature. His large and rotund stomach distinguished him and did not take away from the handsomeness of his physical structure. His skin was pleasantly brown and hair smoothed back in ripples likened to the waves of the ocean. Quite often, he wore a black cut-away formal-type coat with striped pants and bow tie.

When Reverend Perkins prepared to preach, he carried to the pulpit an armload of books. He read from those books whatever the lesson was for the evening. Then, he told the Bible Story as no one else could. After telling the story, he began his whoop. Reverend Perkins had a whoop that was heavenly. In fact, it is said that whenever B. J. Perkins preached, whenever he reached his whoop, it was like heaven descending upon the earth. As he climaxed his sermon, he'd bend backward as though his head could touch the floor. When he came back up, he'd be whooping. The ushers would be carrying folk out feet first, shouting. This was the kind of preacher who sought the services of the rising gospel singer, J. Robert Bradley.

Reverend Brackens was very interested in carrying J. Robert with him to Birmingham, Alabama to sing while he conducted revivals in that area. He convinced Miss Cookie that J. Robert was a great singer and that she should allow him to go with him to Birmingham. He insisted that her son could make all kinds of money with the voice he had. Miss Cookie agreed and permitted her son to accompany the persuasive preacher to Birmingham with the promise of periodically sending money back to her from her son's efforts.

J. Robert began to sing in the Ensley section of Birmingham, Fairfield, and thereabouts. Because of his hard work with Thomas Shelby, his repertoire had increased to include songs such as "This World is Not My Home," "Talk About A Child Who Do Love Jesus, Here Is One," "Go Tell The World To Sing," "God's Gonna Set This World On Fire." He sang these kinds of songs all over the Birmingham area.

It was at this time that J. Robert met the great organist, Mrs. Mabel Williams. She was from Fairfield, Alabama. She was the organist for the National Baptist Convention, USA, Inc. She worked with J. Robert and gave him important pointers on his singing techniques. It so happened that a good deal of time became available for the kind of training Mabel Williams was able to give J. Robert. Unbelievably, Reverend Brackens abandoned J. Robert in Birmingham. He left him without a place to stay or means for food and raiment. Bradley found himself virtually on the doorstep of Mabel Williams. She took him in and kept him. While there, J. Robert sang at her church in order to make a little money until he could pay his way back home to Memphis. He felt a deep sense of indebtedness to Mabel Williams, because she had literally taken him off the streets and given him shelter for his head and food for his body.

Later in life, J. Robert saw her at one of the National Baptist Convention sessions at Buffalo, New York, getting on the elevator at one of the hotels. He said to her, "Mabel, can I buy your breakfast today?" She began to scream and cry as she affectionately patted him on his face. Excited, she said to him, "You know baby, the Bible is true when it says, 'Cast your bread on the waters...'" as she harked back to the investment she had made in him years ago in Birmingham. She had helped him then and now he could buy her breakfast.

After two years in Birmingham, Alabama and vicinity, J. Robert went back home to Memphis. When he got back home, he discovered from his mother that the Reverend Brackens had not sent any money as he had promised. This was a great disappointment. The hurt was written large on his momma's face and in her spirit. For both of them, it was a sobering moment of reality to know that people would use you for all they can get out of you and then leave you abandoned on the side of life's road.

But J. Robert pressed on. He reunited with Thomas Shelby and they began to form anew their team and went about singing all over Memphis, the state of Tennessee, Mississippi, and Arkansas. In a marvelous and dramatic way, J. Robert Bradley had begun to see what was around the bend of the river and to know where the clouds went as they quietly floated past the Mississippi and Wolf rivers.

X.

The Great Discovery: J. Robert Bradley At The National Baptist Convention

It is widely known that J. Robert Bradley was introduced to the National Baptist Convention, USA, Inc., by Miss Lucy Eddy Campbell. He was thirteen years old when she placed him before the Convention at its September, 1933 meeting in Memphis and shocked the gathering with his mature singing. He was hailed as a child prodigy.

Miss Lucy had some cursory knowledge of J. Robert Bradley prior to his introduction to National Baptists. She had heard him sing on the radio. He sang on Radio Station WNBR. He was known as "The little boy with the big voice." She had been acquainted with him through Association affiliations and church activities. Even as a little boy, J. Robert sang all over Memphis. In addition, he had joined in league with Leonard Mitchell and Thomas Shelby and formed a trio. Thomas Shelby had a beautiful tenor voice. He sang that part in the trio and furnished piano music accompaniment. In addition, she had come in contact with him at the city auditorium that Christmas when the children were singing "Silent Night" and the policeman came and got her, telling her that a young man was outside singing as loud as the children inside and if she did not go outside and get him so he could sing with the rest of the children she would be arrested. She heard him sing that night, in a most profound way. She probably even knew of his performance as a first grader when he stood in for the lead singer who contracted laryngitis and flawlessly sang the operetta, **Little Alice Blue Gown.** Certainly, this little one-eyed Black boy from Pinch was no stranger to Miss Lucy Campbell. And, when he showed up at the National Baptist Convention session in Memphis in 1933, she would not disown him.

The National Baptist Convention, USA, Inc., had grown to be a prodigious group. Beginning in 1880 in Montgomery, Alabama, it had come to be a large national organization in 1895 when all of the disparate Negro Baptist groups merged together under the leadership of Dr. Elias Camp Morris of Helena, Arkansas. The throbbing pain that came from the big bump in the road of history in 1915 did not divert this mammoth group from its goal.

It was well on its way to becoming the largest and most impressive Negro religious organization in the world. When this convention came to Memphis in 1933, it had some of the greatest Negro luminaries there were at the time in the Race's galaxy. These converged upon the Bluff City of Tennessee, the Cotton Capital of the world.

These were very fluid, vibrant and exciting times for National Baptists. 1933! The Stock Market had crashed in 1929. Soup lines were formed everywhere. Giant cumulus clouds of despair hung over much of America. Food was rationed. And, making worse things worse, there was a World War going on in Europe. Yet, there was something vibrant and bristling going on in the life of Negro Baptists! It seemed as though none of these earth-shaking things were going on. They were not happening. And, if they were, National Baptists were oblivious to them.

Only some forty years out of American Slavery, Negroes had a vigorous determination to survive and succeed, notwithstanding the Stock Market Crash, food rationing, soup lines, and world war aside. They had to prove to themselves and the world they were first class citizens. Thus, under the leadership of their venerable president, Dr. E. C. Morris, they had rebounded from the nightmare of 1915 when a segment of the group split away from them, they made haste and established a publishing house, which was constructed in Nashville, Tennessee in 1924. They collaborated with the Southern Baptist Convention to establish the American Baptist Theological Seminary. The convention was meeting twice a year in cities around the country in large numbers. Thus, National Baptists were educating and publishing for their own people. A lot of great things were happening among National Baptists. In a very real sense, they were not behaving like disaster plagued the land and want was holding the people hostage. To look at the behavior of these people, you would never know anything was wrong.

It was in this kind of environment that J. Robert Bradley made his entree onto the stage of the National Baptist Convention, USA, Inc. When the group convened for its session in Memphis in 1933, Dr. Lacy Kirk Williams was president. He was an outstanding preacher and pulpiteer who hailed from Texas and had been celebrated as one of the rising stars on the Baptist Horizon. When Dr. E. C. Morris relinquished the helm of the convention and subsequently died, there was no question that Dr. L. K. Williams would be the choice of the convention to assume the reigns of leadership for the people.

When the time came, Memphis was saturated with Negro Baptists. Whenever the convention met in Memphis, there was always a throng of delegates to converge on the city. The city itself was easily accessible from all parts of the country. All trains and highways could get to Memphis. Furthermore, Negro Baptists were strong in Memphis; and, Memphians held prominent positions in the convention. Dr. Samuel Augustus Owens was a stalwart leader of Memphis Baptists and the president of the Tennessee Baptist

Missionary and Educational Convention. Dr. Owens pastored the prestigious Metropolitan Baptist Church. Dr. J. L. Campbell held the pastorate of St. Stephens Baptist Church. Dr. L. O. Taylor, pastor of Olivet Baptist Church, was one of the outstanding preachers of his time. Dr. W. Herbert Brewster pastored two of the finest churches in the city. Pastors McDowell, Howard Perry, and B. R. Bell were among the prominent pulpiteers who played host to the National Baptist Convention, USA, Inc. So, Memphis was the place for National Baptists to be in 1933. And, they were there.

As had come to be the tradition and standard, the convention opened with a musical program. This was a grand affair, attended by thousands of both delegates and local church members as well. The music from the choir rose from the city auditorium as great plumes of smoke saturating the atmosphere with the pleasant and sweet aroma of Gospel Music. Birds on the wing conceded to inferiority at the beauty of the music they heard. Flowers blushed and angels bent from heaven to listen to the reverent strains of hymns and anthems from the bosoms of Africa's children.

It so happened that day that Miss Cookie sent her son, J. Robert, to the river to get some crawfish. She confessed that she had no money for food for dinner. She directed him, therefore, to go to the river to get some crawfish. She said, "If you go get some crawfish, I can make some crawfish stew and we can have a good dinner tonight." Miss Cookie went on to work, after giving the order to her son to go catch crawfish. So obediently, J. Robert retrieved his faithful bucket and with bare feet and tattered overalls went on down to the river to catch crawfish.

Robert had become adept at catching crawfish. He had learned to do it with or without bait. This day, his mother did not have the nickel to give him to buy a piece of liver to put on a string to bait the crawfish. So, he used what he had, his hands. This was a rather courageous act because there were snakes that backed up into the holes where the crawfish lived at the water's edge. J. Robert was fortunate. He never had an encounter with snakes at his favorite fishing spot. He stuck his little fat hand into the water and snatched out one crawfish, then another, then another. He kept this up until he filled his bucket.

But, something strange began to happen. Something mysteriously marvelous had begun to waft about in the air. There was music in the air. It was angelic. It was powerful and magnetic in its effects. Being a lover of music, he could not withstand its magnetic power. Its alluring power drew him as though he were in a trance, as though some hypnotic power had overcome him. He walked in the direction of the music. He was oblivious of himself. His bucket of crawfish was in his hand. His toil at the river's edge had caused Mississippi mud to be spattered about his face. The oozy stuff was between his toes and all over his clothes. But, his senses were numbed. He knew not what he was doing. He was like a robot, being controlled by an electronic beam and drawn to its source. One minute he was busily snatching crawfish from the river's edge, the next he was walking into the city auditorium in downtown Memphis. He walked into the door where freight was brought into the auditorium. He began to notice the gargantuan number of Colored Folk gathered at the city auditorium. He had never seen that large a group of Negroes in one place in his life.

Still as it were in a trance, with his bucket full of crawfish---he was not about to abandon his bucket of crawfish, this was dinner for him, his mother and Van---he unconsciously walked onto a stage where there had been assembled a choir and before them a massive crowd of ten thousand National Baptists. He stood there with his one eye bucked wide open in total amazement. He thoroughly enjoyed the music he heard coming from the sainted throats of these Ebony Sons and Daughters of Africa. A little bit and he would have shouted, as he had become known to do in the Memphis church circuit.

While standing with mouth ajar, one of the ladies in the massive choir shouted, "Look at that little ole nasty boy, he's a disgrace. Put him off this stage, he's disgracing us---disgracing Memphis. Take him down!" Miss Lucy Campbell was standing there and heard the lady's vociferous complaint, for the lady had spoken in a very loud and hateful manner. Miss Lucy turned around to see what the woman was talking about. J. Robert had not paid the lady any attention---his excitement obliterated from his mind everything that was going on about him except the fact of this massive crowd before him and the music he had heard come from the choir. He stood there. Miss Lucy shouted, when she saw who the young fellow was, "Oh no, no, no! Leave him alone. That boy can sing." The folk were alarmed, and said, "What?" Miss Lucy said, "Come here son. This is Robert Bradley. Do you know one of my songs?" Robert said, "Yas'sum, I know all of them." She said, "Do you know, 'Is He Yours?' and 'Nobody Else But Jesus?'" He said, "Yes Ma'am!" She said, "Come over here to the piano." Looking back to the choir, she said, "Ya'll sit down a minute." She sat down at the piano and said, "Sit down here son." She began to take her nice handkerchief to wipe some of the mud off J. Robert's face. She had one of the men in the choir to stand J. Robert in a chair, because he was short and she wanted the people to see him. She began to play, looking up at him as he stood in the chair with mud between his toes, "Is He Yours?" He started singing. National Baptists started shouting up at the top balcony and then all over the place. Dr. L. K. Williams looked over his shoulder and said, "Where did you get him from Lucy?" She said, "Out of the river!" He said, "Well, keep him. He's going to be a blessing to us."

This was the beginning of the career of J. Robert Bradley with the National Baptist Convention, USA, Inc.

XI.

Memphis And Beyond: Discovering What's Beyond The Riverbend

J Robert Bradley's introduction to the National Baptist Convention, USA, Inc., at its session in Memphis in 1933 catapulted him into the limelight from that time on. He was only twelve to thirteen years old, but his career had been carved out for the remainder of his life. It was evident even then that his life was in the hands of God.

Immediately after the National Baptist Convention session in Memphis, J. Robert and Shelby began to sing at sessions of the state convention. He became acquainted with many of the great names of the National Baptist Convention when he was introduced to the state convention, the Tennessee B M & E Convention. Ms. Lucy Campbell, J. Robert's teacher and one who had come to befriend him and saw great potential in him, was responsible for getting him to the state convention. He met Dr. E. W. D. Isaac, Jr., and Dr. A. M. Townsend. Dr. Isaac was over the BYPU Board and Dr. Townsend was the Secretary of the Sunday School Publishing Board. Dr. Townsend served in the state convention as secretary, he took the minutes of all the proceedings. This interaction with the officials, pastors, and luminaries of the Tennessee B M & E Convention later opened up doors of opportunity and acquaintance for J. Robert. The next year, Miss Lucy took J. Robert and Thomas Shelby to the National Baptist Sunday School and Baptist Training Union Congress in Raleigh, North Carolina. He sang before the national audience once again and drew them to their feet. This set off a blitz of appearances as invitations came from all over the country to hear J. Robert sing. It was in this setting that J. Robert met Dr. Arthur Melvin Townsend and established a personal, life-long friendship.

In 1933, Shelby began to play for the state convention. They moved to Chattanooga, Tennessee and lived there for more than two years. They served at Second Baptist Church in Chattanooga, where the Reverend Sanderfur was pastor. Pastor Sanderfur came to adore Shelby and Bradley. He took care of them. After a while, pastor Sanderfur took sick. He was placed in the Colored

Hospital in Chattanooga, just off of East Ninth Street. J. Robert went there each night and sat with him. He had a mature way about himself, even though he was young, which manifested itself in care for older people. After a period of illness, Pastor Sanderfur died at the hospital, in the arms of J. Robert Bradley.

While at Chattanooga, Shelby and Bradley put on musical programs for the people. They did so in order to help the churches. Churches were so plentiful that often they were sitting side by side on the crowded street. Though the churches sat so close to one another, when Shelby and Bradley put on a musical program in one of them, that church would be filled.

At these musical programs, which sometimes were done in conjunction with revivals, wonderful things happened, even souls were brought to Christ. This was the case with a young girl, Samella Walton. At a revival at Mt. Paran Baptist Church in Chattanooga, she was converted, along with about twenty others that night, during the singing of one of the songs by J. Robert. He sang the song entitled, "Drop Your Nets And Follow Me." When she heard the song, and how J. Robert Bradley sang it, she gave her life to Christ. That woman now is the school principal at Martin Luther King Magnet School in Nashville, Tennessee and is herself an accomplished musician. She holds membership at First Baptist Church, Capitol Hill, Nashville, Tennessee.

After the two-year stint in Chattanooga, Reverend Womack invited the two of them to Johnson City, Tennessee. Then they went over to Jefferson City, Tennessee. They stayed at these locations for a week to two weeks. From there, Shelby and Bradley went all over the state and then all over the country.

For sure, J. Robert Bradley was beginning to see what indeed lay around the bend of the river and where the fluffy clouds wound up after they had spent their energy over the laughing waves of the Mississippi and Wolf Rivers.

XII.

The Goodwill Tours

Immediately following the 1933 convention in Memphis, Tennessee, J. Robert Bradley and Thomas Shelby became involved in the the National Baptist Convention, USA, Inc., in a very special way. They began to collect money so they could go to the National Baptist Congress of Christian Education during the summer in the month of June. J. Robert sold bottles and delivered papers, anything that could earn him some money to go to the Congress. Shelby's expenses were provided by his church, Pilgrim Baptist Church, of which Dr. W. Herbert Brewster was pastor. By attending the Congress, these two, who had by now become inseparable, made an impact upon the Convention and the Congress. But for them, it was a thrill and honor simply to be on the Congress program. They never received any remuneration for their singing.

In the meantime, Shelby and Bradley became involved in something else that was most significant. It was something called the Goodwill Tours. There had been a falling off of allegiance of the membership of the National Baptist Convention. Constituents had discontinued using Sunday school literature published by the Sunday School Publishing Board. There was somewhat of a general state of discontent among many of the members of the convention.

The spark that spawned such a state of affairs was something that had happened pertaining to the publishing house. A certain Mr. Pearson from Chicago, Illinois reportedly had gone to Nashville to conduct an audit of the Sunday School Publishing Board. Apparently there had been some nervousness about the publishing house inasmuch as it had been the crux of the problem which split the convention in 1915. There was always caution when it came to the publishing house. Horrible memories of 1915 lurked in the minds of everyone. It appears that while Mr. Pearson arrived in Nashville and performed his work to audit the books, while returning to Chicago, he came up missing. He boarded the train in Nashville but was never seen after that. This stirred a great deal of concern and it was surmised to be the reason for a drastic fall-off of convention support by constituents.

President L. K. Williams thought to appease the people and solicit their support by forming what he called a Goodwill Team. The Team was to tour the country in an attempt to rally the favor of The Faithful. The group consisted of singers and preachers, including Dr. L. K. Williams himself. The members of the Goodwill Team were: J. Robert Bradley, Thomas Shelby, Clevon Derricks, E. W. D. Isaac, Jr., and Odie Hoover. Miss Lucy Campbell joined the team on occasion. Over time, the group picked up Hines from Atlanta, Simms from Texas, and Ruffner from Savannah, Georgia. Toward the end of the tour, Mr. Nelson Senter from Nashville, Tennessee and the Fifteenth Avenue Baptist Church joined them. Dr. L. K. Williams provided most of the preaching, but he was frequently assisted by other great pastors and preachers such as Dr. D. V. Jemison.

During the Goodwill Tour, J. Robert Bradley began to promote the music of Miss Lucy Campbell. From one city to the next, for almost a month, the team went preaching and singing. The effect from city to city was just what was hoped, the spread of good will. At every stop, people who had been estranged from one another were reunited once again through the preaching and singing of the Gospel of Jesus Christ. People were hugging and kissing one another who had not spoken for sometime. They renewed their religion in Jesus Christ and the convention was brought back together. There was a powerful song which was sung during the tour, "He Will Remember Me."

A very unique demonstration of the outpouring of the Holy Spirit occurred in Seattle, Washington. At the People's Institutional Baptist Church pastored by Dr. Fountain W. Penick, a great crowd had gathered for the Goodwill Tour. Pastor Penick was one of the officers in the National Baptist Convention and his wife was secretary for the woman's convention. The governor of the state had been invited. He was in the audience, along with his secretary. The two were caucasian.

During the worship, J. Robert Bradley sang Miss Lucy's "Nobody Else But Jesus." The governor's secretary was taking notes while Bradley was singing. While taking notes, presumably, the governor's secretary became overcome by the Holy Ghost and fell from his table in hysterics. When this happened, the Negro worshippers began to shout. For about twenty minutes, nothing could be done. The Holy Spirit was in complete control. Remarkably, a number of people joined the church as a result of this demonstration of the power of the Holy Ghost.

XIII.

Transitions

The life of J. Robert Bradley was on the verge of taking off into the ethereal realm of greatness. But he could never penetrate that realm alone; he was to be the composite of many persons and personalities who had an impact upon his life. Memphis would forever leave its indelible impression upon the life of this vocal virtuoso, this child prodigy, this marvelous maker of music.

To begin with, there was Lela, his mother, with her sophistication, poise, dignified behavior, and love for fine things. His father, John Bradley, gave him his booming voice and his swarthy, strong, and beautifully proportioned body. Surely Leonard Mitchell provided him youthful impetus and encouragement to sing to the glory of God. Then there was Thomas Shelby, the inimitable. Through his indefatigable drive to train J. Robert in the finer things of music, he helped him to develop one of the most unique bass-baritone voices that ever would be heard. Then of course there were the preachers who shaped the theological mindset of the young man. Pastor B. R. Bell surely nurtured the young man to fear God and flee from the devil. Certainly Reverend W. Herbert Brewster thrilled his little heart with preaching that smoothly flowed to the cadence of poetic rhythm. There were many more preachers who touched the life of this rising star who was about to go shooting blazingly across the heavens.

It goes without saying that the most outstanding personality to impact J. Robert's life early on, as it relates to his total musical development, was Miss Lucy Eddy Campbell. She saw in him his educational precocity. She also saw in him musical genius that others had not discerned. She believed in him! She believed in him so that she entrusted to him her most precious treasure, her songs. She prophetically surmised that one day he would stand at the zenith of fame and traffick among the many gods and goddesses of music known all over the world.

There were others whose stamp rested indelibly upon the life of this young vocalist. Indeed, Professor J. Ashton Hayes of Manassas High School;

Professor E. L. Honesty, of Grant Elementary; Professor Harry Cash, and even Mrs. Lucille Rhine Woods, though she sometimes lacked the confidence in J. Robert that Lucy Campbell had, were all among the many who inscribed their signature upon the life of the little boy with the big voice.

But, still there were others. In Memphis, the blues were sung with gusto. To live in Memphis meant to hear the blues. J. Robert Bradley heard the blues. They had a distinct affect on him. Classical music was also sung in Memphis. At his own admission, J. Robert Bradley said, "Classics always appealed to me. I always sang them."

Ma Rainey, Butter Bean and Susie, Ida Cox, Mammie Smith, Bessie Smith, and Ethel Waters were only a few who influenced J. Robert's life to some greater or lesser degree. From these, he learned as a young fellow songs such as "When Your Hair Has Turned To Silver," "You Will Always Be The Same," and "I Will Always Call You Sweetheart."

As for the singing of Negro Spirituals, there was none as profound as Marian Anderson. It only took one experience at hearing this tall and beautiful woman sing Negro Spirituals to convince J. Robert that this was the way he would go. That experience was in Detroit, Michigan's Cadillac Theater.

Thomas Shelby and J. Robert were travelling and Pastor Maston invited them to Detroit. They had been travelling on the concert circuit in Northern Michigan when their money ran out. At the invitation of Pastor Maston, they returned to Detroit. The Reverend Maston was pastor at the church where the mother of the great boxer Joe Louis, Mrs. Brooks, was a member. Reverend Maston took them to Sis. Brook's home to eat some turnip greens and corn bread and neck bones she learned to cook down in Alabama. She loved her pastor! She would give him anything, money, food---anything. Her love for Pastor Maston was extended to anyone who was his friend. Sitting at the dinner table, he laughed and his big belly shook as he would say, "Thank you daughter, that's why the Lord blessed you to get a boxing son."

It was the cold, winter time of the year. The two lived with Thomas Shelby's aunt. J. Robert Bradley picked up the paper one day and saw that this Black woman, Marian Anderson, was going to sing. Robert did not have the money to go but he began to tell his story around that he wanted to go. The brother-in-law of Shelby's aunt played the numbers. He said to J. Robert, "Bradley, if I hit the numbers, I'm going to give you the money to go hear that woman." Sure enough, he hit the numbers. He never disclosed how much he got when he hit the numbers, but he was true to his word to Robert. He gave him enough to go to the concert.

Shelby's relative only gave J. Robert enough money to get his ticket for entrance into the theater. He did not have the money to get there. So he began to walk from Joyner and Brush Streets downtown to Cadillac Square where the Cadillac Theater was located. It was cold, very cold. But J. Robert walked every step of the way.

When he arrived at the theater and finally got warm and comfortably situated, he waited for the opening of the concert. J. Robert was not aware that Miss Anderson was soloist for the Detroit Symphony and under those circumstances the orchestra normally played prior to her appearance on stage. While sitting there, the curtain opened and the orchestra began to play. Momentarily, he was struck with wide-eyed excitement as he sat anticipating the voice of the famous Marian Anderson. He sat and listened, literally sitting on the edge of his seat---but no Marian Anderson. In disgust, J. Robert started to leave. He said, "Lord, I'm in the wrong place. I have spent my money, but I'm in the wrong place." On the verge of leaving, he noticed the curtain going down. Though terribly disappointed, the song the orchestra played was beautifully unforgettable for Robert. It was "Under The Spring Chestnut Tree" by Peter Ilich Tchaikovsky. With the curtain fallen and everything quiet and dark, J. Robert thought there was more to come and Miss Anderson would sing after all. After a long time, the curtain rose again. All at once, a tall, handsome, brown-skinned woman strolled onto the stage. Everyone was hollering and applauding. They sprang from their seats as metal springs released from tension. J. Robert joined in the hollering and applauding, leaping to his feet like everyone else. He really did not know what he was doing, or why, but he just joined in with the crowd. All he knew was that he had sprung to his feet like everyone else and was applauding and shouting with the crowd.

While Miss Anderson stood on stage, she popped her dress tail, to the delight of the audience. She had an uncanny, unique way of popping her dress so that a ripple would run in wave-like fashion from the bottom of the floor-length dress to the very end of its train. That was somewhat a trademark of hers. When J. Robert saw this, he just hollered. He had never seen anything like it in his life. He thought it was the most beautiful thing he had ever seen. All of a sudden, she bowed her head. When she raised her head, it was the signal for her accompanist to hit the first note. With a rich, resonant, femininely deep and full voice, she sang, "I'm trampin', trampin', tryin' to make hea'm my home." J. Robert shouted out, shattering the reverent silence that had come over the theater, "Yas Ma'am I am!" People turned to look at the young man who could not hold his peace. They quickly turned back to the stage to thrill over the masterful singing that was taking place. They too, wanted to shout like the excited one-eyed young man.

After the concert, J. Robert wanted to go back stage to speak to Miss Anderson. He was afraid, for some reason, and did not do so. But from that night, he vowed to sing classical music and Negro Spirituals like Marian Anderson. He left the Cadillac Theater with a sense of indebtedness to Miss Anderson. It was years before he got a chance to tell her so, but it was so. From that moment, she had placed the spark in his heart to sing classical music and Negro Spirituals, the kind of music critics came to say was his best singing. He tucked the printed program in his shoes so he could not lose it. He took off for home. It was cold, really cold, but he never felt any of it. Every step of the way, he walked briskly singing "Trampin', trampin', trying to make hea'm my home."

From that time, J. Robert followed Marian Anderson wherever she went. He attended her first concert at Carnegie Hall in New York City after she had a very serious operation. She had a growth on her esophagus and her doctor, Dr. Bucky, determined that he had to perform surgery to remove it. He told her, "Miss Anderson, I might be able to save your life, but I cannot promise I can save your voice." The operation was performed. Miss Anderson's first concert after the operation was the one held at Carnegie Hall. Dr. Bucky was there. J. Robert saw him in the hallway with his hat in his hand. He noticed his demeanor. The visage of his persona reflected grave concern. Miss Anderson opened the concert with a tremendous song, "Graus Jehovah De Herod." When she opened her mouth and began to sing, Dr. Bucky shouted gleefully with deep satisfaction, "Yes Ma'am!" He placed his hat on his head and walked out the door and went home. He was satisfied that the surgery had been successful and Miss Anderson could continue her career to sing and inspire the likes of J. Robert Bradley.

As he stood on the launching pad in Memphis, Tennessee, he did so with a "we-ness," a multiplicity of personalities and experiences which would be carried ahead. The world would soon discover herself to be the proud recipient of one of God's most profound blessings, J. Robert Bradley.

XIV.

What's Around The Bend Of The River And Where Do the Clouds Go?

J Robert's debut before the National Baptist Convention, USA, Inc., in Memphis, Tennessee in 1933 spawned a great deal of activity for him. He and Thomas Shelby travelled across the length and breadth of the state of Tennessee singing and promoting the music of Miss Lucy Campbell.

While Memphis was the launching pad for J. Robert Bradley, Middle Tennessee in general and Nashville in particular was destined to become the nuclear center for the development of his great career. It was at this time that Dr. E. W. D. Isaac, Jr., persuaded Dr. L. K. Williams, President of the National Baptist Convention, USA, Inc., to allow Bradley to join the Goodwill Singers to help promote the welfare of the convention. This development caused Nashville to replace Memphis as the home base for this great musical Maestro, J. Robert Bradley. At the invitation of Dr. E. W. D. Isaac, Jr., he made a dramatic move to Nashville, Tennessee to serve as a member of the Goodwill Singers of the National Baptist Convention, USA, Inc. It is little wonder that his now longtime buddy in music, his mentor and disciplinarian, Thomas Shelby, accompanied him. They both moved into the old BYPU building on Gay Street in downtown Nashville and worked for Mr. Isaac for $7 a week. They went on the Goodwill Tours whenever they were scheduled and travelled to the National Baptist conventions and congresses in June and September of each year. The two were incorporated into the musical fabric of the congress and convention sessions. They promoted and sang the music of Miss Lucy Campbell, and all the other creators and writers of music. This was done notwithstanding the presence of the likes of great singers such as Clara Ward and the Ward Singers, Roberta Martin and Sallie Martin and their singers and the great Thomas Dorsey. In the midst of all these, J. Robert Bradley and Thomas Shelby emerged to be the leaders of music for National Baptists. It was a common occurrence for the great musicians, soloists, gospel singing groups, and composers to attend the National Baptist Convention and Sunday School and Baptist Training Union Congress. They purchased booth space in the exhibition hall and displayed their wares. Quite often, Roberta Martin and her singers, Clara Ward and the Ward Singers would appear in the exhibition area singing their songs. Clara Ward and her singers were often heard singing the songs composed by the great Reverend W. Herbert Brewster. The same was true with Mr. Thomas A. Dorsey. He was a known fixture at the conventions and congresses, selling his sheet music and having someone there to sing it.

But the singing of the convention and congress was the sole responsibility of Miss Lucy E. Campbell and her two rising stars, Thomas Shelby and J. Robert Bradley.

XV.

Charles F. Bryan And J. Robert Bradley

While Nashville came to be the launching pad for the brilliant international career of J. Robert Bradley, it was the little towns of McMinnville and Cookeville, Tennessee which claimed prominence in giving a definite intellectual shape which would last for the remainder of his life. McMinnville, Tennessee was one of the Tennessee cities which hosted the revivals for which J. Robert provided music. After arriving in Nashville, J. Robert met up with a pastor who held a charge in McMinnville, Tennessee. This little town lay some seventy-two miles to the southeast of Nashville and about twenty miles to the north of Manchester, nestled in the East Tennessee foothills. Cookeville was a college town which lay about twenty miles to the north of McMinnville and about seventy two miles east of Nashville. These two little towns were the places of a dramatic turn of events in the life of J. Robert Bradley. In the meantime, Detroit, Michigan claimed the status of home for Thomas Shelby because the rising preaching star of National Baptists, the Reverend Clarence LaVaughn Franklin, invited him to become his pianist at the New Bethel Baptist Church where he pastored.

J. Robert had gone to McMinnville, Tennessee to work in a revival with an evangelist from Chattanooga, Tennessee. It was in 1938 when the revival was in session at the St. Mary's Baptist Church. As is typical for revivals in Black Baptist churches, the Holy Spirit was present, high and powerful in the church. One of the persons attending the revival was a cook who worked for white people who were owners of a prominent farm. The Black cook was so ecstatic and carried away with the revival that she walked out of the kitchen of the white folks place on the way to church with a bowl of bread batter in her hand. She walked out of the kitchen on up the hill to the Black Baptist church while her white employers were left waiting for corn bread. They were forced to eat light bread that night, because their cook had walked out with the cornbread batter in the bowl. Their curiosity got the best of them. What made their cook do this to them? They had to find out! The white people for whom the cook worked were Mr. and Mrs. Charles Bryan who owned the Falconcrest

Farm. They had a son, Charles Faulkner Bryan who was music professor at Tennessee Polytechnic Institute (TPI) in Cookeville. He and his new bride, Edith, had come to McMinnville for the summer to live. He was making only about $1,400.00 a year as head of the music department at the college in Cookeville. That was not a lot of money. So, he and his new bride went to his father's place because at least they could get some food to eat.

On that hot August afternoon, the Bryans were out on the front porch trying to fight off the oppressive heat of summer. As they swung on their front porch, someone came passing out flyers about a revival and concert. The flyer stated that the concert part would be conducted by Robert Bradley with Thomas H. Shelby, Jr., as his accompanist. It was to be held August 8-14, 1938 at the St. Mary's Baptist Church in McMinnville. Charles and his new wife Edith decided they wanted to go.

They got ready and went up the hill to the little Black Baptist church. They were the only whites there. Although they sat on the back seat, they stuck out like a sore thumb among the many Blacks who filled the small church building. It was hot that night, so much so that all the church building's windows were open to allow fresh and cooling air to circulate. Along with the admittance of fresh air into the sanctuary, bugs of all sizes, giants, mid-size, and little ones all accepted the invitation. They swarmed around the lights which hung from the ceiling. The worshippers reverently and politely fanned them away while they tried to concentrate on the solemn proceedings. But, the bugs really were annoying.

When Thomas Shelby came to the instrument, he gave a preliminary introduction of the singer who was to come later in the program. He talked of his tremendous voice and that he had been discovered in Memphis, Tennessee. Shelby sat down at the piano and began to play. He played all over the piano. The bugs were still coming. The big ones and the small ones. As they flew in and swarmed around the piano, some landed on the floor about Shelby's feet. It was a humorous scene. He would play awhile, and, in the midst of a song, reach over and squash a bug with his foot.

After Shelby played several instrumental selections, he brought out the featured artist, J. Robert Bradley. To the Bryans, he was a very large man. Probably the blackest Black man they had ever seen. But he had a distinguished air about himself which overrode any of his other features. As he walked to the spot where he was to sing, he gained his composure. He stood erect, head thrown back, hands folded and paused waiting for his accompanist to play. When Shelby began to play, J. Robert opened his mouth and began to sing. When the sound flowed from his mouth in a reverent, rippling, vibrant manner, Charles Bryan almost leaped from his seat beside his wife. Embarrassed, he sat down and looked around inquiringly to see if anyone was looking. He was thoroughly shocked and filled with disbelief at the sound that came from this Black man's mouth! He turned to his wife and said, "I've never heard a voice like that. Ohhhh, I've never heard a voice like that. But, he's ruining it! He is singing wrong! If he continues to sing like that, he will lose it!"

The Bryans sat in rapt silence throughout the program. For them, it was as though heaven had come down to earth and the gods had come to consort with the sons of men and share with them ambrosia fit only for the divine.

Following the program, Mr. Bryan and his new wife went to the front of the little church to try and get a chance to talk with Robert Bradley. They succeeded in getting to him. Charles Bryan said to J. Robert, "We need to talk, I would like to see you in the morning. We need to talk." J. Robert said politely, "That's just fine. What time do you want to see me?" It was then that Mr. Bryan said to J. Robert that he was endangering his voice from the way he was singing. He then asked J. Robert, "Have you ever studied?" Bradley quietly rejoined, "No, Sir." "Would you like to study?" said Bryan. J. Robert looked down and spoke softly and politely, "No, Sir!" Bryan shot back, "You are going to! I can help you!" As though getting a bit excited and plaintive, J. Robert said, "No, Sir! I am alright, thank you." As though oblivious to J. Robert's response, Mr. Bryan shot back sternly, "You be here tomorrow morning at 9:00 o'clock." At 8:00 o'clock, rather than 9:00 o'clock, J. Robert was standing on the front steps of the little church on the hill. When Mr. Bryan arrived at the church, he got down to business. He began by ordering J. Robert to "stand straight!" This was how he started. "Stand straight," he said as he commandeered the role of trainer of one who was to become one of the world's premiere bass-baritones. Then, he instructed J. Robert to say "Ah." This drilling seemed to be rather odd, eccentric, and maybe a bit crazy. But, Mr. Bryan continued, "I want you to say 'Ah' on this note." This went on for more than two hours. J. Robert never realized such was necessary for the development of the human voice. The training was so fascinating and challenging. J. Robert liked it. The two struck a mutually satisfying relationship, so much so that they met each other there at the church each morning thereafter during that week for more training.

At the close of the week, when the revival meeting and concert programs had come to an end, Charles Bryan and his wife talked with J. Robert in an attempt to arrange future times for further training. Mr. Bryan asked J. Robert for his address. It was then they learned that he was illiterate. J. Robert politely said to them, "I don't write." The Bryans knew they really had a challenge on their hands. It was one, however, that they were not willing to back up on. Charles Bryan then wrote out a note with his name, address, and phone number. J. Robert and Shelby were scheduled to appear at other towns about the south, so there was no definite idea of when he would be available for more training. But Mr. Bryan said to him not to lose his name, address, and phone number and when he got the chance, after he completed his tour, to contact him. They parted after that night, not really knowing if they would see each other again.

Indeed, as the Fall of the year came upon the Bryans, school activities consumed their attention and they really lost track of the man with the once-in-a-life-time voice. One night in September, however, about eight o'clock at night, the telephone rang. It was J. Robert calling from the bus station in Cookeville telling them he was waiting to be picked up. The Bryans were pleasantly surprised but delighted that the young man had taken them up on on their challenge.

The Bryans hastily began to make provisions for J. Robert's stay in town. There were not many Blacks in Cookeville and the times were those of segregation, especially in the South. Mr. Bryan and one of his fellow professors, who provided the automobile because he did not have one, went to the bus station to meet J. Robert. They had arranged for him to go to the home of the Gibsons, a Baptist minister and his family who lived in town. He looked more Caucasian than he did Black. They were friends of the Bryans. They welcomed J. Robert and made him feel at home. The home of the Gibsons became home for J. Robert Bradley for the next year or more.

The Bryans got down to business right away. During the daytime hours, Mrs. Bryan, a first grade teacher, began teaching Robert his A B C's. She taught him to read and write as though she were teaching a kindergarten or first grade student. Robert amazed her with his enthusiasm for learning. He had a mind that seemed to soak up knowledge. It was like a sponge, it absorbed all the liquid substance of learning there was. Especially was he enthusiastic about this learning experience, because it had everything to do with his God-called career, singing. So, although he was eighteen years old and being trained to read and write like a child, that did not matter to him. He ate it all up as though it were something good to eat. His voracity for education was of such that one day, while visiting the Bryan's library, Robert asked Mrs. Bryan, "Have you read all those books?" speaking of the many books on shelves which wrapped all around the room. Mrs. Bryan responded that she thought she had read all of them. Robert, as though a little child longing to get grown so he could do what grown-ups do, said, "Someday, I'm going to read every book that's up there."

The Bryans were unusual people. The south was rigid with segregation. Cookeville and McMinnville were no exception. The Bryans were Southerners by birth. But, they were of a breed of Southerner who believed in the humanity of all mankind. Charles Bryan's grandfather was a slave owner. However, his Christian conviction caused him to free his slaves in the

1840's, more than twenty years before the Civil War. He gave each of his former slaves their freedom, a mule and forty acres of land. So, the humanity of all mankind, including the Black man, was a part of Charles Faulkner Bryan's psychological and spiritual make-up. This reality was probably part and parcel of the compelling reason for wanting to train this Black man with such an unusual voice. It explains why he was so willing to take obvious risks, which could have cost him his life, to develop the voice of J. Robert Bradley.

Voice training for Robert began at night. Because Blacks were not allowed on campus at Tennessee Polytechnic Institute (there was only one Black man on campus, the cook), Charles Bryan surreptitiously carried J. Robert on campus to his office during nighttime hours. Once in his office, he closed the door and they got down to the business of going over the basic fundamentals of music and voice training. On one night, while the two were hard at work and oblivious to the world, a noise was heard outside the door of Professor Bryan's office. He stepped outside to see what it was all about. Once outside the door, he saw that the hallway was lined up with students just sitting on the floor listening to what was going on inside his office. There was not a murmur of objection.

But someone obviously did pass the word on to the college president, Dr. Q. M. Smith, that Professor Bryan was teaching a Black man in his office during nighttime hours. One night, while hard at work with Robert, the door of his office suddenly opened. President Q. M. Smith simply walked right into the office. There was nothing for Professor Bryan to do; but of course, he did stop to extend courtesies to the president. His mind took momentary flights of fright. For, here he was with a Black man in his office, teaching him voice lessons. This was prohibited, and he knew it. He did not know what the president was going to say or do. So, he simply said, "I am helping this young man. He needs some help." President Smith said, "I want to hear him sing." Professor Bryan turned and gestured to J. Robert to prepare to sing. Nervously, he said, "Sing one of your peoples' songs for the president." J. Robert sang one of his Negro Spirituals. He sang it effectively and with great pathos and feeling. When he got through, they both looked toward President Smith and saw that he had tears in his eyes. He reached into his pocket and took out some money and gave it to Robert. He never said anything about him being on campus; and, from that time, J. Robert studied in the office of Professor Bryan until his training ended.

Mr. Bryan proved to be more than a friend and kind white man who wanted to help a Colored "Brother." He was one of the rare white men who was willing to endure hardship on behalf of the Cause of Righteousness. It was unusual for a white man to spend time with a Black man in the 30's in the South. It was even the more unusual for him to carry a Black man onto a college campus where Blacks simply were not allowed. However, Charles Bryan did this with J. Robert Bradley. He was even so pretentious to carry J. Robert to the local McMinnville Lions Club in order to have him sing for the people. One evening at the Lions Club, one of the gentlemen there had become a bit inebriated and lost control of himself. The drunken white man shouted aloud, "Charles, they tell me you're in love with niggers now!" Mr. Bryan rejoined unperturbedly, "Yes, I am." He went on playing the piano and J. Robert continued to sing. When they finished, everyone in the Lions Club meeting gave them a round of applause.

While living in Cookeville, neither Mr. Bryan nor the Gibsons assessed a fee for the services they rendered to J. Robert. Mr. Bryan did not charge him for the voice training he provided nor did the Gibsons charge him for lodging and food. Mr. Hobart Martin, a member of the little Black Folks church on the hill, took pride in being the barber for this young rising musical star. God was still making a way for J. Robert Bradley, even in a strange land away from Pinch.

XVI.

Back To Nashville And Preparation For Greater Things

Momentary displeasure seized J. Robert while in Cookeville. He was yet receiving modest pay from Dr. E. W. D. Isaac, of the BTU Board, approximately $7 a week. The pay was for his participation in the Goodwill Singers. Mr. Bradley thought this was woefully inadequate for the kind of services he was rendering. He voiced his disapproval by going back home to Memphis rather than to Nashville. His disgust and displeasure did not last very long, however. Miss Lucy Campbell and Dr. C. R. Williams, the two of whom would take over the Baptist Young Peoples Union Board (BYPU) upon the death of Dr. E. W. D. Isaac, Jr., interceded with Dr. Arthur Melvin Townsend on behalf of J. Robert Bradley. They spent their money to board a train to Nashville from Memphis to speak with Dr. Townsend about hiring J. Robert. They were successful. Dr. Townsend contacted J. Robert and urged him to come back to Nashville to work for him at the Sunday School Publishing Board. He did not mention the amount of pay involved. J. Robert agreed to return to Nashville, Tennessee.

Along with participating in the promotional trips made by the Goodwill Singers, J. Robert was assigned to travel extensively with the persons Dr. Townsend had appointed to promote the sale of bonds for the retirement of debt on the Morris Memorial Building. So, everywhere he went, he promoted the sale of the **Baptist Standard Hymnal.** Dr. Townsend employed him to promote the singing of the hymns of the church. National Baptists had fallen slack in this area. Simultaneously, his travels were dovetailed with the work of the likes of Miss. Edna Bronson, Dr. F. P. Phillips, Mrs. Willa Johnson of West Palm Beach, Florida, Sis. McGowan, who was president of the women's convention in Mississippi in selling bonds. These teams travelled in Arkansas, promoting the work at Arkansas Baptist College in Little Rock. Louisiana, Alabama, and all points in the South were targets of activity. During these meetings, J. Robert set the spiritual atmosphere by singing from the Baptist Standard Hymnal. The singing indeed set the house in order for the ministry of selling bonds to retire the debt on the Morris Memorial Building in

Nashville. As a result of J. Robert's singing, people flocked to these meetings all over the South and large amounts of bonds were sold so the debt could be retired in record time.

Upon returning to Nashville, J. Robert also resumed training sessions with Mr. Bryan. It was at that time that Charles F. Bryan assumed a teaching position at Peabody College for Teachers in Nashville. During that period of time, J. Robert discovered that Mr. Bryan was indeed a musical genius. He wrote songs that catapulted themselves to the top of contemporary popularity. He wrote the "Bell Witch," which became very popular among white people.

When he moved back to Nashville from Memphis, J. Robert lived at the Colored YMCA which was located downtown at 4th and Charlotte Avenue, across from the brand new publishing house building for the National Baptist Convention, USA, Inc., the Morris Memorial Building. For three years, he walked to Peabody College for voice training. The school was located southwest from downtown, about three to four miles. J. Robert, never having the financial wherewithal to pay for public transportation or cab fare, walked every step of the way and then returned to the YMCA. Mr. Bryan sent him through the paces of rigorous vocal exercises, day in and day out. Coupled with his own natural ability, the training he received at Grant elementary and Manassas, Miss Lucy's assistance, and Thomas Shelby's strict discipline, Mr. Bryan's training began to bring a sharp edge to what had been started in Memphis years earlier.

Charles Bryan's effort to train J. Robert was joined by Lewis Nicholas, music critic for **THE NASHVILLE BANNER.** The two trained Bradley intensely for the three year period that the trek was made from the downtown Colored YMCA to the Peabody College campus and return. This was a bold effort because there probably were no other Blacks on the campus of Peabody College in those days. Racism and segregation were in full bloom in Nashville in the '30's and '40's. But these were no competition for Bryan, Nicholas, and J. Robert Bradley. They bolted past traditions and hurtled over segregation and laws of discrimination. They were engaged in something eternal, the furtherance of music and one who was musical. They were about something that was heavenly.

The test came one evening when bravery prompted Mr. Bryan and Nicholas to schedule J. Robert Bradley to sing at one of the chapel services on the Peabody College campus. When he arrived, J. Robert felt the probing unseen fingers of ten thousand eyes feeling all over him. The choking, miasmic, polluted haze of prejudice hung oppressively low in the audience that day. Before stepping to the front of the audience to sing, something obnoxious, distasteful, detestable, and completely hateful happened. The words "Nigger, Nigger, Nigger," could be heard coming from some of the young men in the audience---or, it could have been some of the young women.

The all-white audience simply could not stomach the idea of a Black man appearing before them, on the campus of prestigious Peabody College.

The gibbering and badgering failed to shake J. Robert; neither did it deter him from doing what he passionately had worked so hard to do, sing. On that day, he chose to sing one of Edward Boatner's songs, "I Want Jesus To Walk With Me." Admittedly, J. Robert was nervous. To still him, however, Mr. Bryan drew him to his side and held him reassuringly close. He walked with him to the place where he was to sing. After that, however, someone else stood with J. Robert. It was the presence of God. When he opened his mouth, something profound happened. The house became still, reverently still. When he finished, he had walked almost half-way back to his seat before the audience collected itself to know what had happened. When the audience in the crowded chapel finally realized what had happened, they erupted in thunderous applause. J. Robert Bradley had no more problem on the campus of Peabody, even though all this was happening in the dead heat of the late 1930's, early 1940's.

XVII.

The Romance With Nashville

The Nashville Experience for J. Robert was more than a change of address from Pinch in Memphis; it was the beginning of a romance that lasted until his life would fade into the evening shades of eternity.

The relationship which developed between Dr. Arthur Melvin Townsend and him became rich and robust. The Executive Secretary of the Sunday School Publishing Board, NBC, USA, Inc., became as a father to J. Robert. A musician himself, as well as a physician and publisher, he took Robert under his wing of compassionate care just as a father would his son. Of course, J. Robert united with "Doctor's" church, the historic Spruce Street Baptist Church.

Dr. Townsend was moved by the fact that J. Robert had spent the first part of his life working with National Baptist churches and the convention without receiving anything. He felt Robert had been mistreated. He wanted to demonstrate that there were some Baptists who appreciated his musical abilities and contributions. Dr. Townsend did not intend to try to make J. Robert rich, he wanted him to be comfortable and feel like singing.

One of the nicest things Dr. Townsend did was to call him into his office and give him some money for his mother. He left a note on his desk one day which said, "Robert, before you go home this evening, stop by my office." When J. Robert went to his office, as he sat down Dr. Townsend reached for his checkbook and began to write a check. While writing, he began to talk. He said, "Robert, I want you to take this and go to Memphis and move your momma out of that alley. Move her into one of those apartments. I want you to take some of this money and buy some furniture for the apartment. Then, leave some money with her so she can have some spending change." This was the kind of philanthropic approach Dr. A. M. Townsend had to the relationship between himself and J. Robert Bradley. In fact, he became the sole supporter of Mr. Bradley and sponsor of his musical training for the duration of his career. Throughout the rest of his life, Dr. Townsend provided J. Robert financial support in every way. Without Dr. Townsend, there may never have been a J. Robert Bradley as he is known today.

At Spruce Street Baptist Church, J. Robert became acquainted with the grand old man of the church, Deacon Harvey Clark. Mr. Hudson, the distinguished father and leader of the outstanding Hudson Family impacted the life of the young virtuoso. Mr. Luther Carmichael was another. Sis. Thelma Mason, Sis. Ola Hudson, and others sponsored a concert which J. Robert performed at the Ryman Auditorium in downtown Nashville on behalf of Spruce Street Baptist Church. Endless is the list of members of Spruce Street Baptist Church and, in fact, National Baptists and Christians all over the city of Nashville who befriended J. Robert Bradley and claimed him as such. Many are those in Nashville who were lovingly obliged to have him for dinner, to visit and share family-like intimacies, and to make him feel at home in a city which was away from home. Robert literally fell in love with Nashville, as a result of this kind of hospitality.

There were others in Nashville who became friends with J. Robert and remained so until they departed this life. John Adkins was one of these. John Adkins was a colorful young man, a sagacious man who became one of Nashville's most prominent personalities in the funeral business. He could be credited as one of the great supporters of J. Robert and the development of his career. He was indeed his friend.

John Adkins met J. Robert Bradley at a singing program at his church, Progressive Baptist Church in South Nashville. Dr. E. W. D. Isaac, Jr., had carried the Goodwill Singers to this church to sing. It was a program that lasted all day. They started singing outside the church building. This was to attract a larger crowd for the program which was to take place on the inside. Once the Goodwill Singers had drawn people to the church and the crowd had been drawn inside, they went on with the program. It was a long and arduous ordeal for the singers, however.

After the program had concluded, J. Robert, Thomas Shelby and in fact all of the young men of the Goodwill Singers, had become terribly hungry. They had no food and there was none in sight. But, John Adkins pulled both J. Robert and Thomas Shelby to the side and looked at them. He could see hunger boldly written across their face. They looked rather pitiful as they wrestled with their hunger but tried so very much to demonstrate their dignity. John Adkins, who had a way of speaking to you rather roughly but with a certain compassion and care, said to them, "Man! You guys look like you're hungry! Com'on and go with me!" He took the two young men to his father and mother's house. When he got there, John Adkins said to his mother, "Momma, these two young fellas are hungry, give them something to eat." J.

Robert and Shelby sat down to some of the best cooking they had ever eaten. They smacked their lips on hot fried chicken. They ate well seasoned turnip greens and sopped the pot liquor with corn bread. This experience was the beginning of a life-long friendship between J. Robert Bradley and John Adkins.

The acquaintance with John Adkins opened a door for J. Robert to become identified with one of National Baptists most outstanding families, the family of Dr. James M. Nabrit. Dr. Nabrit served as the Secretary of the National Baptist Convention, USA, Inc., under the presidency of Dr. L. K. Williams and Dr. D. V. Jemison. At the time, he was serving as president of the American Baptist Theological Seminary in Nashville. Being one of the officials of the convention, Dr. Nabrit had heard J. Robert sing over the years since his advent onto the stage. He had developed a fondness for his singing and really liked to hear him.

In the meantime, Dr. Nabrit had several very fine daughters, all of whom were sought after by young would-be male paramours. He was very careful about allowing his daughters to court young men and certainly was particular about the kind of young men with whom they spent time. The youngest was Cecelia and was not at the time supposed to be seeing young men because of her age. But John Adkins had taken a liking to her and was asking Dr. Nabrit if he could call on her.

In the face of John Adkins' persistence and Cecelia's desire to see him, Dr. Nabrit conceded to allow his youngest daughter to spend some time with the young man. There was one provision, however, there had to be supervision. Because J. Robert knew both the Nabrit Family and John Adkins, he became the one person Dr. Nabrit trusted to chaperone John and Cecelia as they spent time together. Dr. Nabrit gave him instructions that if they got too close together, he was to cough and clear his throat. This was a signal to her father that maybe he should go into the room and see what was happening.

It is without question that J. Robert performed his task well; and these two young people ultimately married. This was the beginning of a relationship with two of the most influential people in his life, a relationship which would last a lifetime.

Upon coming to the Sunday School Publishing Board, there was none who befriended J. Robert like Dr. Jacob Tilestson Brown. He found himself staying with him almost all of the time he spent at the Board at Fourth and Charlotte Avenues. He was fascinated with the manner of Dr. Brown's speech. He had preached so that he lost his voice. Because of this, he had to have assistance from a megaphone. Dr. Brown was a theologian. He was the Director of Publications for the Sunday School Publishing Board of the National Baptist Convention, USA, Inc. He knew the Bible on the highest order. Pastors and preachers came from everywhere to discuss the Bible with him and seek information. J. Robert was able to learn much from this luminary of Biblical astuteness.

Dr. Marshall A. Talley was another personality which fascinated J. Robert. He found himself frequenting his office at the publishing house. Dr. Talley was the director of the Christian Education Department of the Sunday School Publishing Board, NBC, USA, Inc. Nashville provided new acquaintances which were destined to affect his life entirely. John Work of Fisk University was one of those. Mr. Work was noted for his relationship with the Jubilee Singers of Fisk University. He also was noted for his arrangement of Negro Spirituals. To capture the pristine music of his people, he often went off into rural sections of the South, to Arkansas and Mississippi, to visit rural churches and listen to the Black congregations. It was out of these travels and visitations that Mr. Work was able to arrange many of the Negro Spirituals which later appeared in **Gospel Pearls,** published by the Sunday School Publishing Board.

When J. Robert Bradley discovered John Work, he found himself walking to the campus of Fisk University to establish a personal relationship with him and to learn from him. It was Fisk University where Robert met R. Nathaniel Dett, the great arranger of Negro Spirituals. He often visited Fisk to hold fireside chats where he would talk about the Negro Spiritual. J. Robert learned so much from Mr. Dett, who had visited the areas of South Carolina, Beaufort, and outlying islands where the aboriginal music of the African slaves was yet being sung and the nascent versions of the Negro Spirituals were born. The relationship with Mr. Dett became strong and lasting. It was of such that the last time Mr. Dett visited Nashville for his fireside chat at Fisk, J. Robert accompanied him to the railroad station. The two of them conversed about various and sundry things, and when time came for the train to depart, Mr. Dett rose to go to the train. They embraced each other and said, "Goodbye." That was the last time J. Robert saw Mr. Dett, for he went home and died.

Anywhere music was being taught, J. Robert made himself available for tutoring. This is the way it was with Mr. John Work. J. Robert often walked to Fisk's campus to solicit whatever help the noted musician could offer. Mr. Work was suffering from heart problems; however, in violation of his wife's complaints, he conceded to J. Robert's request for help. Training sessions with Mr. Work were held day and night in his home. Mrs. Work often entreated her husband to cut short the sessions, but he would not do so, he made J. Robert stay as long as they both could last. John Work was driven to lend himself to the training of this young man, for as he said to everyone he met while walking Fisk's campus with J. Robert, "This is the greatest voice I have ever heard." Thus, because J. Robert could not read music, he taught him note by note how to read. J. Robert learned by pointing one finger and following along note by note and word by word. They worked until ten and eleven o'clock at night in Mr. Work's home on the campus of Fisk University. Indeed, John Work joined the entourage of musical elites who touched and ennobled the life of J. Robert Bradley, the stentorian vocalist from Pinchgut in Memphis.

It could be said that this phase of J. Robert's romance with Nashville literally ended on a high note. His love for music and mankind led him to write the lyrics to a song. The song was "A Physician's Prayer." It was written for a very good friend, Dr. Ralph Revere from Boston, Massachusetts. Ralph, who was from the West Indies, grew up in the New England City of Boston. He gravitated to Nashville to attend medical school at Meharry Medical College. Ralph was musically inclined. He played the piano and organ beautifully. It was this that drew J. Robert to him. But, Ralph loved sports as well. One day he was playing kick ball. He fell on his hand and injured it. Upon examination, it was discovered that his days of piano and organ playing were over. The kick ball injury ended his career as a musician. Ralph Revere decided to pursue his career as a physician at Meharry. Because J. Robert knew him and was so very fond of him, he wrote the lyrics to the song and his teacher, Professor Charles F. Bryan provided the music. The song was dedicated to Dr. Revere upon his graduation as a medical doctor from Meharry Medical College.

The Physician's Prayer

J. Robert Bradley
With determination

Music by
Charles F. Bryan

XVIII.

A Venture To The North

J. Robert Bradley's acquaintance with the president of the National Baptist Convention, USA, Inc., Dr. L. K. Williams, caused him to make another change of location. Now, it was on to Chicago, Illinois.

J. Robert had truly begun to see what lay around the bend of the river of life. A variety of circumstances permitted him to discover where the clouds went when in their fluffy flight they fled across the sky. While in Memphis, he often was carried about by car to short distances such as Arkansas, Mississippi, and up into Tennessee. But, he always returned home. There was that brief stint in Birmingham, Alabama. But even after that, he returned home to his Mother. His trip to Nashville, at the invitation of Dr. E. W. D. Isaac, was the first permanent move away from home, away from his mother who was such a great influence in his life. What a challenge the trip would be. The train ride from Memphis to Nashville was a most memorable experience. The trip to Nashville was the first time he would be on his own; and, truly, he would find that he was in the hands of God.

The train ride from Nashville to Chicago was another memorable experience which carried him to a higher level in his career. The move to Chicago convinced him once again that he was in the hands of God. The train ride took him into a new world, one which he had never visited. He was so excited that he never thought of the far and away city of Chicago, Illinois---the Windy City, cold in the winter time, and the city's demand on the body for physical endurance. He boarded the train at Union Station in Nashville, his mind was intently fixed on what lay ahead. The clickity-clack of the train's wheels rhythmically began to churn up the miles. The steam engine belched black smoke from its stacks, choking the skies with its thick plumes. The North Star train carried J. Robert to Louisville, Kentucky, Indianapolis, Indiana, and on into the city of Chicago and an entirely new experience.

He made the trip to Chicago without the kind of clothing necessary for the hard winters known to that region. He went attired only in a thin black suit and no overcoat to shield him from the wintry blasts that swept in from the sprawling Lake Michigan and blew across the city. One of his friends, whose powers of compassion overruled naivete, carried J. Robert to a State Street pawn shop and bought him an overcoat. With this apparel, Bradley was able to keep warm.

J. Robert Bradley was invited to Chicago by Dr. L. K. Williams. Dr. Williams invited him to Chicago's prestigious Olivet Baptist Church, where he pastored. Mr. Theodore R. Frye was directed by Dr. L. K. Williams to invite J. Robert to be soloist for the Gospel Choir of the Olivet Church. When J. Robert got to Chicago, however, Mr. Frye placed J. Robert over the Gospel Choir as the director.

There were two great choirs at the Olivet Church. One of them was composed of some one hundred and twenty-five voices and was under the direction of Mr. Edward Boatner. Mr. Boatner was the director of music for the National Baptist Convention, USA, Inc. His responsibility was to go to the cities in which the convention was to hold its annual sessions and develop a choir from the corps of musicians in the local churches. He was also a singer, writer and arranger of Negro Spirituals. "Trampin'," "O, What A Beautiful City," "Swing Low, Sweet Chariot," "My Good Lord, Done Been Here, Done Blest My Soul And Gone Away," were only some of his musical renditions and arrangements. Mr. Boatner collaborated with Dr. A. M. Townsend to compile the **BAPTIST STANDARD HYMNAL** and **GOSPEL PEARLS** published by the Sunday School Publishing Board, NBC, USA, Inc. It was in Memphis, Tennessee at a very early age that Robert had met Mr. Boatner. At that time, it was beyond his wildest imagination that he would become a musical consort with this famous musician of national stature.

Mr. Theodore R. Frye was director of the Gospel Choir which consisted of from seventy-five to one hundred voices. Once J. Robert arrived in Chicago, Mr. Frye relinquished both the soloist and directorship positions of the Gospel Choir and gave them to Mr. Bradley.

During the process of the transition of J. Robert and Mr. Frye, Dr. Williams was killed in an airplane crash in Michigan. The plane had been caught in a terrible storm and fell from the sky. Sadness swept across the country as the message of Dr. Williams death was noised abroad. In the meantime, Dr. Branham was made interim pastor at the Olivet Church. It seemed to be a natural decision because he served Dr. Williams for thirty-five years as his assistant. He wanted J. Robert Bradley to help him rebuild Olivet in the wake of Dr. Williams' death. J. Robert was programmed to sing at the funeral of Dr. L. K. Williams.

A strange and well nigh bizarre incident occurred on the day of the funeral of Dr. Lacy Kirk Williams. The Olivet Baptist Church building caught fire. The electrical wires, it is surmised, were old and frayed. It is believed that they contributed to the cause of the fire. Whatever the cause, the funeral was halted and the casket bearing National Baptists' venerable leader was rolled out onto the ice-laden sidewalk in front of the burning church building.

The church building did not burn entirely. The burning was contained to the upper portion of the building. Because of this, the organist was encouraged to play on during the evening and night. The organist played all night long while the bier sat on the icy sidewalk throughout the night. Snow and sleet swept down from the heavens in torrential sheets while the casket bearing the body of Dr. Williams sat outside. People who had come from Mississippi, Alabama, Georgia, and all over the nation, stood in the inclement weather. On the next day, the funeral was carried to DuSable High School where sadly and respectably it was completed. The death and burial of Dr. Lacy Kirk Williams was marked by even more bizarre and unusual circumstances. After the funeral at DuSable High School, the burial was attempted the next day. The weather was oppressively cold and forbidden. The skies were spitting flakes of snow and icy crystals of sleet, and rain. It was bad! People had come from all over the United States, from Dan to Beersheba, so to speak, for the funeral and burial of National Baptists' revered leader. They came by car, buses, and trains to say goodbye to their celebrated leader. The procession made its slow and agonizing snakelike way to the cemetery.

Ironically, when the hearse arrived at the gate of the cemetery, it broke down and could go no farther. Concerned mourners took the casket from the hearse and sadly made their way to the place of burial. Incredibly, when they arrived at the grave site, the six foot rectangular hole was filled with water. They could not bury Dr. Williams that day. In fact, it is not certain when they finally buried his body.

J. Robert Bradley stayed with the Reverend Branham, who had served as Dr. Williams' assistant for 35 years, until Olivet Church called Dr. Joseph Harrison Jackson as pastor. It was during this brief period that J. Robert became acquainted with many outstanding music personalities. As Divine Providence would have it, he came to know Mrs. Bowles, who had moved to Chicago from Memphis. She became known as an entrepreneur in music printing. It seemed natural for him to gravitate to her place on State Street. She operated a music print shop, the kind which she operated in Memphis. Mrs. Bowles' Memphis print shop became a weekly gathering place for twenty-five to thirty preachers who came to preach sermons which they were not able to preach on Sunday. The back of Mrs. Bowles shop became a church of sorts. When she moved to Chicago, it was a natural that she would establish a print shop there as well. Just as in Memphis, the Chicago preachers sought her shop as a place to preach sermons that possibly no one wanted to hear but themselves.

Eventually, Mrs. Bowles began to promote the printing of gospel music and the distribution of the same. It was in this kind of environment that J. Robert found a new and temporary home. Mrs. Bowles made provisions for the fellow Memphian to reside at her Music print shop. For some time, J. Robert lived in the back of the store, sleeping on a narrow cot with only provisions of bare necessities. He never complained; however, he always felt God would take care of him. He was in God's hands. Really, making it on bare necessities was nothing new. In Memphis, he remembered how his mother, who was illiterate but a great provider for the family, used her meager monies earned cooking for white people to purchase bologna and crackers for dinner for Van, his brother, and himself. So, in Chicago, it was nothing for him to make it on the bare necessities of food.

But it was in this setting of scant provisions that J. Robert met some of gospel music's most popular artists. Theodore Frye, Kenneth Morris, Roberta Martin, Sally Martin, and Thomas Dorsey were only some of the great musicians Mr. Bradley met while living in the back of Mrs. Bowles' store. Out of these personalities, Mr. Dorsey published the immortal song, "Precious Lord, Take My Hand," along with others such as, "Peace In The Valley." Kenneth Morris and Roberta Martin formed the company, Martin and Morris, which wrote, published, and distributed gospel music.

It was during this time that J. Robert met the incomparable Mahalia Jackson. The two of them established a very affectionate relationship in the mid to late forties. She lived on the Southside of Chicago, on Indiana Avenue. She owned a hairdressing establishment and lived in the back of the same building. She was an excellent hairdresser, keeping her own hair immaculately styled. It was through her singing and hairdressing that she got on her feet financially. Mahalia was originally from New Orleans, Louisiana and had made an impact in the churches there. When she first went to Chicago from New Orleans, however, the large churches did not allow her to sing because they thought she was too bluesy and boogie woogie with her music. When she got popular, however, these same churches begged her to sing for them.

The Chicago music community was homogeneous and looked out for one another. Mahalia was one who welcomed musicians of all sort to her place. She knew they did not have much money, so she made what she had available to them. She was an excellent cook and fed all the singers who came to her shop. There were times when J. Robert and others bought small portions of chicken, chicken feet, chicken necks, ten cents worth of this and ten cents worth of that and she would put it all in a big pot and feed them. She did the cooking. Mahalia loved J. Robert Bradley. He spent much time with her, in fact lived in her home. Their relationship welded them together so much so that it lasted throughout his departure to New York City and five year stay in London. When he returned to the United States in the 1950's, their friendship was just as strong. In fact, he made frequent trips to Chicago to be with her. She gave him keys to her house. He kept the house for her while she was away. She cared much for Dr. Martin Luther King, Jr., and made a special trip to Washington, D.C., to give a concert with Josephine Baker for one of his rallies. She was bent on raising money for the Civil Rights Movement and did raise a great deal of money in the Chicago area. While in Washington, D. C., she stayed at the Mayflower Hotel. She called J. Robert and gave him the telephone number so if she were needed he could call her. She was especially interested in the condition of Mr. Theodore Frye, who at the time was gravely ill. She wanted to know of his death, if it occurred, so she could return to Chicago for the funeral.

The two had a humorous relationship. On one occasion, she said Bradley, "You don't have no sense. All you want to do is sing. You don't know how to make no money. You just want to sing and shout. I bet you right now, you don't have fifteen cent in your pocket." The cause of such caustic but loving criticism was that she often walked about the house singing, "Silent a'lent night, Ho-a'ly night...." J. Robert, who had gone away to study voice was offended at her lack of culture and training, suddenly said to her one day, "No Baby, that's wrong." He went on to demonstrate the "proper" way to sing the song. "Silent night, Holy night, all is calm, all is bright...," he said. "You see how I am phrasing it?" he said. She turned up her nose and said sarcastically, "Uh Huh!" She then went into another part of the house.

Some time passed before she made her point about J. Robert's criticism of her style of singing. She had added on to her house a new bedroom she called **The New Orleans Room.** She had a giant kingsized bed which stretched from one side of the bedroom to the other. She seized this time as the opportunity to get back at him for his condescending attitude toward her style of singing. She took a pillow from her bed and threw it at him. "Whop," the pillow went as it landed with a solid thud upon his head while he sat in a soft chair dozing. "Bradley," she said in a tone of voice which commanded his attention. He responded, "Now 'Haley, you go on now and leave me alone 'cause I'm sleeping. I'm not bothering you so you go on." She said, "Wait a minute. Whose house is this?" He said, pleadingly, "It's your house." She conceitedly said, "Uh huh!" Whose chair is this?" He said, "It's your chair." "Uh huh," she said. "Whose bed is this?" gesturing toward her giant kingsize bed. Bradley said, "It is your bed!" She said "Uh huh." Then J. Robert shot back, "Now 'Haley, you know everything belongs to you. But, that does not have a devilish thing to do with me sleeping." She said, "Uh huh." "Well," she said, "you remember that 'Silent a'lent night, Ho-a'ly night?' that is how I got all this." She went on, "Look over there in the drawer." J. Robert said, "Alright, Haley." When he went to the drawer, he pulled it out and there lay a check which had not been cashed. It seemed as though she had kept it there just for J. Robert, to teach him a lesson about what she could do without the kind of training he had painstakingly gotten. She said, "What does it say?" Half asleep, J. Robert said, "It says, Two Hundred and Seventy Five Dollars." She said, "Read again, Baby!" When he looked again, he said, "Oh, it reads Two Hundred and Seventy Five Thousand Dollars!" She said, "That's what I got for singing 'Silent a'lent night, Ho-a'ly night."

Mahalia was really not trying to be critical of J. Robert and his training. She was simply trying to get him to go after making some money. But he was determined to sing hymns straight, without any aberrations. He had committed himself to this even though it meant being financially disadvantaged.

The musical careers of Mahalia Jackson and J. Robert Bradley remained constant and strong until her death. J. Robert performed on her program at Carnegie Hall in New York City. He appeared on many programs with her. The two admired and respected each other. "She was my friend," said J. Robert about her. Mahalia told the world that she loved J. Robert and that he loved her. She said of J. Robert that he had the greatest voice in the world. When Mahalia died, the funeral was held at McCormick Center in Chicago, Illinois. J. Robert Bradley sang "I'll Fly Away." The newspapers reported that when he sang,

> "Robert Bradley, the husky gospel singer from Nashville, touched a nerve that caused several women to `feel the spirit,' to shout or faint silently, as a dozen white-clad nurses fluttered attentively."

J. Robert sent his friend away in fine fashion.

Mr. Thomas A. Dorsey was another outstanding music personality Mr. Bradley came to know during his stay in Chicago. Mr. Dorsey had made an indelible impression on the little mind of J. Robert when he was a little boy growing up in Pinch in Memphis, Tennessee. He heard his song, The Little Black Train Is Coming," and was impressed by it. The song went,

> *The little Black train is coming,*
> *Get all your business right.*
> *You'd better set your house in order,*
> *'Cause the train will be here tonight.*

Bradley was impressed by this song because Black people converted it into a Negro Spiritual. The Black songwriter, Hall Johnson, turned the song around and wrote,

> *My Good Lord's done been here,*
> *Done blessed my soul and gone away.*
> *You may be a rich man,*
> *Whiter than the drifting snow,*
> *If your soul ain't anchored in Jesus,*
> *Straight to hell you're bound to go.*
>
> *I tell you,*
>
> *My good Lord's done been here,*
> *Done blessed my soul and gone away.*
> *My good Lord's done been here,*
> *done blessed my soul and gone.*

A great deal of time was spent with Mr. Dorsey. He was music director at Pilgrim Baptist Church in Chicago, where Dr. J. C. Austin was pastor. At the same time, J. Robert Bradley was music director for the Gospel Choir at Olivet under the pastorate of Dr. L. K. Williams. Quite often, their paths crossed and lives dovetailed with one another.

J. Robert became personal friends with the likes of Roberta Martin, Sally Martin, and Theodore R. Frye. J. Robert and friends often went to the home of Kenneth Morris, who wrote "Just A Closer Walk With Thee." Morris' wife, Niecy cooked for the crowd of singers who converged upon their home. Accompanying J. Robert were the likes of Eugene Smith, Robert Anderson, Narcellus McKissack, Bessie Folke, Delores Barrett. These all sang together and gave programs. They did this to live.

J. Robert Bradley was one in a million who struck a receptive chord with the music community in Chicago. Not everyone was able to find reception in Chicago. Not so with J. Robert. Destiny had it so that he was able to go back to that city time and again to sing. Each time, he found a large receptive community.

After the nineteen month stint at the Olivet Church, the Reverend Mr. Branham sought to raise enough money to placate J. Robert and to keep him there, at least to take care of him. He made him a salary of $7 a week. But J. Robert had to walk what seemed to be a hundred miles down Michigan Avenue each time to get to the church. Rain, snow, or sunshine J. Robert had to walk to Olivet so he could get that salary of $7 a week. When Dr. Jackson arrived at Olivet to assume the pastorate, J. Robert approached him about his status. He said to him, "Doctor, Reverend Branham said to me that he would raise my salary." Dr. Jackson shot back, "I have just got here and I do not know the business of the church." Dr. Jackson had served a pastorate in Philadelphia, Pennsylvania and Omaha, Nebraska. J. Robert made himself available to Dr. Jackson to continue the effort to rebuild Olivet. But Dr. Jackson was not that much enamored with Bradley. When he was pressed about what the music program would look like under his pastorate, Dr. Jackson retreated with the statement that he had just arrived and had not the opportunity to see what the church's program was. However, when pressed further, he suggested to J. Robert that a church in Philadelphia, pastored by a Reverend Marshall Shepherd, needed a director of music. Bradley discerned that this was a veiled suggestion that he was not wanted under the Jackson pastorate. The tenure of duty spent at Olivet in this period of flux was nineteen months. Bradley's remaining stay at Olivet was not so pleasant. His pay was hard to come by. Sis. Bessie Alexander attached herself to J. Robert Bradley as a friend and sought to help in the acquisition of his salary. She was a gospel singer, one who knew and sang with Mr. Theodore Frye of gospel music fame. She got on her knees each Sunday morning and went all over Olivet Church collecting monies for the salary of J. Robert. In fact, she was successful in gathering as much as $200 to help him on his way.

In the meantime, the Reverend Branham had absconded. He told J. Robert that he was going to Pasadena, California to rest. It was in Pasadena that Dr. Carter had built one of his churches as he had done up and down the California coast. Unbeknownst to J. Robert, The Reverend Branham went to California to take up with the Reverend and to stay there. He was left in Chicago to fend for himself. Dr. Jackson did not offer any help. Just as painful was the fact that the church, for which he had given nineteen months of his life, did not even say "goodbye" to him as he prepared to take leave to go to New York City.

J. Robert began to make preparations to go to New York City. He had little money. However, he had friends and supporters back in Nashville. He had Dr. Arthur Melvin Townsend and Charles Bryan who cared for him greatly and would see to it that he got whatever he needed to further his vocal training. So, The Lord made a way for him through his friends to make the journey to New York City for training that would prepare him for the world.

XIX.

On To New York City And Life-Changing Experiences

Mr. Bradley's Chicago trials did not leave him bitter and discouraged. This was simply another step toward towering heights of greatness. Rejection at Olivet provided him the rare opportunity to traffick in lofty areas of prominence. Chicago was destined to be a launching pad to the Gotham City of New York.

The journey to New York City really began with Mr. Charles F. Bryan and Dr. A. M. Townsend. Both of these men believed that J. Robert Bradley was ready for serious preparation and vocal training. Their natural instincts informed them that Bradley was not to be relegated to one type of music, that of the Negro genre, Negro Spirituals, hymns, and gospel songs. They knew he had the capacity to sing anthems, classics, and even opera. This demanded knowledge of languages such as German, French, Italian, and maybe Russian. These men had a basic confidence in the capability of this rising virtuoso. Mr. Bryan and his friend Mr. Nicholas knew the eminent Madame Edyth Walker of New York. She was one of the foremost trainers in vocal music in the world.

Once again, J. Robert Bradley took a long train ride. This time it was from the Windy City of Chicago to the financial center and art capital of the world, New York City. His widening experiences were acquainting him all the more with what lies around the bend of the river and where the fluffy clouds go when they pass over the river-bound rendezvous he found as a young boy.

Always at home wherever he went, J. Robert Bradley arrived in New York City and quickly found a place to stay at the YMCA located at 135th Street and 7th Avenue. He really did not know where to go or what to do upon arriving in New York, he could only attribute his direction to the providence of God. But he had always had a knack for being friendly and making himself known to people. No matter where he went, people liked him. Because of this innate gregariousness, immediately Mr. Bradley became acquainted with Dr. O. Clay Maxwell, who had pastored in Memphis, Tennessee, Dr. Gardner

Taylor, and other powerful pastors who came to his assistance. These pastors, apparently apprised of Mr. Bradley's presence and business in New York City, became his supporters. They invited him to sing at their churches on Sundays. It was nothing for him to sing and receive an after offering of as much as $500.00. In the hands of God, Mr. Bradley did not have to suffer for want, even though in a strange land.

It so happened that at the time, Hall Johnson's Choir was preparing for a play entitled, "Run Little Children." This is the choir which did the music for the play, "Green Pastures." Coincidentally, the choir was rehearsing for the play in the basement at the YMCA where Mr. Bradley had taken up residence. Things were so tough for performers like the Hall Johnson Choir that they had to rehearse anywhere they could find space. While going down the hall at the YMCA, Mr. Bradley was singing at the top of his voice. It may have been that he found out about the choir rehearsing at the "Y" and wanted them to hear him. Well, for whatever reason, it worked. A little red woman who heard him singing as he frolicked down the hall, reached out and grabbed him. She was Juanita Hall from South Carolina. She was Hall Johnson's assistant. She grabbed him and pulled him into the room where the choir was rehearsing and told him to sit down. It was then that J. Robert joined the Hall Johnson Choir. It was incredible that becoming a member of the prestigious choir of Hall Johnson would happen so quickly and effortlessly.

Mr. Bradley did not have any particular lead parts in the choir. He simply sang as a choir member. However, he did participate in the play, "Run Little Children." His musically pensive nature delivered respectable dividends. He always paid special attention to the method of the music, the way it was played and sung. Of concern for him was the peculiarities of the music. There was one song the choir sang with 27 beats on a big drum. At every rehearsal, J. Robert counted those beats. He carefully counted them as though there was something important hanging onto each beat. At each rehearsal, Mr. Johnson used his skillful hands to direct the choir. He had powerful hands. Their mystical, musical movement wrung from each singer such sounds that caused the heavens to stand at attention and bend a listening ear. Angelic observers mused that something great was going on when Hall Johnson directed his choir. J. Robert had studied Mr. Johnson's hands, their mystical, magical, marvelous movement so that he knew the meaning of every motion from the downstroke. He knew the music so intensely that he knew every beat, syllable and word.

On one occasion while the choir was rehearsing, Mr. Johnson was directing the choir on the song with the 27 beats of the big drum. The choir was singing and Mr. Johnson was directing. When the 27 beats of the big drum came down, and the director pointed to the man who was to come in with a part, the man failed to come in with his part because he was looking off at something else. As if struck by some great power of compulsion, J. Robert Bradley came in the man's place singing correctly the part that was due at that time. The result of J. Robert's dramatic musical rescue was that he was retained as a permanent member of the choir. Mr. Bradley's involvement in the Hall Johnson Choir was a simultaneous development and compliment to the inception of vocal training that would bring him to stand before Kings and Queens.

XX.

Training Under The Incomparable Edyth Walker

The professional training of the vocal ability of J. Robert Bradley was uppermost in the mind of Dr. A. M. Townsend. But just as interested in his musical development was Mr. Charles Bryan of McMinnville, Tennessee. Mr. Bryan had taken personal interest in the vocal training of J. Robert and had carried him through more than two years of training in Cookeville and later at Peabody College in Nashville, Tennessee.

When the conditions came about when it was time for J. Robert to leave Chicago, coincidentally, Mr. Bryan manifested his passion and concern for his further development. He conceded that he had taken J. Robert as far as he could in terms of top grade vocal training. It was time now, he concluded, for Robert to go to New York City to train under a master teacher.

One day Mr. Bryan had a meeting with one of his friends, Mr. Lewis Nicholas. Mr. Nicholas was a music critic for one of the local newspapers in Nashville. He had expressed his knowledge of a person in New York City who might be able to help. He said her name was Edyth Walker, a Wagnerian soprano and a protégée of J. P. Morgan, the great philanthropist. Nicholas explained that Ms. Walker had lived in Germany for over 30 years. She had sung in the New York Metropolitan Opera House up to 1903. At that time she was on stage with the great Caruso, the two were performing together. It so happened that Edyth Walker held a note longer than Caruso and he kicked her on the leg in jealous protest. Edyth slapped him in disgust. Her Opera superiors told her that unless she apologized to Caruso and did the same on her knees before the great Vol Kirk, she would not be able to continue in the Metropolitan Opera. She became incensed and refused. She went to her home, packed her bags and left for Europe. She made Germany her home for the next sixty years. While in Germany, Edyth learned all the great operas and became one of the great teachers of opera. She became the head lady at the Munich Opera House and remained in that position for some time.

While in Germany, Edyth became an advocate for justice and a vocal opponent of the atrocities perpetrated against the Jews by Hitler during World

War II. Hitler expressed his rage against her for speaking in opposition to him. He knew her to be an American and that she had a wealthy supporter in J. P. Morgan. Nevertheless, Hitler put out an order to have her killed. Sal Hurok, Marian Anderson's manager, had kept up with Edyth all the time she was in Germany. When he learned that she was in trouble, he sent for her and brought her home to New York City.

When Edyth Walker arrived back home, she decided to take a few students. One was the renowned Marian Anderson, of course. Her manager had arranged for the rescue of Edyth when she faced some very dangerous circumstances. It was naturally an act of gratitude for her to take as a student the person who was managed by the one who saved her life from certain death. Another student she took was Blanche Thebom. She was the madame of the Opera House in Atlanta and even now operates the Opera House in that city. Other students were Harold Bordon and Y. L. K. Sze, Jan Pierce, and Richard Tucker. Mr. Bryan and Lewis Nicholas believed that if she were to ever hear J. Robert Bradley she would agree to accept him as one of her students as well.

When J. Robert pondered what was about to happen, he was indeed baffled. Here he was with all of his deficiencies preparing to appear before one of the premiere vocalists of all times and a professional instructor of the first magnitude. He had not completed school of any sort, he could not read music, and had no knowledge of languages at all. This woman was working with first class artists, sight readers, and those capable of speaking and singing in a variety of languages. But the time came for his opportunity to take another step in his development. He prayed that he would do well.

He had thought of how he would present himself when he appeared before Ms. Walker. He would employ the body posture Thomas Shelby had taught. He would throw his head back, draw in his stomach and sing from the diaphragm, stand erect with his feet together as they do in the military when they stand at attention, and he would open his mouth and let the words flow like the Mississippi and Wolf Rivers. The diction and word pronunciation Shelby had drilled into him would find currency when he stood before this giant of a woman in the world of music.

When J. Robert went to make his first presentation before Ms. Walker, he found her to be a woman stricken with years. She had large blue eyes. Her body was cast in frailty. Quietly, J. Robert thought to himself that because of her health problems alone, she had no business taking on another student, let alone someone of such background as his. But, he sighed, took a deep breath and thought to himself, "I really am glad to be here."

The moment of testing finally came. He had brought his little repertoire of music, not really knowing what would be appropriate. But he went on, trusting in The Lord who had never let him down. Ms. Walker sat in a chair, as straight and rigid as an army general, paying particular attention to this potential member of a peculiar kind of army, an army of musicians of the vocal sort. When the two had exchanged normal courtesies, J. Robert prepared to sing for this world renowned virtuoso. He knew he would be under the microscope of scrutiny. He knew that this evaluation of his potential could mean possible propulsion into another realm of life, or, it could mean that he would be moribund forever among musical mortals of a mediocre sort. But, here was his opportunity!

J. Robert began to sing. He sang with all that was in him. The finesse and refinement that his momma had taught, albeit living in the squalor and stench of Pinch in Memphis, the articulation and pronunciation that Thomas Shelby had drilled and instilled in him, the studiousness and diligence that Ms. Lucy had taught, and his own power of memory and determination to be somebody someday, began to issue forth as he opened his mouth in song. He sang as never before. Ms. Walker sat riveted to her seat. Her eyes popped wider and wider in utter astonishment. She listened to this musical phenomenon, her mouth fell ajar in stark amazement. She could not believe what she was hearing and presently experiencing in her home. She convinced herself that she was listening to something very unusual, a once in a lifetime voice. She thought to herself, "There is something to this young man which must be developed."

When J. Robert completed his presentation, silence gripped the room. He stood in place with a childish plea writ large upon his face. Edyth Walker did not know much of what to think. She sat in silence for what seemed to be the space of one half an hour. Finally, a look of approval began to etch itself across her face. With the deep resonating sound of the voice of J. Robert Bradley ricocheting against the chambers of her mind, she threw her hands up to her face. Her weathered and drawn hands began to tremble as they clutched her face. J. Robert looked and saw tears streaming down her face, cutting rivulets through her fingers, and heard her as she began to exclaim with approval, "Yes, yes, yes! I will do it."

It was incredible! J. Robert had just been assured that he would begin his training, training which would prepare him to sing to the world. He had no money. Other great performers were paying Ms. Walker $25 a week. But, he had no money and no way to get the kind of money needed to pay for his training. But in spite of that, his training was just about to begin.

Edyth Walker was a world renowned trainer of the first magnitude. She had a track record that was far reaching, including many of the top named musical performers in the industry. J. Robert Bradley would be added to her record. She began her task by introducing her cane to J. Robert. The cane was her ever-present companion. But it was more than a stabilizer and support for her unstable and failing physical frame. The Edyth Walker Cane was to be used to pop her newest student, J. Robert Bradley, when he went wrong in one of his assignments. If he forgot to roll his "r's", she would pop him with her cane and demand that he perform the task correctly. He had to work on it until he got it right.

Ms. Walker started J. Robert out on German *lieder* and would say German phrases and have him repeat them to her. If he did well, she was pleased. If he made a mistake, she would strike him with her cane as her demonstration of displeasure. Progress was being made. J. Robert was a good student and Ms. Walker found herself sharing musical intimacies with him. She shared with him her knowledge of outstanding musicians such as Chopin, Liszt, and the great German poet, Goethe. She told J. Robert many wonderful stories about her experiences with these people. She strove with all that was in her to lift the cultural level of J. Robert. In addition to teaching him the German language, the alphabet and words with which to build his vocabulary, she taught him to interpret German songs as he learned them. She taught him to translate them in such a way that he could fit them into his American, Western, and Southern mind. She really raised his cultural level to become an intellectual.

Some two years into his training with Ms. Edyth Walker, she threw fear into J. Robert by insisting that he have his tonsils removed. One day she told him to open his mouth. He did not know what to think, but reluctantly did as he was told. When she finished her examination, Ms. Walker said, "Well, you are going to have to have your tonsils removed." J. Robert panicked. He thought he would never sing again if he did that. Immediately, he called Charles F. Bryan to see if he should or should not have his tonsils removed. Ms. Walker was adamant, however, about the removal of his tonsils. She said, "Either you take those tonsils out, or you don't study with me any more." She sent J. Robert to Graduate Hospital in Philadelphia, Pennsylvania to a doctor who had worked on her throat in Munich, Germany. He looked into his mouth and agreed that his tonsils needed to be removed. The next day, the procedure was done and J. Robert was put to bed for the evening. The next day, he left the hospital and went to the home of Mrs. Figgs in Philadelphia, who was a member of Dr. William J. Harvey's church. His recovery was without incident, with the exception of terrific hunger which was caused by his inability to eat solid food. But J. Robert made adjustments so he could get food in his belly. He prepared some grits and sort of threw it down his throat, in some way that it did not touch his tonsils, until his belly was completely full. Once again, he was happy, his belly was full.

Ms. Walker began to speak of J. Robert as a Miracle Child. She was so pleased that she began to teach him a select number of German songs. There were times when she became very discouraged with the progress of J. Robert; but, she did not give up. Because she did not give up and worked with the innate abilities which J. Robert brought to the task, she began to observe phenomenal progress. J. Robert worked hard every day. He practiced from early in the morning to late in the evening. She even thought he was progressing so that, in her mind, she believed Robert was good enough for Carnegie Hall.

New York 23. **VII** '48

Dear Bradley!

Thank you most sincerely for your fine letter and the noble sentiments which you express. I am sure that you will attain what you deeply desire---to glorify God with your beautiful voice.

What about coming with SZE or alone, Tuesday afternoon? that I may hear the progress you are making. Call me up Tuesday.

Most cordially

Edyth Walker

Ps.: Many thanks for the lovely card from the South.

On one occasion, Mr. Charles Bryan from Cookeville, Tennessee came to New York to see J. Robert. In fact, there was a dual purpose for his coming. He had a friend there who was to conduct one of his compositions. Mr. Robert Shaw was an outstanding musician of the time and was located in New York City. He was a good and close friend to Charles Bryan. The two had communicated and agreed that Mr. Robert Shaw would direct a folk opera Bryan had composed, entitled, "The Bell Witch." Bryan and Shaw had arranged for the folk opera to be performed by the New York Philharmonic Symphony, under the direction of Mr. Shaw.

While Mr. Bryan and Mr. Shaw were together, they both discussed J. Robert's progress. They had been in consultation with Ms. Walker and had talked with her about his progress. They all considered that J. Robert had been in training now for four years. Their mutual agreement was that it was time for him to make a student debut at Carnegie Hall. All having agreed on this, fitful preparations were begun for the event. The date was set and plans were begun for the concert. Notices were prepared and mailed out to persons who would be interested in attending.

For the epochal event, Dr. A. M. Townsend was notified of J. Robert's student debut. With glad hearted anticipation, he prepared to make the journey to New York City. Dr. Townsend was the one person who had always supported Mr. Bradley with finance and encouragement. He sent a monthly check to pay for rent, food, and training. There were times when he sent a letter of encouragement, something that served as a catalyst of determination for J. Robert. He was intensely interested in the development of this young virtuoso. It was little wonder that he wanted to be present when his pride and joy made his debut at the famed Carnegie Hall.

The time came for the concert. Carnegie Hall was filled to capacity. It is the place where performing arts are truly at home. Whenever anything or anyone of significance is featured there, the connoisseurs of music make it theirs to be present. There was great wonder, however, about this unknown singer. No one had heard of J. Robert Bradley. He had not attended Juilliard School of Music, his name was not familiar in that community. Some of those who bought tickets to attend the concert did so out of force of habit. However, curiosity accompanied most of those who came; because, they simply were unfamiliar with this new voice in town. The only real currency J. Robert had was that he was a student of the renowned Edyth Walker. Everyone in music knew that Edyth Walker was the top of the line in music instructors. They also knew that she only dealt with the cream of the crop in musical talent. So, it stood to reason that this unknown vocalist had something to offer.

Robert took the stage. His dress was immaculate and his poise was impeccable. His thoughts were of Thomas Shelby and how he taught him to "Stand up straight. Throw that head back. Stick out that chest. Think about what you are doing. Spit out those words." His thoughts were of Ms. Lucy Campbell and how she gave him every chance he needed to sing before important and massive audiences. He thought of how he had memorized her songs and how he had to do the same thing to stand on the stage at Carnegie Hall. All these thoughts raced through his young mind as he prepared to lift his voice at the down stroke.

He began to make his contribution. It was smoothly delivered and warmly drew a supportive applause. As he offered up his repertoire in crescendo, J. Robert drew escalating applause. By the time the concert ended, the audience was drawn to its feet and enthralled in some kind of ecstasy, a gripping sense of awe. It was all because of this young man from Pinch in Memphis, Tennessee, the son of an illiterate father and mother, and a school dropout---J. Robert Bradley.

After the concert, Dr. Townsend was pleased. He bristled with happiness and pride at what J. Robert had done. Ms. Walker had told him of his progress, that he was a miracle child. She had also told him that she would do all in her power to help him. J. Robert accompanied Dr. Townsend to the train station. Dr. Townsend talked endlessly of what he had heard at Carnegie Hall. As he forced his way through a crowded train station with J. Robert struggling hard to keep up with him, his face gleamed with a radiant glow, a reflection of divine reverence and righteous pride. But as he approached the track where he was to board the train back to the south land, he turned to J. Robert and took him the by shoulders. He looked him in the eyes. He began to pour onto him words of thanks and praise for what he had done at Carnegie Hall. But he fastened his eyes onto J. Robert's and said to him, "Robert, I want you to learn all you can and do the very best you can. Do what your teachers tell you. But when you get through, come on back to the convention and sing hymns for the Baptists!" His thick arms and hands began to tremble as they lay heavily upon the shoulders of the young man in whom he had invested so much. His eyes were riveted to the eye of J. Robert. In his usual humble and obedient manner, J. Robert responded, "Yes sir." Dr. Townsend gave Robert some money, sufficient to tide him over for a good while, and stepped onto the train. He waved goodbye. The train pulled out of Grand Central Station and, belching black smoke and groaning, disappeared out of sight and went on back to Nashville. The news of J. Robert's success at Carnegie Hall swept across the nation and especially the world of National Baptists. In Nashville, at his home church, Spruce Street Baptist Church, his popularity flourished. There was a swelling tide of passionate interest to have him return to Nashville for a concert. Some of the members of Spruce Street Baptist Church, his home church in Nashville, led by persons such as Sis. Thelma Mason, began to plan for such an event. They thought to have the concert at the War Memorial Auditorium. They inquired into the possibility and discovered that they could do it. The next matter was to arrange to get J. Robert to Nashville. They then sought to secure train tickets for his trip to Nashville and back to New York. The date was set for the concert and things were set in motion.

The time arrived when J. Robert came back to his newly adopted home, Nashville, riding on the waves of his success at Carnegie Hall. The concert had been scheduled for Friday night October 12, 1951. The auditorium was completely packed. The Nashville church community had turned out to hear this rising star who had gone away and made good. The church membership at Spruce Street was present in full force. They were tremendously excited about this young man, whom they now claimed as their own.

At the time of the concert, Dr. A. M. Townsend was seated on the front row, waiting to hear the one who had come to be like unto him as a son. Everyone, indeed, sat on the edge of their seats, stood on tiptoe, as it were, in anticipation, waiting for the curtain to rise. The hour came with great drama and excitement.

When J. Robert took centerstage, he bowed gently to the crowd, which received him with a warm embrace which could be felt with spirit and mind. He was immaculately dressed. His shoes gleamed in the spotlights which shone down from the top of the stage. His posture was perfect and his one eye peered at the crowd with reverent devotion and wide-eyed appreciation for the warm hearted reception. In the audience was Mr. Charles Bryan, who had taught J. Robert so much of what he had learned. There was a visible pride **writ large** across his visage. He demonstrated a quiet enthusiasm with a face aglow at the fact that he was about to listen to one whom he had found so low but now had soared so high.

J. Robert had carefully selected his repertoire for the evening's concert. The Program Selections were as follows:

PROGRAM I

To Lo Sai .... Torelli 1651-1708
  (Well Thou Knowest)

Vittoria Mis Core .... Carissimi 1604-1674
  (Victorious, My Heart)

Hear Me, Ye Winds and Waves .... Handel 1685-1753

PROGRAM II

Gruppe aus dem Tartarus .... Schubert 1797-1828
Lied eines Schiffers an di Dioskuren .... Schubert
Aufenthalt .... Schubert

III

O Isis .... Mozart 1756-1791

PROGRAM IV

Blow, Blow, Thou Winter Wind .... Quilter
Come Away, Death .... Quilter
O Mistress Mine .... Quilter
The Blind Ploughman .... Radclyffe-Hall

PROGRAM V

Hear de Lambs A Cryin' .... Arranged-Brown
Goin' to Ride in de Chariot .... Arranged-Brown
Dere's A Man Goin' 'Round .... Arranged-Brown

PROGRAM VI

He Knows Just How Much You Can Bear .... Martin
Just To Behold His Face .... Campbell
King Jesus Will Roll All Burdens Away .... Morris

LESS WILLIAMS, Accompanist

All these he performed meticulously. Whirling through the minds of so many of the audience were thoughts of the background of this young man. Some knew of the rough life he had in Memphis' Pinch District with an illiterate father and mother. Many of them knew he had never completed school of any kind. But to their amazement, glee, and delight, here he was on stage in one of Nashville's prestigious performing arts settings singing classical music only known by the masters. On this night, background aside, they took delight that he handled himself like one of the masters.

Toward the end of the concert, an emotional moment stirred the audience. Whenever Baptists come together in a church setting, there is always the desire "to feel something." J. Robert had sung classical numbers, many of which were done in foreign languages. He had shown mastery of these languages, as though he had attended Fisk University and had taken a Ph.D. in foreign languages. Although the program had not concluded, Dr. Townsend arose and went to the stage and beckoned to J. Robert. He paused and out of deference to this man who had come to be like a father to him went over to hear what he had to say. When he bent down to hear Dr. Townsend, he saw fire and fervor in his eyes. His eyes gripped his and did not let them go. Then "Doctor" said to J. Robert, "Robert, sing 'Amazing Grace'…for me!!!" As "Doctor" finished his impassioned request, he held both of his fists to his chest and drew them briskly to his bosom, thumping his bosom two or three times, and drew a deep breath as he said, ". . .for me!!!" J. Robert said obediently, "Yes, sir" and went back to the center of the stage. When he lifted up that familiar bass baritone voice with the familiar "Townsend arranged" "Amazing Grace," the audience went to pieces. The Holy Ghost came down and filled the whole house.

XXI.

The Death Of Edyth Walker

Ms. Edyth Walker meant so much to J. Robert Bradley. She had taken him from nowhere and set him on the course to somewhere. She had taken a voice which had been rough-hewn out of the ghettoes of Memphis, Tennessee and fashioned it to face the world of music. But now, a horrible reality appeared on the horizon of the life of J. Robert Bradley---the loss of Ms. Walker.

Shortly after J. Robert's success at Carnegie Hall, Ms. Walker took sick. Age had taken its toll on her. She had demonstrated evidence of the encroachment of sickness. She was lethargic and favored her cane more than usual by placing more of her weight on it. This development proved to be disastrous for J. Robert. He had not been around anybody who had done so much for him, gotten sick, and then died. But, he was about to experience that harsh reality.

Suddenly, Edyth Walker was stricken with a paralyzing stroke. She was hit very hard by the stroke. She had everything going against her. Her age, her poor health, and lack of physical strength simply could not give her what she needed to override the ravages of a stroke. She sensed that she had been hit with a lethal blow. J. Robert was struck with fear that the one person who had delivered him from the pit of mediocrity and the ranks of also rans was on the verge of death. He saw this as the harbinger of worse things to come. J. Robert had never been as close to anyone who had meant so much to him and his development as Edyth Walker. To lose her would be devastating to J. Robert Bradley. The announcement of her sickness left him in a state of shock.

On her sick bed, Edyth Walker called all her students to her bedside. With the exception of Marian Anderson, who was in Connecticut, all went hastily to her bedside. With death lapping at her soul, she assured support of her students. But for J. Robert, she had a very different but important message. Before going into her sick room, J. Robert thought of the many things Ms.

Edyth Walker had done for him. She had told him so many wonderful stories of the great musicians of the world. She had taught him how to sing in the Germanic language. She had taught him the meaning of opera songs, what was behind them. Just as importantly, she had taught him culture and lifted the level of his life to the intellectual. He was not sure if he could take the sudden transition that seemed so imminent.

When it came his time to go in to see Ms. Walker, he really was not prepared. When he went in, he immediately began to cry. He thought of what she had meant to him. He wept uncontrollably. On her sick bed, however, she sat up and shot back at J. Robert to desist from his weeping. She said, "Don't you dare look in my face and cry!" "Don't you dare!" she said, as she tried to raise up her emaciated body, vibrating with passion. Already frail from the burden of the years, her arms, hands, and body showed the protrusion of her skeletal frame, with loose and emaciated flesh hanging lifelessly thereon. Again she said, "Don't you dare look in my face and cry. You had everything against you. You are Black! You have no money! You cannot read and you do not know music. It is going to take everything you have to pull this train up to the top of the mountain and I am depending on you. You hear me, Robert?" That was the last time J. Robert Bradley saw his instructor, Edyth Walker. She drew her last breath and died.

The death of Edyth Walker was devastating to J. Robert Bradley. He never knew the extent of the influence this woman of women had on his life.

J. Robert simply could not get over the death of his friend and mentor. He was not the same after her death. He could never get over her death. To exacerbate the situation, the body of Ms. Walker was cremated. This was rather shocking because he had never known of the cremation of one of his friends. But, he watched as his tutor and friend was cremated. It was not a pleasant scene. Realizing this was a method by which some people exited this life, he resigned to the practice. It was a new experience, one from which he could not easily overcome. After the cremation, some of his friends took him home and put him to bed.

Mr. Bradley was so affected by the death of Ms. Walker that he was unable to sing. For almost one year, Mr. Bradley was unable to sing. The death of Ms. Edyth Walker was so devastating that he simply was unable to bring himself to utter a note. Robert could not sing, whether in church, in school, or anywhere. It took what seemed to be forever for him to recover from the staggering loss. There was none in New York who had given the time and attention to the development of J. Robert other than Edyth Walker. He was paralyzed at the thought of her being gone. In time, he came to realize that death was a part of life. But, the question of what would happen now that Ms. Walker was gone became uppermost in his mind. She had answered the question before her death. She had said to him, "I am going to leave you in the hands of the bass from China, one of my students. His name is Mr. Zee." She said, "You will be a bass and Mr. Zee is a bass now. He will help you." Ms. Walker thought she could leave J. Robert in the hands of Mr. Y. K. Zee. It was thoughtful of her; for, he was an excellent singer and possibly would be an excellent instructor. He was an excellent artist and knew much about the craft. Mr. Bradley tried to work with Mr. Zee for about six months. But, it did not work. His Chinese background did not blend with this Black man from Pinch in Memphis, Tennessee. He really did not think much of working with J. Robert. He felt to work with him was a step down, he was not on the same intellectual level as himself. In time, Mr. Bradley left Mr. Zee. It was fortunate, indeed, that J. Robert remembered what his mother had taught him at home. Somehow he knew that he was in the hands of God who would make a way for him.

XXII.

The World Becomes A Stage: Preparation For London And Beyond

Charles Bryan came back to New York to look in on J. Robert. When he came, he was told of the experience with Mr. Zee. But, J. Robert told Mr. Bryan about Lawrence Brown. Lawrence Brown was the accompanist for Roland Hayes and for more than five years with Paul Robeson. Lawrence Brown had been in London, England working with Roland Hayes. He was an excellent pianist and accompanist. But Mr. Hayes' unpredictable personality caused him to fall out with Mr. Brown. In one of his fits of rage, Mr. Hayes went off and left Lawrence Brown in London without any money at all. Mr. Brown was left to fend for himself. Coincidentally, Paul Robeson was brought to London to do "Showboat." For political reasons, he was not allowed to sing any longer in America. Mr. Robeson had not had a personality such as Lawrence Brown, that calibre of musician, to play for him. Upon arriving at London, however, Roger Quilter told him that there was a fine Black American living in London. He was referring, of course, to Lawrence Brown. The two met. It was a perfect match. Lawrence Brown was out of work and Paul Robeson needed an accompanist. They immediately became partners. Mr. Robeson learned that Lawrence Brown, who was from down south in America, knew how to play Negro Spirituals and knew how to accompany him. Lawrence Brown stayed with Paul Robeson for thirty-eight years. Initially, he played for him in London for "Showboat." He travelled all over with the famous singer, accompanying him on concerts all over Europe. During the ensuing years, Mr. Robeson took sick and died, and left Mr. Brown with no one, at least of Robeson's calibre, to accompany. He went back to New York, vowing not to play for anyone else.

It so happened that J. Robert learned of Mr. Brown's presence in New York just as he and Mr. Zee parted company. J. Robert and Mr. Zee simply came to a great divide in the road. They could not get along. But a bad experience opened the door for a good experience. Mr. Brown as an instructor would be a boon indeed.

Mr. Bryan was supportive of J. Robert's desire to seek out Lawrence Brown as an instructor. There were a couple of times subsequent to his conversation with Mr. Bryan when J. Robert saw Mr. Brown. He watched the building where Mr. Brown lived and waited for him to come out. When J. Robert approached him, he said, "Go away, go away, I do not want to be bothered," obviously irritated. On another occasion, when Brown saw Robert coming, he turned and quickly walked the other way. Each time J. Robert saw him, he called out to him, "Mr. Brown, you have got to help me!" However, each time Mr. Brown ran off in the other direction. J. Robert was later to discover that Lawrence Brown had considered himself to be finished with singers. He had been with Roland Hayes and Paul Robeson and wanted nothing to do any longer with singers. Finally, J. Robert successfully accosted Lawrence Brown. He apprehended him so he could not get away. It was then that he pleaded his case and laid his plight before him. Brown gave him the directions to come to his apartment the next morning. Robert went up to his apartment and sang for him. Brown did not know what J. Robert had done prior to meeting him and what he had to offer. He had never heard of him. But once hearing him, he agreed to take him on.

This new relationship opened up new avenues of opportunities and relationships with personalities previously unknown to J. Robert Bradley. Lawrence Brown lived at 138 West 135th Street in an apartment on the very top floor. His apartment was just across the street from the Red Rooster, a lounge. Also in the vicinity was Small's Bar. At the intersection of 135th Street and 7th Avenue, thousands of people made transfers on the bus lines. Among the thousands making their transfer each day was the eminent Harry T. Burleigh. He was making his way down from his home in The Bronx to Mid-Manhattan. Mr. Burleigh was so prominent and outstanding as a vocalist that a rich philanthropist built a massive cathedral in downtown Manhattan in which he was to be the featured singer. He sang there until he was full of years.

On occasion, J. Robert Bradley met Mr. Burleigh at the transfer intersection. The two greeted each other amiably and, normally, went on their way. There were days when Mr. Burleigh was very irritable. When J. Robert approached him to shake hands, he'd withdraw almost angrily saying, "Don't touch me! Don't touch me! I'm hurting all over." He walked away in what seemed to be great anguish and pain. J. Robert did not know what to make of it at first. As time went on, however, he noticed that if he met Mr. Burleigh after he had made a stop at one of the local establishments, he would be very cordial, excited, and would almost shake his hand off.

Navigation to and from the apartment of Lawrence Brown proved to be quite hazardous. There were dangers unseen far more threatening than the jolting handshakes Harry T. Burleigh gave when he was not "hurting all over."

On one occasion while walking along to go to Lawrence Brown's apartment, suddenly a large object dropped from above and landed immediately in front of him. Had he made another step forward on the crowded sidewalk, he would have been hit in the top of the head and killed instantly. The falling object was an appliance motor which someone dropped from an apartment window. No one was hit, fortunately.

New York presented another brush with death for J. Robert. While walking through Central Park, he came upon a garden with flowers or maybe weeds which affected his breathing. He found his breathing labored and the more he tried to breath, the more it became difficult. He suddenly thought he was going to die, because he could not get his breath in any way. He began to run. That was all he knew to do. He remembered a doctor's office close by the park, so he ran for his office. When he got there, they quickly began to work on him, administering medication to alleviate his condition. He finally was all right, but not before he had been told he had a close brush with death. J. Robert Bradley reckoned that the path to musical preparation and maybe prominence would be through many dangers, toils, and snares, even through the valley and shadow of death.

The union with Lawrence Brown was entirely beneficial for J. Robert. Lawrence Brown taught him the English way of singing, the English repertoire, and all the finer touches and tones he needed to be accepted in London later on. In fact, when Mr. Bradley went to London, he was immediately accepted to sing for the British Broadcasting Corporation. Lawrence Brown indeed prepared J. Robert Bradley for the life of classical music in London. Mr. Brown coached J. Robert on the whole gamut of music. He trained him in the classics and Negro Spirituals as well. The more J. Robert worked with Lawrence Brown, the more Mr. Brown was impressed with the voice of this young vibrant neophyte in the music world. Everyone who heard J. Robert was impressed with his voice. Mr. Hurok, the manager of Ms. Marian Anderson, was immensely impressed. Harold Holt in London was immediately impressed with his voice.

Once Lawrence Brown cultivated Mr. Bradley to the point where he thought he was capable of handling more advanced training, he suggested that J. Robert go to London. Mr. Bryan in Nashville agreed with this assessment. Lewis Nicholas in Nashville also conformed to this conclusion. Dr. Townsend agreed to continue his financial support for J. Robert. He had been sending monthly checks to him out of his own personal account to support him up to this point. All of Robert's room and board, his personal expenses, music lessons, etc., were paid for by Dr. Townsend. He agreed willingly to continue that support in London.

RITES HELD FOR LAWRENCE BROWN, FAMED COMPOSER, SINGER, PIANIST

NEW YORK - Private funeral services were held recently for Lawrence Brown, composer, vocalist and pianist who was for many years accompanist to Paul Robeson.

Brown, 79, who resided for the last 47 years at 138 West 135th St., died Dec. 25, at Harlem Hospital.

One of the foremost arrangers of Negro spirituals, he was born in Jacksonville, Fla. His father, like Robeson's, had been born in slavery.

In 1914 Brown moved to Boston where, while working as an elevator operator, he studied music and later won a scholarship for full-time study.

In 1920 he went to London where he studied composition at Trinity College and published the first of more than 400 arrangements he made of Negro folk songs.

* * *

In London, Brown was

LAWRENCE BROWN

tutored in music and voice by Amanda Ira Aldridge, daughter of Ira Aldridge the Afro-American who won fame in Europe as a Shakespearean actor and was the first black man to play the title of "Othello."

While living in England, Brown met Roland Hayes, the noted black tenor, for whom he was accompanist at a Buckingham Palace command performance in 1921, and then for four years on Hayes' concert tours.

Brown's partnership with Robeson, which lasted for 38 years, began in 1925 when the two young performers made musical history at their first concert recital with program comprised entirely of Afro-American songs. The influence of Brown on Robeson's singing career was noted by the latter in his book, "Here I Stand, " where he wrote of his "great good fortune" in having teamed up with Brown.

"Lawrence Brown," wrote Robeson, "was firm in his conviction that our music---Negro music of African derivation---was in the tradition of the world's great folk music. And so for my first five years as a singer, my repertoire consisted entirely of my people's songs."

Brown, who retired in 1963 when illness brought an end to Robeson's career, was a bachelor. He left no immediate survivors.

[Note: This article is from the personal effects of Dr. J. Robert Bradley. It is from an unidentified newspaper which has no date written on the clipping. However, it has been established that Mr. Brown's death was 1972.]

On the eve of the voyage, J. Robert pondered the inestimable good that Dr. Arthur Melvin Townsend had been for him. He mused that nobody had meant as much to him as Dr. Townsend. All the while he was in New York, checks came in the mail as faithfully as the sunrise. These were not checks drawn on the account of the Sunday School Publishing Board; they were drawn on his own personal account. In a dream, J. Robert saw Dr. Townsend as reflective of his love and care for him. Robert saw Dr. Townsend with two blankets. He said, "Here Robert!" and took a blanket and threw it over him. Robert knew then that "Doctor," as he affectionately called his boss, did not want him to be cold. J. Robert knew Dr. Townsend loved good music and appreciated what he had done and anticipated what he was going to do for National Baptists; so in the dream, it was little wonder that "Doctor" would take one of the two blankets he had to cover him to make sure he would not get cold, or, to be sure he was covered and taken care of---that all of his needs were taken care of. Those thoughts satisfied J. Robert that he would be taken care of in London and anywhere else he would go. But he also knew that he would ultimately go back to Nashville and to "Doctor" to make good his pledge to sing hymns for National Baptists.

The noted pianist and accompanist for Marian Anderson, Billy King, was planning a trip to London. He often vacationed in London. This was one of those times when he was going to London for his vacation. Plans were made for Mr. Bradley to accompany Billy King on the Atlantic voyage. While awaiting the exciting time of departure, a going away party was arranged for J. Robert by one of his very special friends, Marie Sampson. If ever there was a woman with whom J. Robert fell in love, it was Marie Sampson. She was a beautiful woman. She was angelic in her physical features, her face and figure, and she was exquisite in her dress. Her long hair often fell across her face and enhanced its Italian features. J. Robert loved her.

Marie wanted to do whatever would strengthen J. Robert's possibilities of developing his music career. The least she could do at this point, she thought, was to provide for him a **bon voyage** party. And so it was. She invited all of his friends to her place at 574 St. Nicholas in New York City. She greeted them with fine foods, exotic fruit, tantalizing vegetables, and all the accoutrements to make a memorable evening and highlight the departure of her special friend, J. Robert Bradley.

The time came in 1952 for the big trip. Passage had been booked for J. Robert Bradley on the Queen Elizabeth from New York to London. It was an exciting time for him, but foremost in his mind was that he was going to London for help. But getting on that giant ship was an euphoric experience. J. Robert had never been in such a setting. So many people! People from around the world. Speaking different languages. And the boat. It was so large. It was immaculately clean. He found himself wanting to go all over it, to examine it, to explore it, to experience it.

Standing on the deck of the ship, J. Robert looked at the disappearing skyscrapers of New York City. This was a city bustling with excitement. It was a new and vibrant city. It had introduced him to a much different and faster lifestyle than that which he knew in Memphis and Nashville, Tennessee. His eye was enlarged with excitement. He looked with a sense of disbelief at the tall buildings on Manhattan, amazed that he, of all people, would be taking such a journey. As he beamed at the city disappearing behind the ocean's horizon, a faint smile of disbelief but deep satisfaction was etched across his face. He wheeled around and frolicked across the deck, the cool summer ocean breeze briskly brushing joyfully and playfully across his face. His young body was bursting with energy. With that energy, he bounded up steps as though he were in Pinch or somewhere in Memphis paddling his car tire as though it were his own Cadillac. As he conquered one level after another, he turned about to view the surroundings. They were all different and beautiful. He went to the galley where an abundance of food was served. He toured the gaming area. He came upon the place for exercise and games of athletics. All over the boat he found himself. From the top of the boat to the bottom. From one end of the boat to the other, he had business. It was like a child exploring a brand new world. It was like reliving his youth as he branched out from Pinch into the larger world of Memphis, Tennessee. At the close of the day, he had a sumptuous meal. He had never been in a place where he could eat all the steaks he could hold. When he made that discovery, he ordered them two at a time. He raided the giant fruit trays, filled with large, luscious peaches and plums from Jerusalem. When he had finished and gotten his fill of food, he burped as he did on the banks of the Mississippi River when he had gotten full on the sweet rolls from Snider's bakery washed down with a drink from his water jug. He then went to his suite for a good night's sleep.

During the three to four day trip, J. Robert was privileged to render a concert on board the Queen Elizabeth. Billy King was familiar with procedures onboard the boat. He arranged to have J. Robert render the concert. He went to the purser and told him there was a young singer on board and the people would do good to hear him. He told the man that he had an unusual voice and wondered if they would want to have him render a concert. They responded, "Yes, gladly so!" J. Robert sang for the people. He did Handel's "Where Ere You Walk," the Negro Spiritual, "Swing Low, Sweet Chariot," and about two or three other selections. The people received him beautifully. After the concert, he gained immediate popularity. Admirers invited him to join them in their gatherings. In fact, he was invited to join one party in the first class section of the steamliner and was privileged to spend time there, even to recline in peaceful sleep amidst lavish and sumptuous quarters.

Arriving in London was to experience a world unlike anything J. Robert Bradley had ever known. It was an older world; a slower world; a settled and staid world; a world steeped in history; and, a world truly given to the arts. Early on he experienced the laid-back attitude of British life, the slower-than-slow style of living in England. He immediately made friends in London. He was always able to make friends anywhere he went. The same was true in London. His friends invited him to accompany them to Northern England. They were to make the trip in a chauffeur-driven automobile. J. Robert needed some money, so he went to the bank at Trafalgar Square in which he had placed some of his money. There was a sense of urgency to things, he was in a rush and needed to make the money transaction at the bank quickly. Knowing his friends were waiting for him---they needed to get on the way because of the distance of the trip---he rushed into the bank and stepped up to the tellers station, panting, and blowing, out of breath. "Five Pounds, please! Five Pounds, please!" was his urgent request. The stoic teller simply stood there, as though at military attention, with his head straight up, looking over the head of J. Robert. When Robert finished making his out-of-breath request and had settled down, realizing the man was not responsive, the man finally looked down at him and said, "England is a way of life!" That was his way of saying that in England, people do not get in a hurry for anyone or anything. With those kinds of experiences, he really began to know what was beyond the riverbend on the Mississippi and where clouds go when they are wafted by the wind beyond the eye's view on the banks of the Wolf and Mississippi Rivers. But common to himself, he immediately was at home, even in Foggy London Town.

NOTE: The following is an article which appeared in <u>THE MEMPHIS COMMERCIAL APPEAL</u> by Eldon Roark. The article, under the general rubric, "Strolling," was the first to follow the career and development of J. Robert Bradley. The article appeared in the August 2, 1952 edition.

STROLLING
with Eldon Roark

Recollection of Tragic Days

A short, neatly-dressed, heavy-set man, smiling and flashing the prettiest set of even white teeth we've seen in many a day, came in to see us yesterday---and took us back in memory to one of the most dramatic moments of the great flood of 1937.

As the waters rolled down the Mississippi Valley that year, thousands of people in the lowlands had to flee for their lives. Memphis on the bluffs was a haven, and they came in a steady stream, a pitiful procession of weary, bewildered, mud-splattered, homeless people. The Auditorium was turned into a huge receiving station. There the refugees were registered, vaccinated, given meals and temporary shelter before they were assigned to camps at the Fairgrounds and elsewhere.

One of those tragic days I was strolling at the Auditorium when I was attracted by singing in the south hall. It was crowded with negroes. Red Cross officials had sent them there to sit and wait their turn at being processed. It was a good place to rest and it kept them from getting scattered all over the place.

Officials also had suggested to negro volunteer workers that they might get the refugees to sing. That would help to take their minds off their troubles.

Sweet Chariot Was Swinging Low

So, as I entered the hall, a negro boy, about 17, was leading the singing, which was gaining steadily in volume, fervor, intensity. They were singing hymns, well-known negro spirituals, making the sweet chariot swing low. The boy not only had a good voice, buy he had the power to whip them up to a spiritual frenzy. Soon he had them---men, women and children---throwing their heads back, opening their mouths wide and aiming their voices right at heaven. All of God's 'chillen' might not have shoes, but they could trust Him.

The fervor kept swelling, the singing kept getting louder and louder. Then some of the refugees started shouting. Hallelujah! Praise the Lord! The whole building reverberated with the music and the wailing and the shouting. And the boy who was leading them urged them on. Let yourself go. Throw back your head and sing what's in your heart.

All of a sudden a Red Cross official charged thru a rear door and ran down an aisle toward the stage, waving his arms and shouting, "Just a minute, just a minute! Hold it, hold it! Just a minute!"

The singing stopped. "It's all right to sing," the official said, "But we can't have this. Let's calm down a bit. You're disturbing everybody else in the building. People can't talk." Then he hurried on out.

But there was no more singing. The spirit was gone. The young director wasn't interested in any halfhearted effort. When he led singing he wanted people to let themselves go if the spirit moved 'em.

There was much mumbling in the audience. "Can't he'p shoutin'. When you feel like shoutin', you got to shout."

They sat in glum silence and awaited their turns at the processing desks.

The Beginning of a Career

That young singer and director was a Memphis boy---J. Robert Bradley. And altho only 17, he had already attained some local fame in negro church circles. A few years before he had been discovered by Lucy E. Campbell, teacher at Booker T. Washington High and hymn writer. It happened at a Press-Scimitar Goodfellows party for negro children at the Auditorium.

As the party progressed, the children at the party were led in Christmas songs.

Outside the Auditorium was a group of negro children whose relatives and friends had neglected to get tickets for them. So they just showed up, hoping. Among them was 12-year-old Robert Bradley. And when he heard the children inside singing, he, too, started singing. He sang so loudly and so well that he made himself heard inside. Lucy Campbell was thrilled by his voice. She went out to him. She took him in to sing for everybody.

She had discovered an artist.

From Memphis He Went Places

So that's the background of the heavy-set, smiling man who came in to see us yesterday. We had forgotten the singing incident of the flood, but he brought it all back. We hadn't seen him since that day, 15 years ago and we learned he has gone places since then. He told us all about it.

When he left Memphis, he joined the late Dr. L. K. Williams, president of the National Baptist Convention, Inc., which has 4,000,000 negro members across America. He traveled with him 18 months as a soloist and singing director till Dr. Williams was killed in an airplane mishap.

Then Bradley went to New York with the Hall-Johnson Choir, and was in the Broadway show, "Run Little Chillen."

He came back to Memphis for a while---his mother and brother still live here---and got into church music. Charles F. Bryan, head of the music department at Peabody College, heard him sing in a revival at McMinnville and offered to help him train his voice. He studied privately under Prof. Bryan for a few years, and then Prof. Bryan sent him to New York to study under Madame Edyth Walker, famous Metropolitan opera soprano. She was reluctant to take him, because she already had all the students she could teach. But when she heard Bradley sing "Let Us Break Bread Together on Our Knees," she told him, with tears running down her cheeks, that she would teach him. "You will become a great singer."

He studied with her till her death, making his living thru his singing at revivals and church concerts. And when he was hard up, he also made some records---but he isn't proud of them.

Now he is director of music for the National Sunday School Baptist Training Union Congress and soloist for the National Baptist Convention, Inc., with headquarters in Nashville.

And He Will Study in Europe

He is, however, taking a two-year leave and will soon be on his way to study in Europe under the most famous voice teachers in England and on the continent. This great opportunity has been arranged for him by Dr. A. M. Townsend. Dr. Townsend is secretary of the National Baptist Sunday School Publishing Board, but his sponsorship is on a personal basis.

Critics say Bradley's voice, baritone-bass, has great resonance, power, beauty. He, however, attributes his success to the Holy spirit as well as to his voice---to the prayers he learned to say at his mother's knee.

"I'm against jazzing church music," he says.

He also attributes his success to the help and encouragement he has received from friends, white and colored. He believes people of all colors and creeds in America will help a boy or girl with ambition if they are approached in the right spirit.

His ambition? Well, when he returns from Europe, he would like to give his first concert here at the Auditorium---up there where Lucy Campbell discovered him singing his sad little heart out on that Christmas long ago.

XXIII.

The Crucible Of London: Training For Greater Things

Once in London, Billy King introduced J. Robert Bradley to Mr. Roger Quilter, a renowned instrumentalist and musician **par excellence**. In preparation for J. Robert's visit to London, Lawrence Brown had made contact with Roger Quilter on his behalf. Upon their arrival, Billy King simply took him to formally meet with Mr. Quilter. When his mission was over, he left J. Robert in Quilter's care. Roger Quilter was a world renowned musician and instructor of the first magnitude. He was such a musical genius that he took Shakespearean poems and phrases and set them to music. "Drink to me only with thine eyes," was one of his masterpieces. He befriended Blacks from America, and helped them develop their musical talent, probably one of the few who did. Among the Black Americans he had assisted were Roland Hayes, Paul Robeson, and Marian Anderson. These had gone before J. Robert Bradley. They had gone before him in many ways. Academically, they exceeded anything he brought to the experience. Roland Hayes was a graduate of Fisk University in Nashville, Tennessee; Paul Robeson had completed his schooling at Rutgers University in New Jersey; and, Marian Anderson had completed college in Philadelphia. It just so happened that as J. Robert was settling down in London, the world renowned Fisk Jubilee Singers from Nashville, Tennessee were scheduled to make a September 26, 1952 appearance at the Royal Festival Hall. They were extolled by the British for their contribution to the world of music since 1865. The Fisk Jubilee Singers were at home in London and England. They were a part of the intellectual landscape. J. Robert had none of these academic accomplishments to bring to the experience. He had not completed grammar school or high school. But, he brought to the experience the grit of determination to make something of himself and the most unique and powerful voices the world had ever heard. These two qualities were compelling enough for Roger Quilter to take on J. Robert as a student.

Upon settling down from his grueling and exciting trip on the Queen Elizabeth, Mr. Bradley took up residence in Paddington, a section in London.

Then he met a member of the Royal Family, Lord Barry Wayne McHughes. He moved in with the family at 32 Gloucester Place in London. God fixed it so that this large door of opportunity was open to him. Because of the location of his residence in London, J. Robert was exposed to some of the world's outstanding personalities. At 32 Gloucester Place, he met Sir Randolph Churchill. He was the son of the noted statesman, Sir Winston Churchill of Great Britain. Ralph Von Williams, the director of the London Philharmonic Orchestra was another person with whom Mr. Bradley had the pleasure of meeting and becoming close friends. Mr. Williams was Mr. Music in the city of London in that time. Saul A. Gorlinsky, the impresario of London was another personality J. Robert came to know. He was responsible for bringing outstanding musicians into the city. This is the man who ultimately was persuaded to open the door for his appearance at the Royal Festival Hall. Jack Samuels was another outstanding personality J. Robert came to know while living at the residence of royalty. Mr. Samuels was the owner of a chain of jewelry stores all across Europe. He came to be very kind to Mr. Bradley. If it happened that Dr. A. M. Townsend's check to J. Robert was late or something happened that placed him in a bind, Mr. Samuels had his bank to send a check to Robert's bank to be put into his account to tide him over. He came to be a true friend.

Most prominent of all personalities he met as a result of residing with the Royal Family was that of the noted theologian, physician, evangelist, organist, and missionary, Albert Schweitzer. Lord Barry Wayne McHughes, being of the Royal Family of England, quite naturally had a great many friends around the country and the world. One of these was Ms. Clara Urquhart. Clara Urquhart, a prominent millionaire, knew a great many notables in the world, including Dr. Albert Schweitzer. It so happened that Ms. Urquhart had come to London for the summer of the year 1953. Being a friend of Lord Barry Wayne McHughes, she was welcome to be house guest with the Royal Family at 32 Gloucester Place. Coincidentally, Dr. Schweitzer had scheduled the delivery of a speech on the West End of London. Dr. Schweitzer was well known in several areas of life. He travelled all over the world just to play the old pipe organs in the chapels and cathedrals of great cities. His theological acumen caused him to be in demand all over the world as well. It was such an occasion that brought him to London.

A Ms. Anderson, a photographer from New York City, had been attempting to get to Dr. Schweitzer to take pictures of his mission work and hospital in Africa and to write stories about the same. She had been unsuccessful, and as a last resort called on Ms. Clara Urquhart for assistance. Ms. Urquhart suggested that she come to London and prepare to meet Dr. Schweitzer while he was there.

When time came for the visit to the West End location where Dr. Schweitzer was to appear, Ms. Urquhart invited J. Robert to accompany her. He gladly agreed. He had heard of Dr. Schweitzer, his missionary work, his theological involvement, and his musical prowess as well. He was elated that he was to see such an outstanding personality. When he arrived at the auditorium where Schweitzer spoke, he finally was introduced to the man. He was a charming man. J. Robert had known that Dr. Schweitzer was not a man who was easily accessible. But, Ms. Urquhart had opened the door of opportunity to meet this world class individual.

When the opportunity presented itself, J. Robert met Dr. Schweitzer at which time he was given a picture of the theologian/physician. Much later, Dr. Schweitzer sent him an autographed slip of paper at J. Robert's request because he had failed to autograph the picture. Clara Urquhart sent the slip of paper back to J. Robert with his signature and a little note written thereon, **"Das est das,"** or "That is that." In the correspondence, Clara Urquhart said, "Dear Bob, accept this as a wonderful gift from 'Doctor' because he is slowly sinking. Don't feel bad that he did not say anything else, be proud." The joy of meeting Dr. Albert Schweitzer was that of the joy of a little child receiving a piece of candy. It was like magic. J. Robert later in life thanked God and cried aloud for allowing him to meet such great people. These were the kind of prestigious personalities J. Robert was privileged to meet due to his residency at 32 Gloucester Place in London.

J. Robert plunged immediately into study. He had single-minded concentration on the purpose of his journey. He was there to study and train to develop what God had given him in Pinch, a voice that would take him around the world. He was not there to frolic about and play. He was there on a specific and sincere mission. Roger Quilter got him underway in serious study, but at the same time he pointed J. Robert in the direction of other tutors who could help him. He enrolled at the Trinity College of Music in London where he studied for a period of about three years. He studied there under the tutorship of Mr. Levy.

Mr. Quilter gave J. Robert invaluable training. Initially, he assisted him in his pronunciation of simple phrases and parts of speech. Robert had a problem pronouncing his "ings." Mr. Quilter said to him, "Robert, you are from the South and you are having trouble pronouncing your `ings.' You have got to pronounce your `ings' properly." "See if you can get this," he said. "A man was calling his butler and said, 'Where is Mr. Plunk<u>ing</u>?' The butler said, `Why Mr. Plunk<u>ing</u> is in the kit<u>chen</u> pluck<u>ing</u> the chic<u>ken</u>.'" Then he said to Robert, "You get that?" "Work on pronouncing those 'ings!'" Mr. Quilter recognized he did not have the intellectually astute product he had in Hayes, Robeson, or Anderson, but he knew he had a far more superior voice than any of the three. Thus, he was painstaking with J. Robert toward the development of his full potential.

Although he enrolled at the Trinity College of Music, London, Robert continued to study under Mr. Roger Quilter. He also was guided by Mr. Quilter to Amanda Ira Aldridge. At this time, she was about eighty-five years of age, but still a virtuoso of the first magnitude. She was the daughter of a Polish mother and Black American from Florida. Her father, Ira Aldridge, was a great Shakespearean actor. His statues are located all over Europe. When he died, he was buried in Poland. His daughter, Amanda, was a prote'gee' of the great Swedish nightingale, Jenny Lynn. She had sung all over in the great concert halls of Europe and England. In addition, when Paul Robeson was to play the part of **Othello The Moor** in London, Amanda let him use her father's sword. This was the Amanda Ira Aldridge with whom J. Robert Bradley was to study. Others under whom he studied while in London were Roy Henderson, Frank Titterton and Mr. Levy at the Trinity College of Music, London. These were the people with whom Robert studied and from whom he learned myriads of lessons in music. One taught him English methods of music, another taught Germanic language, still another taught French, and another taught Italian. One taught diction, another taught Handel's style, and still another taught Schubert's style. He spent about an hour with each of his teachers each day. This kind of multifaceted study constituted the daily rigorous training for J. Robert. It was like a man getting up every morning going to a job. This, for him, **was** a job! It was his work---to learn to sing so he could represent his Momma, his family, Ms. Lucy, Thomas Shelby, Professor Charles F. Bryan, Dr. Townsend, and the Black people of the National Baptist Convention, USA, Inc.

These experiences were not without their pain and agony. J. Robert experienced great pain in the trials and tribulations of learning this new repertoire of music. He underwent severe distress as he strained to learn the languages, an accomplishment to some lesser degree he had wrought with great difficulty in New York. But now, in a completely strange place, a long way from home, the stress was even greater. From the pressure, many nights he went to his living quarters and cried, cried until he went to sleep. His tears were not those of resignation but determination. For each morning, he arose to give it another new and vigorous try.

J. Robert progressed so well that his mentors sought to get him on BBC, the British Broadcasting Corporation. He went there highly recommended from all his teachers. But this experience, as well, was not with so much glamour. It was work and a thankless task. Each morning, he reported to the BBC at 7:00 A. M. At the beginning, they placed him in a single room, alone. There was a piano and a stool, for the musician. There was nothing for him to use as a chair. He had to stand all the time while rehearsing. He went over his music time and time again. He worked on his voice modulation and enunciation. He drilled himself on the articulation of the languages he had worked so hard to learn: French, German, and Italian. He worked hard in preparation for his BBC debut.

Finally, the musician came into the room where J. Robert was. The room was really cold, not in the sense of an absence of heat but the absence of furnishings and the presence of indifference. The little indifferent man came into the cold and indifferent room for the moment of testing. He was a drawn, austere man. He had cold, icy blue eyes and the business of music was written all across his visage. He took the music from J. Robert's hand and, without a word spoken, began to play. J. Robert began to sing. If he made a mistake, the musician corrected him and went on. It was all a matter-of-fact. Fortunately, there was not too much to be corrected. J. Robert had prepared well for the moment. When the music was over, when the man finished playing and J. Robert finished singing, the austerity gripped man stood up, gave him his music and, almost without a word of thanks, turned and walked out of the room. J. Robert had learned in New York City that there were not too many pats on the back or personal applause from fellow musicians and critics. There, he learned to weather the frigidity of indifference and calculated coldness of peers and partners. So, this was simply another episode in the life of a vocal artist who was trying to make it up the rough side of the mountain of the music industry.

In a week's time, J. Robert received a letter from the BBC radio station. He was eager to open it, but fear and trepidation overcame him with the feeling that he had failed the test. Hands shaking and heart palpitating wildly, he finally opened the letter. When he read the contents, he could have shouted and run as he once did in church down in Memphis when he got happy. The letter said he was to sing the entire home program at a particular time on the radio station, the BBC. This was the beginning of his singing on the BBC and introduction to all of Great Britain and Europe. All over the listening area of the BBC, which covered an enormous area across Europe, people began to hear this resonant, sonorous voice emanating from the soul of J. Robert Bradley from Memphis, Tennessee.

The arduous training in which J. Robert engaged paid off in other significant ways. One of significance was participation in a concert with the oldest male chorus in London. His popularity and respectability had reached such astronomical heights that everyone was in pursuit of him and his talents. The London music community saw him as the successor to Roland Hayes and Paul Robeson.

On Sunday, October 4, 1953 at 8:00 P. M., the Rossendale Male Voice Choir, under the direction of Fred Tomlinson, Esq., was scheduled to perform a concert at The Picture House, Rawtenstall in London. The two featured soloists were to be Joan Butler, Soprano, and Robert Bradley, Baritone. They were accompanied by Herbert Fox. Mr. Harold Holt, prominent in the world of music in and about London, arranged for J. Robert to sing with the Choir.

The Rossendale male Voice Choir had more than seventy voices. The musical selections and program composition were as follows:

PROGRAMME

The Queen

CHOIR
"The Fishermen of England" arr. Montague F. Phillips
"Marching Song" -------- Matyas Seiber

"The Fishermen of England"

Around the shores of England, that stretch towards the sea
There dwell an ancient people, And they labour mightily.
In havens unfrequented that a busy life forgets,
The fishermen of England are working at their nets.

In tiny vessels they defy the perils of the deep,
And scan the water's dreary waste with eyes that never sleep
And when at night you safely lie in blankets snug and warm,
The fishermen of England are riding out the storm.

And when the foes of England assail in fury blind
The children of the storm arise and leave their nets behind.
With merry oath and laughter and a smile upon their lips,
The fishermen of England go down to sea in ships.

-----Gerald Dobson.

"Marching Song"

Soldier, soldier, to Rumania marching hear the wind blow hollow.
Weeping willows o'er the river arching hang their leaves in sorrow.
Weep, ah, weep you weeping willow, bending o'er the shoulder of my love,
Whisper softly so that she may hear you:
Woe, woe, woe, is my heart, my darling, now that I'm no longer with you.
Round the doorway of my mother's cottage rose and vine are twisted,
But I'll never see my mother's cottage now that I've enlisted.
Ninety bullets round my shoulder, ninety wounds of sorrow in my heart,
We'll be in Rumania tomorrow, then my heart will die of grief, my darling,
then my heart will die of sorrow.

---English words by A. L. Lloyd.

SOLOS---
"Ah! was it he" (La Traviata) -------- Verdi
"All are aware" (Daughter of the Regiment) Donizetti
Joan Butler

SOLOS---
"Lord, I can't stay away" - - - - - - - Roland Hayes
"Nobody Knows the trouble I seen" - -- Lawrence Brown
"T'is me O' Lord" - - - - - - - - - - H. T. Burleigh
Robert Bradley

CHOIR----
"A Toast - - - - - - - - - Luigi Cherubini (1760-1842)
"Ave Verum Corpus" - - - -L. G. da Viadana (1564-1627)

"A toast, let's drink"
A toast! let's drink with hearts all merry,
A toast, come let's drink, death to traitors all;
The Loyal for ever flourish!
Mirthful with wine be honest hearts,
Come, come, a toast, come, come, a toast,
Come, a toast.

"Ave Verum Corpus"
Ave verum Corpus, natum de Maria virgine;
Vere passum immolatum in cruce prohomine;
Cuius latus perforatum unda fluxit sanguine,
Esto nobis praegustatum in mortis examine.
O dulcis, O pie, O Iesu, fili Mariae,
Miserere nobis. Amen.

INTERVAL

CHOIR---
"Tiger! Tiger!" - - - - - - - - C. Armstrong Gibbs
"Widow Machree- - - - - - - - - - - -arr. S. E. Lovatt

"Tiger, Tiger"
Tiger, tiger, burning bright in the forests of the night,
What immortal hand or eye Could frame thy fearful symmetry?
In what distant deeps or skies Burnt the fire of thine eyes?
On what wings dare he aspire? What the hand dare seize the fire?
And what shoulder and what art Could twist the sinews of thy heart?
And when thy heart began to beat, What dread hands and what dread feet?
What the hammer? What the chain? In what furnace was thy brain?
What the anvil? What dread grasp Dare its deadly terrors clasp?
When the stars threw down their spears, And watered heaven with their
    tears,
Did He smile his work to see? Did He who made the lamb make thee?
Tiger, tiger, burning bright in the forests of the night,
What immortal hand or eye Dare frame thy fearful symmetry?
-----William Blake.

"Widow Machree"

Widow Machree, 'tis no wonder you frown,
Och honee! Widow Machree:
It ruins your looks, that same dirty black gown,

Och honee! Widow Machree.
How alter'd your air, With that close cap you wear,
'Tis destroying your hair
Which should be flowing free,
Be no longer a churl To its black silken curl,
Och honee! Widow Machree.
Widow Machree, now the winter's come in,
Och honee! Widow Machree.
To be poking the fire all alone is a sin,
Och honee! Widow Machree.
Sure shovel and tongs To each other belongs,
And the kettle sings songs Full of family glee;
Yet alone with your cup Like a hermit you sup
Och honee! Widow Machree.
Take my advice, darling Widow Machree,
Och honee! Widow Machree,
And with my advice, faith, I wish you'd take me,
Och honee! Widow Machree.
You'd have me to desire Then to stir up the fire,
And sure Hope is no Liar In whisp'ring to me
That ghosts would depart With me next your heart,
Och honee! Widow Machree.

-----Samuel Lover

SOLOS----
"O could I but express in song" ---- Malashkin

"Killarney" ------------------Balfe
Joan Butler.

SOLOS----
"Swing low sweet chariot" ------ Lawrence Brown
"Every time I feel the spirit" ----Lawrence Brown
"City called Heaven" ----------Hall Johnson
Robert Bradley

CHOIR---
"Lock the door, Lariston" -- arr. Granville Bantock
"Lock the door, Lariston"
Lock the door, Lariston," lion of Liddesdale,
Lock the door, Lariston, Lowther comes on;
The Armstrong's are flying, Their widows are crying,
The Castle town's burning, and Oliver's gone!

Lock the door, Lariston, high on the weather gleam
See how the Saxon plumes bob on the sky;
Yeoman and carbinier, Billman and halberdier,
Fierce is the foray, and far is the cry!

Bewcastle brandishes high his broad scimitar,
Ridley is riding his fleet-foot grey;
Hidley and Howard there, Wandale and Windermere,
Lock the door, Lariston, hold them at bay!

"Why dost thou smile, noble Elliot of Lariston?
Why dost the joy candle gleam in thine eye?
Thou bold Border ranger, Beware of thy danger;
Thy foes are relentless, Determined and nigh."

Elliot raised up his steel bonnet and look-it,
His hand grasped the sword with a nervous embrace;
Welcome, brave foe-men, On earth there are no men
More gallant to meet in the foray or chase!

"Little know you of the hearts I have hidden here,
Little know you of the moss-trooper's might,
Linhope and Sorbie true, Sundhope and Milburn too,
Gentle in manner, but lions in fight!

I have Mangerton, Ogilvie, Raeburn, and Netherbie,
Old Sim of Whitram and all his array;
Come all Nurthumberland, Teesdale, and Cumberland,
Here at the Breaken tower end the affray!"

Scowled the broad sun o'er the links o' green Liddesdale
Red as the beacon light tipt he the wold.
Many a bold martial eye Mirror'd that morning sky,
Never more op'd on his orbit of gold.

Shrill was the bugle's note, dreadful the warrior's shout,
Lances and halberds in splinters were borne;
Helmet and Haulberk then Braved the clymore in vain,
Buckler and armlet in shivers were shorn.

See how they wane, the proud file of the Windermere,
Howard! ah, woe to thy hopes of the day!
Hear the wide welkin rend,
While the Scots' shouts ascend:
Elliott of Lariston, Elliott for aye!"

----James Hogg.

Piano supplied by
Messrs. Read, Franklin and Heywood, Bury.

o0o

JOAN BUTLER

At the end of the War this talented young coloratura soprano began her Professional career when she joined the Royal Carl Rosa Opera Co., having been offered leading roles. Given four weeks to learn the opera, she made her debut as Gilda in "Rigoletto," in which she was immediately extremely successful, performing the role in its finest traditional manner.

Her introduction to radio was very exacting, being called upon in her first broadcasts to perform works such as "Hymn to the Sun" from Rimsky Korsakov's opera "Coq D'Or," Queen of the Night arias from Mozart's "Magic Flute," "Fairy Song' from Verdi's "Falstaff," etc., in the "Ring Up The Curtain" and other operatic programmes. She has with equal success appeared in the lighter type of programmes, namely "Grand Hotel," "Rainbow Room," "Those Were The Days," etc., and is now one of our regular broadcasters. She also appears on the Television screen.

Last year she had the pleasure of fulfilling one of her ambitions when making her debut with the Halle Orchestra in Manchester, and has recently realised another by appearing at the Royal Albert Hall, where she sang with the London Symphony Orchestra.

She is now in great demand for Opera, Oratorio, Concert work, etc., and it is certain that her beautiful voice of over three octaves range, together with her charming personality, will keep her in the top flight of singers to the delight of her audiences for many years to come.

o0o

ROBERT BRADLEY
BARITONE

In the great Mississippi Valley Floods of 1937, thousands upon thousands of weary, terrified, mud-spattered people fled for their lives and took refuge in the high-level town of Memphis.

The vast auditorium there became their temporary home where Red Cross officials fed, clothed and eventually provided new accommodation for them. As they sat there, sad and exhausted, one of the officials suggested that someone should lead them in singing---just to cheer themselves up.

A 17-year-old negro (sic) boy jumped up to his feet and began leading them, and soon the vast auditorium swelled with the sound of hundreds of voices, all finding release for their pent up emotions. They sang spirituals, hymns and songs, and through all the singing came the strong, richly clear tones of the young boy, refreshing and inspiring them with the natural beauty of his voice.

The boy was **ROBERT BRADLEY**, and although he had achieved local fame in Memphis singing in church choirs, this was the first time he had faced such a vast public audience.

Since that day he has travelled widely across America. He has a following of some 4,000,000 negroes---members of the National Baptist Convention, Inc., and after country-wide concert tours, he went to New York where he studied with the famous Metropolitan Opera singer, Madame Edyth Walker. To-day he is famed throughout the United States for his well-known and well-loved spirituals.

For some time associated with Lawrence Brown, who was for many years personal accompanist to Paul Robeson, Robert Bradley, the possessor of a magnificent natural voice, is rated by thousands as a worthy successor.

He has recently returned from a highly successful concert tour in South America and is to visit important music centres in Italy.

XXIV.

Doors Which Open Into Europe And South America

The hard work J. Robert Bradley invested in study and training did not go for nought. It more adequately prepared him for the renowned and internationally acclaimed BBC, the British Broadcasting Corporation. His successful debut over the BBC introduced him to European countries, all of whom were connoisseurs of fine classical music. Moreover, this exposure allowed him to give his renditions of the American Negro Spiritual. Roland Hayes and Paul Robeson both had swept the land and enthralled the people with their versions of Negro Spirituals. They had won acceptance and credibility with their intellectual finesse and musical ability. But they had not heard such renditions of this young, vibrant, vivacious, and sonorous voice which had suddenly burst upon the scene with amazing natural ability. Subsequent to the BBC broadcast, invitations poured in for J. Robert to go to Norway, Denmark, Sweden, Holland, Finland and other countries in Europe. In all these countries, the Baptists invited him to sing in their concert halls. They opened the door for J. Robert to visit their countries and sing. Knut Andersen of Norway invited him to visit that country. In Denmark, Oscar Graus, a great leader in the Baptist church invited him to come to them. Josep and Maude Abrahamson made it possible for him to visit Sweden. He sang in Hamburg, Germany and Paris, France. All over Europe, he sang classical songs, plying his musical trade, employing the many languages he had learned from his mentors.

Each summer, after residing in England for a couple of years, J. Robert was invited to make circuit-type visits to these countries. Whenever it was announced that he was to do a concert in their country, the people completely filled the concert hall where he was to sing. All over Europe, especially in the Scandinavian countries, he won the hearts of the people. They loved him with a deep and abiding love. They counted him as a special guest and considered it a signal honor to have him in their country. In Sweden, Norway, Denmark, and Finland, they hosted dinners in his honor. A private automobile was even provided so he could have transportation about the country while there.

While in London, another wide door of opportunity opened for him to go to another field of service. Dr. Jernigan sent word that he wanted J. Robert to represent the National Baptist Congress of Christian Education at the Baptist World Alliance Youth Congress. Dr. Jernigan sent J. Robert the money for him to make the trip to Rio de Janeiro, Brazil. He set sail for Brazil in the summer of 1953. With a stop in Argentina among other places, it took seventeen days at sea to complete the voyage. The giant oceanliner docked in the very heart of the city of Rio de Janeiro, in the very sight of the capitol. He stayed in Brazil for one month. Including the return trip of seventeen days, Robert's stay away from London was a bit more than two months.

J. Robert's one month stay in Brazil was peppered with spates of appearances before the Baptist World Alliance Youth Congress. He led a group of about twenty-five National Baptists who provided the singing for the Baptist World Alliance Youth Congress. Among them were Pauline Campbell, Grace Burt Taylor and her husband Reverend Burt, and other National Baptists who participated with the youth of the convention in providing music. In fact, on one occasion, he sang before the largest audience he had appeared before in his life. It was in the massive colosseum, The Maracana, that a crowd of about two hundred fifty thousand gathered for worship. J. Robert had the honor of leading the singing and rendering music. The stadium was built by a German Jew who had been expelled during the time of Hitler's assault against Jews in that country. When J. Robert saw those two hundred fifty thousand Baptists from around the world, he was stricken with fear. He suddenly wanted to die. But, he measured up to the occasion. One of the most memorable experiences was when he was requested to sing for the president of Brazil, President Getulio Vargas. This man had the notoriety of being a dictator. He also had the reputation of killing people or having them killed. He was known as a terrible man. But there was something about J. Robert that won his heart. J. Robert had the privilege of singing on Brazilian radio and President Vargas heard him. He invited him to come to his presidential quarters. Some people thought he was being summoned in order for the president to have him killed. But that was not the case. J. Robert was unaware of what may have been the slightest danger. He went to the president's quarters, walking with his chest out and head thrown back. President Vargas reached out to him and embraced him with all the might he had. The people did not know what to think. There was a sigh of relief, because they saw that J. Robert's harm was not on the president's mind. They all could see that President Vargas was moved by the singing of this artistic genius and musical maestro.

When the trip was drawing to a close, the music critic of Brazil, Donna Alder, said, "This man will come back many times to Brazil to sing for us." In her music column, she went on to speak of J. Robert's voice, how God had endowed him with a vocal gift of musical excellence.

XXV

Bradley And The Bryans In London

From the time he left New York City, J. Robert was in constant touch with Charles Bryan and his wife, Edith. They were determined to monitor their student's progress in his profession. He was their prize, their joy. They were proud of the one in whom they had invested so much.

Late in 1953, Charles said to his wife, "We are going to London." She protested, saying they did not have the money, nor did they have anyone to keep the children. Mr. Bryan insisted that they make the trip. He outlined how they could do it. He had wound up a tenure of duty at a little school in Alabama, Indian Springs. He really thought he needed a serious rest from all his work. So, he pressed for the trip.

They made arrangements for the children, and off they were to London. They took an airplane flight to New York City and on to Montreal, Canada. From there, they took a boat for London. Mr. Bryan wanted to relax a bit, and at the same time, do some composing. The five-day boat trip was just the thing for this. It served three purposes in one, rest and relaxation, a time for composing new music, and transportation to London.

They had written J. Robert and told him when they anticipated arriving in England. They expected to see him right away once they had gotten to their destination. Once they arrived in London, they settled down in a very sedate old English hotel, across from Kensington Gardens. Immediately, they tried to get in touch with J. Robert but were unsuccessful. They stayed in London for some time, but still did not hear from Robert. They decided to go on to Edinburgh, Scotland. Mr. Bryan was involved in the process of researching the origin and history of the ancient dulcimer. When they returned to London, there was a note at the hotel which stated that Robert Bradley had called and would call that night at 4:00 o'clock. J. Robert called at 4:00 o'clock, just as he had said in his note. In the conversation, he said, "I want you to be my guest for The Trouping of the Colors." This was the celebration of Queen Elizabeth's birthday. Robert said, "I will be there in a taxi for you." Excitement filled their hotel room. They got themselves ready and debated whether they should wait in their room or go on out to the porch of the hotel and wait there for Robert to come in the taxi. They decided to go out to the porch and wait, sitting on the little benches provided for hotel guests.

After awhile, a British taxi whirled into the hotel's driveway. Out stepped this gentleman with a French Beret perched sideways on his head and a modern suit and a cane and spats. J. Robert was displaying his newfound British aire, dress and demeanor. He said to the doorman, "See that these flowers are taken to Mrs. Bryan's room." He had brought a big beautiful bouquet for Mrs. Bryan. This was a tradition which he had begun in Cookeville. It was an expression of his sincere appreciation for what they had done to wipe out the crippling illiteracy which would have prohibited him from ever being in such a place as London, England.

The Bryan's chuckled to one another as they listened to J. Robert's manner of speech. Probably unaware of it himself, he had taken on the British aire and mannerism of speech during the time he had been in London. As they listened to J. Robert speak, Charles punched Edith in the side. It was a humorous experience, but one that was totally and thoroughly satisfying to the Bryans. They had watched this young man grow from an illiterate, struggling to nurse an incredibly unusual God-given gift of a voice only heard once in a life-time. Mrs. Bryan had evaluated J. Robert as a young man who possessed a mind akin to a sponge which absorbed anything and everything there was to be learned. Here he was now mastering English of the British sort. They were exhilarated.

While they rode in the taxi, they discussed J. Robert's progress in England. As he talked with them, he spoke in very precise English. He had actually taken on British ways. The Bryans could not resist asking him how the people were accepting him. He told them, with a sparkle in his one eye, "They think I graduated from Harvard." They all broke out in a laugh that shook the little taxi as it rumbled through the crowded streets of London on its way to the Clarence House.

The Clarence House is the location of the home of the Mother Queen of England. It was there that they were headed on the first leg of their trip for the evening. The taxi delivered them to the driveway of the Clarence House. They got out of the taxi and stood on the driveway to await the Royal Family. While they were standing there, the Mother Queen, Prince Charles, and Princess Ann arrived. J. Robert had Mr. Bryan and his wife to wave at the family. Mr. Bryan was short and because of this, J. Robert had him get on his shoulders so he could see the parade of Royalty. Mr. Churchhill, the Queen, and entire family of Royalty all passed by on the way to the Houses of Parliament for The Trouping of The Colors.

The three of them remained around for more of the Royal festivities. The Queen was scheduled to come out onto the balcony at Buckingham Palace and wave to the people. They wanted to see that. Suddenly, a standard English shower, a veritable summer downpour came down upon them. J. Robert had his umbrella with him, so he let it up and all three gathered together close to one another to keep from getting wet while they waited. Charles and Edith Bryan simply could not get over the "Britishness" that had overcome Robert. They thought they would have a bit of fun with him, because they could not help but remember when their prize student was very much "Ghettoish" out of Pinch in Memphis, Tennessee. While huddled under the umbrella, trying to keep from getting drenched with rain, Charles whispered to Edith, "I'm going to break him down." By that, he meant he was going to take J. Robert back to the time he was not so British. He knew just the way to do it. They often liked to see J. Robert when he forgot that he was who he had become, a musical virtuoso and rising star in the world, and went back to the little boy with the big voice out of Pinch in Memphis. Charles Bryan said to his wife, "I'm going to break him down." He then spoke out and said, "Lordy, me, Robert, I just would give anything for some good old turnip greens and some cornbread." J. Robert shot back, "Lordy mercy, I starving." All of a sudden, he had gone back to that nineteen year old boy the Bryans met in McMinnville, Tennessee. Momentarily, J. Robert had forgotten his British brogue.

They went from there to a French restaurant. They sat down to a full course dinner and J. Robert ordered each meal. They marveled that he was able to read the foreign language on the menu and order therefrom. It was indeed a treat to watch their student effectively operate in a world that was far removed from what he left back home. Especially was Mrs. Bryan thrilled when J. Robert climaxed the meal by having the waiter bring her "…the largest and best strawberries in all of England." That closed out the meal.

Following the meal, J. Robert took Mr. Bryan to Trinity College of Music to meet Mr. Levy, his instructor. Mrs. Bryan was put in a taxi for the ride back to the hotel to rest before the evening. Later that evening, J. Robert took the Bryans to the play, **THE KING AND I,** starring Yul Brynner. Robert had secured a box seat and had tea brought to them. After the play, he took the Bryans backstage and introduced them to the cast, whom Robert knew, especially Murial Smith of America who had one of the leading roles. During the evening, they talked freely about J. Robert's up-coming debut at Royal Festival Hall and the opening of the Baptist World Alliance.

The visit of Charles and Edith Bryan with their prize student in London was filled with excitement and thrilling moments spent together. But it ended on somewhat a solemn note. Following the evening watching **THE KING**

AND I, the three of them agreed that J. Robert would not need to go back to the Bryan's hotel. Instead, the three formed a circle and began to talk guietly together. J. Robert asked sincerely, "Mr. Bryan, will you write a piece of music for my debut?" He said he would. The conversation developed more and more into a sentimental experience. It really bordered on sadness. Mr. Bryan charged J. Robert to take the music of his people, The Negro Spiritual, to the world. This, he felt, was the greatest thing he could do for his people. Neither one, Charles, Edith, or their student, J. Robert had the faintest idea that it would be the last time they would see each other as a three-some. A year later, Charles Faulkner Bryan was dead at the age of forty-three. When J. Robert looked at him as they formed the little circle in London, it was to be the last time he would see the man who made such a difference in his life as a vocalist. The next time he would see him would be in "The City Called Heaven" about which he had sung so many times.

Charles Faulkner Bryan left one of the greatest contributions to the world he could think of, a trained J. Robert Bradley. Of this young man, Charles Bryan said,

"*In my humble opinion, Robert Bradley sings better than the Negro baritone of this day.*"

XXVI.

Preparation For The Festival Hall Debut

As time went along, J. Robert intensively returned to his studies to prepare for the debut at the Royal Festival Hall. His days were spent training with Quilter, Henderson, Aldridge, Titterton, and Levy. In a very fitful manner, his mentors sought to prepare him for his debut at the Royal Festival Hall.

The times were becoming charged with great anticipation. That anticipation was for the pending concert J. Robert was to render at the Royal Festival Hall. There was a sense of incredulity over the fact that such an unknown personality as J. Robert Bradley was to make a debut at the historic Royal Festival Hall. Strange as it was, however, the time was drawing nigh for the young man from Pinch in Memphis, Tennessee to grace the historic hall of the celebrities in the world of classical music in the ancient city of London.

Notice was made of this historic occasion to all of the friends and acquaintances of J. Robert back home in America. Of course, it was not expected that any should make the long trek across the large expanse of the Atlantic Ocean to appear at the concert. It was a matter of excitement and common courtesy that people he knew and loved, people who had supported him all along in his life, would be notified of this historic step in his life.

He continued to work on repertoire. He polished and preened his enunciation and pronunciation. He found himself vocalizing all of the time, wherever he was. He spent time rolling his "r's" and crisply pronouncing his "ings." He did this when he was away from his study quarters. He vocalized in public and people noticed him. He did not mind, however. He knew what he wanted. So, he worked hard to get it. Strangely enough, it was this vocalizing that won him sponsorship of his concert at the Royal Festival Hall. It so happened that vocalists scheduled to perform at the Royal Festival Hall in a debut fashion, had to furnish the expense for that event. Robert had not made arrangements for such expense to be paid. He had not notified Dr. Townsend that he needed the money necessary to pay for the hall. But this was a bridge he would cross in due time, a need he felt confident God would supply.

It happened that J. Robert went to Paris, France to study. He often had to make these kinds of trips to European cities. As a student, he could not remain in London for an indefinite period of time. He had to leave London and go away for a period of time before he could return. So, when he left London, it was arranged for him to study while away.

In Paris, just as in Norway, Finland, Denmark, and all of Europe, J. Robert had made many friends. He was not only a talented man, adorned with vocal ability of an unusual sort, he was gregarious, one with whom it was easy to associate. In Paris, many, many friends were drawn to him. He felt a kinship with them. Toward the end of his stay in Paris, he was confident that he was ready for his debut in London. He had studied tirelessly, some days 12 to 14 hours at a time, days on end without stopping. He got the feeling that he was approaching his peak of preparedness. Because of the approaching time for the London debut and heightening anticipation of that epochal moment, J. Robert thought to share his glee and excitement with his friends. A party, he thought, was the appropriate thing for his friends.

What J. Robert had was an abundance of good intentions. But, he soon came to realize he did not have enough money to match his good intentions. He threw a lavish party for his friends at his hotel. He was unaware of what it would really cost. He had several hundred dollars, but discovered that was not enough.

When the party was over, hotel management personnel approached him to go over the bill and arrange for payment. When they presented the bill to J. Robert, his eye almost popped from his head. He had not imagined the bill to be so enormous. It was so much more than all the money he had. Shock and alarm seized him and completely numbed him almost to the point of panic and paralysis. But, the people wanted their money. The only thing J. Robert could think of was to call on his friends for help. The one friend he thought would help was John Adkins, but he was thousands of miles away in Nashville, Tennessee.

Ever since his days of courting Cecelia Nabrit, John Adkins had established an inseparable friendship with J. Robert. In the wake of a very difficult dilemma, he could only think to call his friend because he would help him. No matter what amount of money he asked of John Adkins, he would give it. Ten dollars, a hundred dollars, a thousand dollars was there just for the asking. So, for J. Robert, this was his only recourse. He got on the phone and called John Adkins. Of course, there were seven hours difference in the time; so, to call Nashville, Tennessee from Paris in the early evening meant it would be very early in the morning, maybe four or five o'clock the next morning.

When the phone rang at the Adkins residence, it broke the night's silence and stunned John and Cecelia. Who would be calling at such an ungodly hour? The voice on the other end of the phone was almost indistinguishable. The operator spoke in thick-tongued French and said, "Mr. John Adkins, please. Mr. J. Robert Bradley calling." The operator spoke so swiftly in her French dialect that John Adkins could not make out what was being said. Cecelia noticed the difficulty her husband was having, so she asked that he give the phone to her. When she took the phone, the operator once again attempted to communicate. "Mr. John Adkins, please, Dr. J. Robert Bradley calling," she said. Cecelia caught on to what she was saying. She then consented to accept the call. When J. Robert came on the line, after exchanging some necessary niceties, he laid his dilemma before her. The story he told was that he was in Paris and the people had lost his luggage with all his money in it. His appeal was that he needed some significant money, the staggering amount of which he gave over the phone. As Cecelia talked and drew from J. Robert what his call was all about, John almost became irate and vociferously complained. "What is he doing over there in Paris anyway? He had no business going over there in the first place," leaped out of his mouth and his resonant rich voice filled the house. It was not that he was angry with J. Robert Bradley for the request he was making, they were friends. It simply was that it was very early in the morning and the disturbance of his sleep had made him irritable. Sensing the desperation and urgency of the moment, Cecelia mentally began to make arrangements for getting the money to their friend. She secured the pertinent information from J. Robert. Later that morning, she had John to take her to Western Union. She wired J. Robert the money he needed. Unbeknownst to them, they had bailed Robert out of a very embarrassing situation. Such was the magnitude of their friendship.

Once all the farewells had been exchanged, J. Robert made preparation for his departure from Paris to go back to London. He arranged for travel on the boat train. This was a mode of transportation where travelers rode the train from Paris, for example, to the coastal place of embarkation. The place of embarkation for the trip from France to Dover, England was Boulogne-Sur-Mer. While vocalizing on the boat train, a Mr. A. E. Johnson, who was the president of the Grundig Corporation, heard him. The Grundig Corporation owned a large number of radio and television stations in Britain and across Europe. Mr. Johnson went over to speak to him and pass on words of encouragement. Incidentally, he gave J. Robert one of his calling cards but he really did not pay any attention to it. Unbeknownst to Robert, this was a very wealthy man.

When he arrived home at 32 Gloucester Place, he emptied his pockets of their possessions. His friend from the Royal Family, Lord Barry Wayne McHughes, looked at what he had placed on his furniture and saw the card with the name of the great philanthropist. He asked J. Robert, "Where did you get this from?" J. Robert said, "Some man gave it to me." Lord McHughes shot back, "Some man? This man is a multi-millionaire. Furthermore, he is of royalty," pointing out the green and gold band which encircled his calling card, a symbol of royalty in England. "You call him right now!" Robert called the man and immediately he said, "Oh yes, I do remember." He said, "Come down this afternoon for tea." Mr. Johnson's office complex was located in Old London, close to the residence of Queen Mary. He had to travel through Cheapside and Bank Street to get there. He showed up for tea at the compound of Mr. Johnson. It was on a cold, dreary and foggy evening, as it is most of the time in London. When he gained entrance, he went through one office after another. From one complex of offices, he went into another, through pools of secretaries and clerks until he reached the office of Mr. Johnson. Finally, Mr. Johnson came from his office which was nestled comfortably and lavishly back behind another pool of secretaries. "Mr. Bradley," he said, excitedly. "Come on into my office." J. Robert followed him into the office, all the time wondering what was to become of this conversation. Mr. Johnson took the pleasure of pointing out to J. Robert the residence of the Old Queen Mother, Queen Mary. It so happened she was out in the flower garden at the time they were looking over into her compound. Mr. Johnson chuckled as he gestured to J. Robert to look at the Old Queen Mother. As she walked about the garden, she used her cane to assist in maintaining her balance. Each time she passed her gardener, she'd hit him with the cane because he would forget to bow to her. She passed him so many times that it appeared he tired of all that bowing, or in his senility, simply forgot to do so after the first time or two. Both J. Robert and Mr. Johnson got a laugh out of the times she whacked the gardener for not bowing when she passed by.

Once they had exchanged courtesies and had those moments of levity, sat down in very comfortable and stylish office chairs, Mr. Johnson got down to particulars. He dispensed with formalities and addressed J. Robert as though he had known him for years. "Robert," he began, "What do you want?" J. Robert said humbly and quietly, almost inaudibly, "Nothing." Mr. Johnson looked puzzled and stunned. This young man had such a tremendous voice. He possessed one of the most marvelous vocal instruments he had ever heard, he must allow him to do something for him. Mr. Johnson implored, "Do you want a home here in London for ever?" Robert said, with a kind of blank stare that was framed with sincerity and forceful fervor, "No, Sir!" "Oh, you must want something!" he shot back. But Robert insisted, "No, Sir!" "Do you want money?" Mr. Johnson urged, leaning forward in his chair in a most reverent entreaty. "No, Sir!" Mr. Bradley almost shouted, thinking he would be taking advantage of the man if he accepted money from him. Mr.

Johnson continued to reason with J. Robert. "Well, what would you like to do?" He suddenly thought of his debut at the Royal Festival Hall and the fact that he needed to find a sponsor. "Oh yes," he said with a sudden surge of enthusiasm. J. Robert's thoughts were suddenly flush with the memory of his frantic efforts to contact the impresario of the United States to Great Britain, but without success. The U. S. impresario was the brother of a man at the Metropolitan Opera in New York and J. Robert had been attempting to see him for the past two years. However, he had not even so much as returned his call, let alone talk to him. Excitedly, thinking that this man sitting before him could be the means by which he could perform the concert at the Royal Festival Hall, he said, "Sir, I would like to make my debut at the Royal Festival Hall before I go home." He told Mr. Johnson of how he had unsuccessfully attempted to contact the impresario to get help from his office. Mr. Johnson leaped from his chair and called the office of the U. S. impresario. He reached him immediately. The impresario informed Mr. Johnson that he was scheduled to return to America the next morning but that he would have one of his staff persons to get in touch with him to work out the particulars and make arrangements for the concert.

The next day, in a mere matter of hours after J. Robert had met with Mr. Johnson, Saul A. Gorlinsky and another representative of the U. S. Impresario office paid him a visit and said, "We want to talk to you about your recital." They all but assured him that his concert was inevitable, Mr. Johnson had instructed them to make it so. As a bit of precaution, they wanted to see the music he was to sing, to confirm that it was concert music. Mr. Bradley said, "Oh yes, it is concert music." He pulled out the whole file of music and they said, "Yes, Schubert, Handel, Mozart. You do all this?" Mr. Bradley responded, "Oh, yes! I do all these. Oh, yes!" From all that could be seen, Mr. Gorlinsky and his companion determined that J. Robert was prepared for his debut. When they had left, he could not help but cry, knowing Mr. Johnson had the gentlemen sent to his apartment and had made arrangements for the concert. In a state of disbelief, he wired Dr. A. M. Townsend to inform him of what had taken place. Immediately, preparations were begun for the recital of Mr. J. Robert Bradley at the Royal Festival Hall. Mr. Johnson, president of the Grundig Corporation, paid for all expenses. In addition, although he made every attempt to persuade J. Robert to remain in London, he gave him one thousand dollars and paid all his bills to go back to America once the recital was over.

Herein was another graphic example of the fact that J. Robert Bradley had always been in the hands of God. All the other Black Americans who had gone to England had to find people to help them. They had to sing at teas to become known within the music circles. Mr. Bradley simply walked into circles of people who seemed to act on cue to do things for this man who was in the hands of God. He had not academic achievement in the music community as Hayes, Robeson, and Anderson. However, he found friends who stood ready to open doors of opportunity for him. Hayes, Robeson, and Anderson were among the first Black Americans to study in Great Britain. J. Robert Bradley was the last Black American to be trained in Great Britain. They came by way of academic prowess and ability to sing. But, J. Robert Bradley came by way of the grit of Pinch in Memphis, Tennessee and the grace of always being in the Hands of God.

XXVII.

The Recital At The Royal Festival Hall

It was 1955 when the climax of an arduous journey would come for J. Robert Bradley. Three years ago, he had gone to London in quest for training in voice to sing the music of the world and to prepare to go home to sing for Black Baptists. The zenith of his achievement was approaching. The highlight of every musician who trains in London is to render a concert at the Royal Festival Hall. It is the place where The Masters sing. It is the dream of every young vocalist. It was about to happen to this young Black man from Pinch, the arch-ghetto, in Memphis, Tennessee, the one who had defied educators in elementary and secondary school and did not attend their schools nor complete their requirements. He now was on the verge of proving that he was a citizen of the world, a student of the universe.

There was one haunting reality which consumed his every thought, while preparing for his historic recital---that was his rendezvous back home with the likes of Dr. A. M. Townsend. Dr. Townsend had written J. Robert a passionate letter just before his recital at the Royal Festival Hall. In that letter, he pleaded with J. Robert to return home to the United States so he could sing hymns, Negro Spirituals, and Gospel Music for National Baptists. That appeal, the passionate request "Doctor" had made at the War Memorial Auditorium just after his student debut at Carnegie Hall, and the fact that "Doctor" had paid for all of his musical training and experiences from Chicago until now, made him set his mind on going home. There was no question about his response to Mr. Johnson when he offered to buy him a home in London forever; it had to be "no" because he had to go back home to serve Baptists.

But as for now, however, the business at hand was that of preparing for the great historic recital. As God would have it, the Baptist World Alliance was scheduled to be held at the Royal Albert and Queen Victoria Hall in London. It had been requested of him by Dr. Townsend and other officials of the National Baptist Convention, USA, Inc., to open the meeting with song. It so happened that the great recital at the Royal Festival Hall was scheduled for Sunday evening, July 17, 1955, with the Baptist World Alliance scheduled to open the next morning. Thus, many of the people who were coming to England for the Baptist World Alliance would be able to attend the recital as well.

To assure that adequate numbers of Baptists, white and Black, attended the Royal Festival Hall recital and the opening session of the Baptist World Alliance, Dr. A. M. Townsend had printed ten thousand copies of brochures advertising J. Robert's appearance at the opening session of the Baptist World Alliance. Dr. Townsend had sent Mrs. Sammie Tate, of the Spruce Street Baptist Church, of which he had been pastor for many years, to travel on the boat to be sure the brochures were distributed to Baptists travelling to the meeting and to distribute them upon arriving in London. Of course, when people discovered that he was to render the recital at the Royal Festival Hall, they made it their business to be present. The recital was scheduled for a Sunday evening in the middle of the short British summer. What a time it was. Excitement charged the air, as if it were electricity. The publicity of the recital, along with the surge of curiosity within the community of musicians, made it all but certain that the Royal Festival Hall would be filled to its capacity of two thousand five hundred. When the time came for the first selection, there was no room for even an extra person to squeeze into the Hall.

Many National Baptists made arrangements for the journey to London to attend the Baptist World Alliance. Among them was Ms. Lucy Campbell. Of course, with her student rendering a recital at historic and prestigious Royal Festival Hall, it was her obligation and delight to be there. J. Robert had arranged to have a special seat provided for her right on the front row. Customarily, the Queen and her family occupied the Royal Box on occasions such as the debut of some special artist at the Royal Festival Hall. All indications were that the Queen and her family would be in their box when J. Robert Bradley took center stage for the recital.

The day of the recital was very special indeed. J. Robert took pains to get himself ready in every way. He had become a meticulous dresser. So, he took great pain to select from his professional wardrobe the most tasteful outfit he could. Throughout the day, he paid periodic visits to his music to polish a portion of each song, as he worked on them one at a time. One delightful development that simply tickled J. Robert was that through the good graces of the wealthy philanthropist, Mr. A. E. Johnson of the Grundig Corporation, The Lord had provided him with one of the foremost pianists as his accompanist for the recital. Gerald Moore was an outstanding pianist. He was known widely in the world of music, especially in London, but also in Europe as well. He was ascribed as "The Unashamed Accompanist." It was quite an accomplishment to have it arranged so that such a musician would play for anyone; and, certainly it was a tribute to J. Robert Bradley. With this distinction, he approached this epochal event with confidence and assurance that all would be well and that God would bring him through.

J. Robert's evening repertoire was replete with Schubert, Mozart, and a variety of classical works suited for the occasion. He had carefully chosen his selections, with the help of his mentors. So, when the evening came, he was truly prepared for the event of events in his life. His trip to the Royal Festival Hall was uneventful. All the way, his only thoughts were on his music and how he would perform it. He had made the determination that he would do the very best he could. Upon arriving, he saw that the auditorium was completely filled, two thousand and five hundred strong. And what was more, the Royal Box was occupied. Ms. Lucy Campbell was on the front row.

The time came for the curtain to rise. J. Robert drew a deep breath and rose to the occasion. His mind was clear. He had taken a mental picture of every song, all of their nuances and shifts. He was comfortable and confident that all would be well. There was no introduction. This was traditional. Everyone there came to hear him. This was a foregone conclusion; thus, there was no need for an introduction. But indeed there was an introduction, and dramatic it was. The announcement of J. Robert's recital at the Royal Festival Hall had elicited response from all over Great Britain and Europe, especially the Scandinavian countries where he had developed such deep and abiding relationships. The Scandinavians were so moved at J. Robert's achievement that they chartered a boat and made plans to fill the boat and make the trip to attend the recital. Indeed, they did. They completely filled the boat and made the trip across the North Sea and up the River Thames to the Royal Festival Hall. Royal Festival Hall is located on the river itself, thus making it accessible to boats and boat traffic. Before embarking for London, the leaders of the tour directed their young men to go to the mountains of Denmark, Sweden, and Holland, etc., and pick flowers for J. Robert Bradley. The plan was to present them once he took the stage. They placed the flowers in the boat's refrigerator to keep them fresh until they got to London.

At the appointed time, he took the stage and prepared to deliver his repertoire of music. While standing at centerstage, with the renowned Mr. Gerald Moore positioned at the piano, suddenly the rear of the stage opened up and hundreds of Scandinavian children and adults rushed through the massive door waving mountain flowers and shouting for glee as they rushed in. When they got to a startled J. Robert Bradley, they showered him with the flowers, throwing them at his feet and all about him. He was outdone! He did not know what to say! Or, what to do! He had never expected anything like this to happen to him. This, was an experience of a lifetime.

After all the excitement, J. Robert settled down to the business at hand. He nodded to his accompanist to begin. The first selection flowed smoothly like a gentle stream. The next selection flowed just as smoothly, but each subsequent number brought with it a bit more ease in his performance. He demonstrated a tremendous command of the languages for those songs which could only be done in French, German, and Italian. The recital was truly an ecstatic experience. Those connoisseurs of classical music marvelled that this Black American mastered the material so well. But still others who knew J. Robert marvelled that he was on stage at all, knowing the meager background of illiteracy and poverty from which he came. They could only attest that truly he must have been in the hands of God for this to happen to him.

During the course of the recital, when he got down to the place where the program called for Negro Spirituals and Gospel Music, J. Robert broke protocol. Hardly was he to pause in the midst of the concert for anything. But, he did. He stopped completely and gestured to Ms. Lucy and called for her to stand. Referring to her as one of his teachers during the days of his youth in Memphis, Tennessee, he had her to stand upon the stage. Robert addressed the Queen and the Royal Family and said, "Your Highness, My Lord, I would like to introduce the lady who has done so much for me and who has created most of the Black Gospel music in America and the world. She is a teacher at Booker T. Washington for over forty years. She is the lady who introduced me to the National Baptist Convention." He cited some of her songs, "Touch Me, Lord Jesus," "He will Understand And Say Well Done," and "In The Upper Room." He gestured to the Royal Box where the Queen and her family sat in austere regality. Then he gestured to Ms. Lucy, who with great dignity and pride, did her little curtsy to the Queen.

When Ms. Lucy went back to her seat, J. Robert proceeded to sing some of the selections she had written. This was the first time Negro Gospel music had been introduced in London or any part of Great Britain or Europe. From then even till now, J. Robert Bradley came to be known as the one Black American singer who braved severe criticism and verbal excoriation in order to introduce Negro Gospel music to people of culture, finesse, and love for classical music. Hayes, Robeson, and Anderson had sung Negro Spirituals with fervor and great power. But it was J. Robert Bradley who had the courage to introduce Negro Gospel music as a genre to Great Britain and Europe. When the people at the Royal Festival Hall heard J. Robert Bradley sing Gospel Music written by Ms. Lucy Campbell, the audience began to feel the passionate, rhythmic swing and sway of his musical renditions, and power of The Holy Spirit which captured the soul and wafted it away to heaven.

ROYAL FESTIVAL HALL

(General Manager: T. E. Bean)

SUNDAY, JULY 17TH, 1955

COMUS ART SOCIETY LTD.
Presents

ROBERT BRADLEY

with

GERALD MOORE
(Piano)

Management
S. A. GORLINSKY LTD.
35 Dover Street, London, W. 1

Programme

I

In questa tomba oscura   Beethoven (1770-1827)

This is a setting of a poem by Giuseppe Carpani. "Leave me to rest in this dark tomb: when I was alive, you should have thought of me. At least let the bare shadows enjoy their peace and do not pour poison on my ashes. Leave me to rest in this dark tomb, ungrateful one."

II

Air from "Elijah"   Mendelssohn (1809-1847)

It is enough! O Lord, now take away my life, for I am not better than my fathers. I desire to live no longer, now let me die, for my days are but vanity.

I have been very jealous for the Lord, for the Lord God of Hosts, for the children of

Israel have broken Thy covenant, thrown down Thine altars and slain all Thy prophets, slain them with the sword. And I, even I, am left and they seek my life, to take it, to take it away.

Tu lo sai
Torelli
(1650-1708)

Thou knowest how much I loved thee, I desire no other favour than that thou remember me, though despising me as unfaithful.

Vittòria, vittòria!
Carissimi
(1605-1674)

Victory, my heart! Weep no more, the vile servitude of love has been banished. The meaning looks, the deceitful tricks, the cheating, the sorrows are ended, the ardour of its crude fire is spent. No arrow strikes my breast to wound me mortally. All ties are broken, all my fears have fled.

III

Hear Me, Ye Winds and Waves
Handel
(1685-1759)

Aria: *Il lacerato spirito* (Simon Boccanegra)
Verdi
(1813-1901)

Fiesco hears the wailing cry of "Miserere" from his palace and realises that his daughter, Maria, is dead. This aria is the lament of an anguished heart. The proud palace is now the sepulchre of his beloved angel; her father's spirit is now weary and broken. Heaven has given her a martyr's garland, and he implores her to pray for him in Paradise.

IV

Aufenthalt
Schubert
(1797-1828)

I linger by the rushing stream, the rustling wood, the precipitous rocks. As wave follows wave, so my tears flow eternally, my heart beats unceasingly. And like the age-old ore of the rocks, my grief remains unchanging.

An die Musik (To Music)
Schubert

Gentle art, how many times, when life's wild whirl has overwhelmed me, hast thou made my heart glow with warm love, hast thou borne me away to a better world! Oft a sigh from thine harp a sweet and holy chord from thee, have opened the portals of better times. Gentle art, for this I thank thee.

Gruppe aus dem Tartarus
Schubert

Hark how the angry sea murmurs, how a brook sighs in a rocky hollow. A deep and tortured sigh is heard. Grief distorts the face of the mountains, their jaws gape in despair, their eyes are hollow. They ask softly and anxiously, will there not be an ending? Eternity throws circles above them and breaks the scythe of Saturn in two.

Aria: **Oh! Isis and Osiris** ("The Magic Flute")
Mozart
(1756-1791)

V

Come away Death *Roger Quilter*

Come away, come away, Death, and in each cypress let me be laid.
Fly away, fly away, breath, I am slain by a fair cruel maid.
My shroud of white, stuck all with yew,
O prepare it: my part of death no one so true did share it.

Not a flower, not a flower sweet, on my black coffin let there be strewn.

Not a friend, not a friend greet my poor corpse, where my bones shall be thrown,

A thousand sighs to save.
Lay me where sad, true lover never find my grave,
To weep there, to weep, to weep there.

O Mistress Mine *Roger Quilter*

    O mistress mine, where are you roaming,
    O stay and hear your true love's coming,
    That can sing both high and low,
    Trip no further, pretty sweeting,
    Journey's end in lover's meeting,
    Ev'ry wise man's son doth know.

    What is love? 'tis not hereafter
    Present mirth hath present laughter,
    What's to come is still unsure,
    In delay there lies no plenty
    Then come kiss me, sweet and twenty,
    Youth's a stuff will not endure, not endure,
    Mistress mine, where are you roaming?

Drink to me only *Roger Quilter*

    Drink to me only with thine eyes
    And I will pledge with mine,
    Or leave a kiss within the cup,
    And I'll not ask for wine.
    The thirst that from the soul doth rise
    Doth ask a drink divine,
    But might I of Jove's nectar sup,
    I would not change for thine.

    I sent thee late a rosy wreath,
    Not so much honouring thee,
    As giving it a hope that there
    It could not withered be.
    But thou thereon didst only breathe,
    And sent'st it back to me.
    Since when it grows and smells, I swear,
    Not of itself but thee.

Oh, no John, no John *English Folk Song*
    This well-known song was collected in Somerset and arranged by Cecil J. Sharp.

Short'nin Bread *Negro Folk Song*
(Adapted by Jacques Wolfe)

VI

(a)   TRADITIONAL NEGRO SPIRITUALS

Dere's a man goin' roun' takin' names	Lawrence Brown
Didn't my Lord deliver Daniel	Lawrence Brown
Sometimes I feel like a motherless child	Lawrence Brown
Ride on, King Jesus	Harvey B. Paul

(b)   TWENTIETH CENTURY SPIRITUALS
    (These songs by the younger Negro composers are being heard for the first time in London.)

He knows just how much we can bear	Phyllis Hall
King Jesus will roll all burdens away	Kenneth Morris
God's amazing grace	Roberta Martin

  (The right is reserved to change the programme if necessary.)

In accordance with the requirements of the London County Council:
(i) The public may leave at the end of the performance or exhibition by all exit doors and such doors must at that time be open.
(ii) All gangways, corridors, staircases and external passage ways intended for exit shall be kept entirely free from obstruction, whether permanent or temporary.
(iii) Persons shall not be permitted to stand or sit in any of the gangways intersecting the seating, or to sit in any of the other gangways. If standing be permitted in the gangways at the sides and rear of the seating, it shall be limited to the numbers indicated in the notices exhibited in those positions.

ROBERT BRADLEY was born in Memphis, Tennessee in 1920, and started singing as a boy in his Sunday school. It was while he was acting as a volunteer to help the Red Cross during the disastrous Mississippi floods in 1935, that he first sang to audiences, and his moving sincerity brought solace to the victims.

The next step in his musical career was when the Sunday School and Baptist Training Union Congress invited him to be soloist at their Congress in Raleigh, North Carolina, in 1937. He was subsequently appointed Associate Music Director of the Congress, and then joined a group of religious teachers to tour the principal States of America, where his voice was an inspiration to all his listeners.

For many years he knew only poverty, but this strengthened his will to win through, and finally his good friend, Dr. A. M. Townsend, sent him to New York to study under the great Wagnerian soprano, Edyth Walker. She was convinced that one day the world would recognize his qualities, and he has since worked to justify her faith in him.

He has sung in Brazil, Mexico, Scandinavia, and other European countries, and recently made a successful television appearance.

The Royal Festival Hall recital was a colossal success. Never in his life had J. Robert Bradley felt such a sense of euphoria. He felt the strong sense of victory. He had ignored all the debilitating reasons for failure, an illiterate father and mother, poverty, a dysfunctional school experience which resulted in personal illiteracy, being used and misused by evangelists and pseudo-friends, all of the hindrances and horrors, devious maneuvers and dilatory tactics encountered along the way, to arrive at the pinnacle of achievement. There was no description of how he felt at this moment of personal victory and success.

The stage of the Royal Festival Hall was inundated with well-wishers when the final selection was rendered. National Baptists who made the long trek across the ocean lined up to give words of panegyrics and expressions of encouragement. Along with Ms. Lucy, others who joined the long line of enthusiasts passing out panegyrics were the Reverend H. Clarke Nabrit and his wife. Reverend Nabrit is one of the sons of the late Dr. J. M. Nabrit, Secretary of the National Baptist Convention, USA, Inc. Many of the older members of the convention said to J. Robert that they were proud of him, that they had watched him develop from the time he was a boy. British and Scandinavians alike lined up to shake hands with this new musical genius. J. Robert was excited, he was so emotionally charged that he could not really come down from the experience.

The euphoria of the Sunday evening Royal Festival Hall recital had not subsided before J. Robert was catapulted to another mountain-top experience. As he exited Royal Festival Hall, he could not help but allow his mind to be crowded with thoughts of what he may have done wrong, what he did right. He went home thinking and wondering what mistakes he made and what newspaper critics would say the next morning. Between his emotional high and nagging wonderment of what he may have done right or wrong, he found that he could not sleep. Murial Smith, a fine American singer was living in London at the time. She was appearing in the musical, "The King And I," starring Yul Brynner. She and J. Robert got together and went to the pool at Trafalgar Square to talk and wait for the morning newspapers to see what music critics said about his concert. He spent a sleepless night. The two of them sat about the pool at Trafalgar Square until the morning hours when the newspapers hit the streets. While they waited, J. Robert cried and then Murial Smith cried, they embraced one another while they waited, wondering what the critics would say. Finally, morning came and **The Manchester Guardian** came out saying:

> J. Robert Bradley made his debut at the Royal Festival Hall here in London. Mr. Bradley's programme consisted of Handel, Mozart and Debussy, Roger Quilter and, of course, his native Negro Spirituals. We shall be watching and giving more attention to the New American Gospel Music that was programmed by Mr. Bradley for the first time in London on the concert stage. Mr. Bradley reminded us of Paul Robeson when he first came to London some years ago. We look forward to hearing more from Mr. Bradley.

The London News reported that:

> J. Robert Bradley sang an interesting concert at Festival Hall.

On that hot July Monday morning, streams of Baptists, white and Black from America and all over the world, made their way to the Royal Albert and Queen Victoria Hall, the Great Hall. In the jostling crowd were luminaries from the National Baptist Convention, USA, Inc. Among them were Ms. Lucy, Reverend and Mrs. H. Clarke Nabrit, and Mrs. Sammie Tate, Reverend and Mrs. T. M. Chambers and their little son and Sallie Martin. The capacity of the hall was more than ten thousand people. From all indications, that capacity was reached.

Once J. Robert got himself together after waiting all night for the newspapers, he proceeded to go to The Royal Albert and Queen Victoria Hall. He had already dressed the night before, but he paused long enough to refresh himself and bathe. He caught a taxi for the trip to the meeting hall of the Baptist World Alliance. He remembered he had gotten a letter from Mrs. Edith Bryan in McMinnville, Tennessee. He had the letter with him, but had not had the time to open and read it. In the envelope was a present Mr. Charles Bryan had sent him as a gift for his recital at the Royal Festival Hall. Mr. Bryan had meant so much to J. Robert. While training him in McMinnville, Tennessee and later at Peabody College in Nashville, he had to explain the meaning of some of the words of songs he was teaching the young Black student. J. Robert was illiterate at the time and simply could not read. Mrs. Bryan taught him how to read while Charles Bryan schooled him on the finer points of classical music and the refinement of the Negro Spirituals. J. Robert had flashbacks of these precious moments while he rode the taxi to the hall. After looking fondly at the picture Mr. Bryan had sent to him as a gift, he took out the letter to read. He began to read:

> Dear Robert:
> Charles and I are very happy for you. Charles passed on.... I want you to be strong because this is what he would want you to do. He knew that you could do it. You have my prayers. You have my love and good wishes to every great move that you will make in your life....
>
> Edith Bryan

While riding in that taxi, J. Robert lost control of himself. He cried with abandon because these two people, Mr. Charles and his wife Edith Bryan, had meant so much to his early development. Now, he was gone. His teacher, his mentor, his tutor who encouraged him, who believed in him was dead. His heart was broken. He wept and wailed with abandon. The driver was befuddled at the emotional eruption happening in the back of the cab.

When he arrived at the Royal Albert and Queen Victoria Hall, he saw the thousands of people who had gathered so early in the morning. He had pulled himself together by that time. When he walked into the Hall, the usher carried him down the aisle to the giant stage. The Secretary of the Baptist World Alliance met him at the edge of the stage. Ms. Lucy Campbell joined J. Robert there. When Sallie Martin saw Ms. Lucy on stage, she joined her. The time to begin the program was nigh. At the appropriate time, the Secretary spoke to the massive audience and said, "Ladies and Gentlemen, J. Robert Bradley made his debut at the Royal Festival Hall yesterday. He will open this convention this morning." Applause resounded thunderously throughout the Hall. He stood and sang a Lucy Campbell song, accompanied by none other than his childhood mentor, Miss Lucy E. Campbell. He remained throughout the week as the Baptist World Alliance soloist. This was the conclusion of a brilliant experience in London for a man who had come to be known as having the voice of a lifetime. Having accomplished that for which he had come, J. Robert made ready to return home to see his Momma and friends and to become the "Voice of National Baptists."

For the next few days, J. Robert prepared for the long journey home. There was not a lot of hoopla about his departure. Friends stopped by and paid respects to him and wished him the best. For J. Robert, the decision to leave London was colored with a bit of caution. He had the opportunity to remain in London and make it his home. He had established many strong relationships, any of which could have been reason for staying. Mr. Johnson, the owner of the Grundig Corporation certainly wanted him to remain in London. He did all he could to persuade J. Robert to make London his home. Mr. Jack Samuels, the owner of a chain of jewelry stores across Europe, used his influence to elicit from J. Robert the decision to remain in London. Mr. Samuels had provided some very important financial assistance for J. Robert. Whenever Dr. Townsend's check was late or he simply ran out of money, he would have his bank to send money to Robert's bank. He also did what he could to persuade J. Robert to remain in London. He was truly a friend.

He had come to be a close friend of Lady Crossfield, the daughter of the ruler of Greece. She was a stately woman. He had the privilege of having brunch at her home in St. John's Woods, a suburb of London. He had gotten very close to the Royal Family. He had the privilege of singing before the Crown Princess, Mary Louisa, at a Christmas party. And, he sang at the Queen's birthday party. Though intriguing the idea of remaining in London, nothing was powerful enough to keep him from making the trip back to be with his people, to render service for National Baptists and show appreciation to his friend and sponsor, one who was like his father, Dr. A. M. Townsend. Arrangements were made for his trip back to the United States aboard the steamliner, The Queen Elizabeth. The return trip to New York was just as exciting as the one to London, the only thing was that this trip carried with it a sense of deep satisfaction that he had done what he set out to do. In the hands of God, he truly had reached a high plateau in his life.

XXVIII.

Return To The U. S. A. And National Baptists

The Queen Elizabeth pulled into New York Harbor with her compartments bulging with jubilant but weary tourists. J. Robert Bradley was among them. He too was weary from the journey, but his mind was bristling with thoughts of home, seeing his mother and Dr. Townsend. Pressing every corner of his mind was the thought of his debt to Dr. Townsend. While in London, there were times, though not many, when he thought to stay in England. But overriding those kinds of thoughts was the haunting voice of Dr. Townsend beckoning him to come home. He heard his voice from the letter he had received while there, "Robert, I want you to come home, and I want you to help keep the hymns and our music in the church. Help our people to sing the spirituals, hymns, and gospels." Because of this, he felt himself a debtor to Dr. Townsend. After all, he had financed all his study and training out of his own personal monies. From the time he left Nashville to go to Chicago, then to New York City, and finally on to London, Dr. Townsend's financial support was there. So, uppermost in his mind was to go back home.

When he disembarked at New York Harbor, J. Robert did not pay courtesy calls on some of his friends or pastors who had befriended him while in the city; e.g., Dr. O. Clay Maxwell, Dr. Sandy Ray, and Dr. Gardner C. Taylor. He rushed to the airport and arranged for air transportation to Nashville. His travel was non-eventful, he only thought about what it would be like when he got home. When he arrived at Vultee Field, it was not as though some renowned celebrity had come to town. Well, it had, but bands and drum and bugle corps were not on the scene filling the air with songs of praise. Dr. Townsend instead was there with a cadre of friends and fellow workers from the Sunday School Publishing Board.

When he had settled down back at his home, he went to the Sunday School Publishing Board where Dr. Townsend presented him to the administration and staff. Dr. Townsend announced that he was naming Bradley to the position of Director of Music Promotion for the Sunday School Publishing Board. This was a period of respite, a restful calm just before a great storm of activity for J. Robert Bradley. It was that stage of rest on the launching pad when a giant powerful rocket prepares for a rendezvous with stellar planets in an extra-worldly orbit. Some tremendous things were waiting to happen in the life of this young man who always said, "I have never had anything in life, but I have always been able to sing."

Immediately, J. Robert began to receive invitations from National Baptist churches from all over the country. Just as excited about J. Robert's return were Southern Baptists around the country. They had become familiar with Mr. Bradley's accomplishments by way of the Baptists of the Scandinavian countries in which he had sung. Along with being in great demand by National Baptists, he also was in great demand by Southern Baptists. He was called upon to sing at the First Baptist Church in Birmingham, Alabama. Belmont Heights Baptist Church in Nashville, Tennessee invited him to sing there. Southern Baptist Seminary in Louisville, Kentucky invited him to journey there to sing to the students. The Southern Baptist seminary in New Orleans invited him there as well.

The 1955 annual session of the National Baptist Convention, USA, Inc., was scheduled for Philadelphia, Pennsylvania. J. Robert Bradley made ready for the trip as the newly appointed Director of Music Promotion for the Sunday School Publishing Board, NBC, USA, Inc. Everyone was proud of J. Robert. They wanted to hear him sing, now that he had achieved such noble and lofty accomplishments in the field of music. Dr. Marshall Shepherd, one of the leading pastors in Philadelphia, Pennsylvania and Recorder of Deeds in Washington, D. C., suggested that Bradley be guest soloist for the pre-convention musical. His suggestion was well received by most everyone. Subsequently, J. Robert was programmed as such. Just as was the tradition of the larger numbers of National Baptists at the time, J. Robert Bradley took the train, along with Dr. Townsend and hundreds of thousands of other National Baptists.

During J. Robert's absence from the country, there had been a change in the leadership in the National Baptist Convention, USA, Inc. When he left for England, Dr. D. V. Jemison was president. When he returned, Dr. Jemison had died and Dr. J. H. Jackson had been elected as the new president. Dr. Jackson was not favorable to J. Robert when he became pastor of Olivet Baptist Church in Chicago, Illinois. He had suggested that some pastor in Philadelphia needed a singer and that J. Robert needed to consider going there. He insisted that he did not have budget enough to hire him. That kind of tension in relations and demonstrated disfavor toward J. Robert followed him even into Dr. Jackson's presidency of the convention. Although he had achieved the highest distinction in music as anyone before or after him, J. Robert never enjoyed the prominence of being the leader of music in the National Baptist Convention, USA, Inc., as long Dr. J. H. Jackson was president.

The night of the pre-convention musical, however, belonged to J. Robert Bradley. The pre-convention musical had long since established itself as the pace-setter for the week's convention session. Because of its popularity, there was a tremendous crowd on hand to hear the musical. J. Robert Bradley was presented to the massive audience to sing. He was presented as having studied in London and given his recital at the Royal Festival Hall and had sung at the Royal Albert and Queen Victoria Hall to open the Baptist World Alliance. He rose to sing. He sang classical music he had done in London. Finally, he sang Negro Spirituals and of course, Negro Gospels. When he got to the Negro Gospels, the Holy Spirit simply swept through the house. When he finished and the fervor and fire subsided, the crowd rose to its feet and gave him a standing ovation.

One of the classical songs he sang was Schubert's "Aufenthalt," which means "The House I Live In," "My Dwelling Place." Dr. Kirkland, the pastor of Marian Anderson at Union Baptist Church in Philadelphia, came backstage to see Bradley once the program had ended. He was intensively moved by J. Robert's rendition of the song, "Aufenthalt." He did not expect that kind of offering to be on the program. He was accustomed to Marian Anderson, his church member, singing this song. It was a delight to know there was someone else who sang it just as effectively and with passion and feeling.

Everyone was relaying the word to J. Robert that Dr. Kirkland was looking for him. He really did not know who Dr. Kirkland was. The informers apprised him of who the man was, "That's Marian Anderson's pastor," and pointed him out in the jostling crowd. J. Robert took the initiative and went to the pastor and said, "Dr. Kirkland!" "Yes," he said, as he spun around, "Are you looking for me?" J. Robert said. He said, "Are you the man who sang that first song? That 'Aufenthalt?' " "Yes Sir," J. Robert said with a sense of humility and respect for the pastor. "You did it so well. I commend you for singing it so well. It is one of Marian Anderson's favorites. She programmed it many times and it is so wonderful that a young fellow like you has gone deep enough into music that you can sing great songs like the great artists. Do you know Marian Anderson?" Robert said, "No Sir." He said, "Well, we are going to do something about that." With this, J. Robert Bradley was on his way to becoming a friend to the world renowned singer, Marian Anderson. He was destined to appear on program with her and appear in photo sessions with her.

The week was spent reacquainting himself with longtime friends of the convention. He had a tremendous experience doing this. As he renewed relationships, he also established himself with pastors around the country who wanted him to come to their church to teach their choirs and congregations to sing the hymns of the church. This is what Dr. Townsend wanted him to do. He was delighted that things were working out so that he could fulfill the debt he owed to "Doctor." When the week was over, there was a deep sense of satisfaction that he had made the right decision to come back home. Considering all things, he knew his people needed him.

XXIX.

To Serve Is To Sacrifice, Sacrificing Is To Serve

When Dr. A. M. Townsend became Executive Secretary of the Sunday School Publishing Board, NBC, USA, Inc., he coined the phrase, "To Serve Is To Sacrifice, Sacrificing Is To Serve." This became the motto of the publishing ministry of the convention as it was carried out at the Sunday School Publishing Board in Nashville, Tennessee. But this was more than a motto for Dr. Townsend, it was a way of life for him. A medical doctor, the first graduate of Meharry Medical College to serve on the Board of Trustees for that school, a former president of Roger Williams University in Nashville, and former pastor of the prestigious Metropolitan Baptist Church in Memphis, Tennessee, he gave all of that up to become Executive Secretary of the publishing house which he had to start with "nothing." This indeed was a sacrifice.

His operational philosophy of "sacrifice" was contagious. He prevailed upon everyone to give something to the convention in order for the convention to become what it should. This was the philosophy he carried each day he operated the Sunday School Publishing Board. Sure enough, he passed this philosophy on to J. Robert Bradley. Once he had returned from London and reestablished himself at the Sunday School Publishing Board in Nashville, and attended the first National Baptist Convention session since his return, in Philadelphia, Pennsylvania, it was then that he began to know what it meant to sacrifice.

Sacrifice for J. Robert did not come in the form of absence of money, it came in the form of not having lots of it. In contrast, the artists with whom he associated in London; **viz.,** Roland Hayes, Paul Robeson, and Marian Anderson all were destined to become very wealthy as a result of their musical talent. But this was not to be for J. Robert Bradley. He was duty-bound to Dr. A. M. Townsend and to his convention to serve at a sacrifice. It was the National Baptist Convention, USA, Inc., which provided a platform for him to demonstrate his musical talent. He had no formal training. He had no formal education, he had not completed public school education and never thought of college. However, the convention looked beyond all this, saw some good in him, and gave him the opportunity to be heard. In addition, Dr. Townsend had personally financed his training, from Chicago, to New York, to London, and now back to Nashville, Tennessee. He was a debtor! He had to sacrifice, as his chief benefactor had done for him. For him, sacrifice came to mean travelling all over the country, often-times without the money he would like to have. But this kind of sacrifice ultimately meant immortality of his name in the mind of every member of the National Baptist Convention for ever and ever.

The days following the Philadelphia session of the National Baptist Convention in 1955 found J. Robert fanning out over the nation rendering concerts and encouraging congregations to sing the hymns of the church from the **Baptist Standard Hymnal.** He participated in revivals at the request of pastors all over the country. All this was with the intent of promoting hymns and anthems, congregational singing, Negro Spirituals and Gospel music of the genre of Ms. Lucy E. Campbell.

He travelled north and south. He was invited to sing for weeks at a time at the Mt. Olivet Baptist Church in New York City. The Reverend Dr. O. Clay Maxwell was pastor of the church and had known J. Robert from the days of his youth in Memphis when he pastored the St. Stephens Baptist Church. J. Robert was invited to Ft. Worth, Texas to be with the eminent Dr. T. S. Boone, pastor of the Antioch Baptist Church. The Reverend Franklin of Brooklyn, New York was another pastor who invited J. Robert to sing. It was there that he sang before going to Toronto, Canada to sing for the Baptist World Alliance Youth Congress. J. Robert had become friends with Pastor Franklin during the time he was studying in New York City. Pastor Franklin called to say he needed his help. He was worshipping in an old Jewish Synagogue and his congregation had dwindled down to one big room. When Pastor Franklin called J. Robert, he said, "Would you come to a one room church and help a man out?" J. Robert answered, "Yes, Sir!" This was the first of a long-standing friendship. When J. Robert returned from London, Pastor Franklin, having come upon better and more fruitful times, invited him to come to New York and sing again for him. It was from this church that J. Robert left to go to Toronto, Canada for the Baptist World Alliance meeting of the youth.

First Vice President Thomas Harten, pastor of the Holy Trinity Baptist Church in Brooklyn, had invited J. Robert to New York City. His church burned and he was out of a church building. A Dr. Cadman had built a cathedral in New York. He had built these kind of cathedral-type church buildings in various places in the world, one in New York, one in London, and one in Paris. When it was learned that First Vice President Thomas Harten was out of a church building, arrangements were made to give the Cadman Cathedral to him for one dollar a year. The building was so large that it had four organs in the sanctuary. The structure took up a full square block. J. Robert Bradley remained with Dr. Harten while he was out of his church building, trying to rebuild, until he was able to go into the Cadman Cathedral.

Pastors in Washington, D. C., were interested in securing the services of J. Robert Bradley. Prior to his stint in London, when he learned that Bradley was staying in New York City, Pastor C. Q. Hickerson of the Gethsemane Baptist Church of Washington, D. C., made arrangements to have J. Robert transported to Washington by airplane every Sunday morning. This was a rigorous schedule, one that was demanding on the body and mind but it was his assignment by Dr. Townsend and Bradley had to be faithful to the calling. This relationship provided the opportunity for J. Robert to establish a life-long friendship with one of the world's greatest evangelists, Dr. C. A. W. Clark. Dr. Clark was invited by Pastor Hickerson to conduct revivals at Gethsemane Baptist Church in Washington, D. C. The two of them, Dr. C. A. W. Clark and J. Robert Bradley, formed a team in the annual revival services at Gethsemane. This relationship continued for some time following his return from London. Since his return to the U. S. A., J. Robert and Dr. C. A. W. Clark have been allies in revival campaigns all over the country, including Kansas City, Missouri, and Nashville, Tennessee.

Also in Washington, D. C., Dr. C. T. Murray, pastor of Vermont Avenue Baptist Church engaged J. Robert in revivals for many years. Joining the entourage of Capitol City pastors who engaged the services of J. Robert Bradley was the eminent and eloquent, pastoral, and powerful Dr. Earl L. Harrison. Dr. Harrison was the long-time pastor of the Shiloh Baptist Church in Washington, D. C. Dr. Harrison could stand flat-footed and without breaking a sweat mesmerize his audience with the Gospel Story. He and J. Robert Bradley had a very special relationship. He was for him a counselor and confidant. On one occasion when J. Robert was rather dispondent and complained over some pain and problems he had encountered, Dr. Harrison took his hand---which had lost some of its fingers when mangled in a sorghum mill in Texas---and rubbed it over his face and said, "Robert, you've blessed the world, haven't you? O. Yes, you've blessed the world! But, Robert, are you Jesus?" J. Robert would never forget this experience because after that day, Dr. Harrison went home and died.

J. Robert worked with Dr. Sandy F. Ray while he pastored the Shiloh Baptist Church in Columbus, Ohio. This relationship continued when Dr. Ray was called to the Cornerstone Baptist Church in Brooklyn. Dr. Ray, who was often jocular in his demeanor and had a tremendous sense of humor, often joked with J. Robert about his financial condition. Dr. Sandy Ray said of J.

Robert that he would often call and say, "Dr. Ray, The Spirit has led me to come to your church this Sunday morning to hear you preach." He said in response, "Come on, Bradley." He knew he was out of money. So he said, "Come on, Bradley. I know you are out of money. Money is the spirit that led you to come to my church." This kind of amiable relationship continued after London.

Dr. Jim Adams, the pastor of the Concord Baptist Church in Brooklyn, where Dr. Gardner C. Taylor pastored for many years, was responsible for having J. Robert to conduct revivals for him for three years in a row. Dr. Ross in California invited J. Robert to render service there. Dr. Ross was one of Dr. L. K. Williams' closest friends during his life-time. Dr. Carter of Pasadena, California invited J. Robert back to his church. He had J. Robert to visit his church shortly after the Goodwill Tour had gone in that direction. The Reverend Joe Branham of San Diego invited him there. Dr. Evans of Miami, Florida invited J. Robert to serve his people there. All of these were mainline church congregations of the National Baptist Convention, USA, Inc. They all renewed that relationship after his triumphant return.

Mississippi was a state which adopted J. Robert Bradley as a favorite son. He had spent many memorable years in service with the venerable Dr. B. J. Perkins in Clarksdale, Mississippi and Dr. Gayton as well. Upon his return from England, he opened up a wonderful relationship with even more Mississippians. The Reverend Dr. Perry "Si" Smith of Mound Bayou, Mississippi often invited J. Robert to that all-Black town to render service. Dr. Perry Smith was father to the late and great Dr. Kelly Miller Smith, Sr., who was the long-time pastor of the First Baptist Church, Capitol Hill in Nashville, Tennessee. The Reverend Albert Jenkins, a student and follower of the late great Dr. H. H. Humes of Greenville, Mississippi often invited J. Robert to his church, the Olivet Baptist Church of that city to participate in revivals.

Through the Reverend Dr. S. L. Bowman, pastor of the Greater Clark Street Baptist Church of Jackson, Mississippi, J. Robert Bradley was voted as guest soloist and song leader for life for the Mississippi General Baptist State Convention's Congress of Christian Education. For an endless number of years now, J. Robert has served in that capacity.

Michigan was another state where J. Robert made an indelible impression with his music. He and Thomas Shelby had made musical sorties into the northern hinterland of the state as well as metropolitan cities such as Detroit. Certainly his musical circuitry included some of the stellar congregations in the Motor City. He sang often at Tabernacle Baptist Church, then pastored by the eminent scholar, Dr. Jesse Jai McNeil and later by Dr. Frederick J. Sampson. The great Bethel Baptist Church, which was pastored by the great Dr. C. L. Franklin, was often frequented by J. Robert Bradley. In fact, Pastor C. L. Franklin often invited him to Detroit and Bethel to sing. While there, Pastor

Franklin treated him to a free medical examination by his personal physician to be sure he was in good health.

In the state of Tennessee, J. Robert renewed his relationships with pastors and congregations upon returning from London. Tennessee had been very special to him. After all, this was his home. He had established long-standing relationships with outstanding pastors and congregations. One of these was the prestigious Dr. W. T. Crutcher, pastor of the Mt. Olive Baptist Church in Knoxville, Tennessee. This was a relationship which was begun prior to his departure to London and the world. He was obliged to continue it upon return. He honored such a relationship with Dr. W. T. Crutcher and the Mt. Olive Church for fifty years. An interesting development was that while J. Robert travelled around the country singing, he caused the people to make use of the **Baptist Standard Hymnal** which had been published by the Sunday School Publishing Board. Dr. Townsend made it a point to produce a hymn book for the convention. In 1924, the **Baptist Standard Hymnal** was published and the copyright placed in the Library of Congress in Washington, D. C. It had been presented to the convention as "the standard" for singing in the National Baptist church. However, some of the churches, in fact, an increasing number of them, had ceased using the hymnbook.

When J. Robert went to a church, he always took a **Baptist Standard Hymnal.** When he sang from the hymnbook, the people were so moved that they immediately ordered two and three hundred hymnbooks as a result of his singing. Many of the churches which had utilized the **Baptist Standard Hymnal** had quit using it; but, when they heard J. Robert Bradley, they renewed their covenant with the convention and ordered the hymnbooks.

J. Robert's travels took him back home to Memphis, Tennessee where it all began. He visited with Dr. W. Herbert Brewster and his Pilgrim Baptist Church and E. Trigg Baptist Church. It was a delight to go back where he had sung so many times as a boy. He sang for St. Stephens Baptist Church where Dr. J. L. Campbell and Dr. T. O. Fuller served as pastors.

One of his fondest desires was to go back where it all began. J. Robert's wish was to sing at Ellis Auditorium where Miss Lucy discovered him and let him sing before ten thousand National Baptists in 1933. He did! On the Fourth Sunday in April 1956, after he received his training in New York City and London, he gave a concert at the place where it all began. Eldon Roark, a reporter for the Memphis newspaper, **The Commercial Appeal,** reported the event.

HOMEFOLKS WILL HEAR FAMED NEGRO SINGER

A Memphis-born negro, J. Robert Bradley, who has sung before the crowned heads of Europe, will give his homecoming concert at 3:30 p.m. Sunday as (sic) Ellis Auditorium.

He studied with Blanche Thebom's teacher, Edith [sic] Walker in New York, after preliminary study with Lucie E. Campbell, retired Memphis teacher who is nationally known in music.

Bradley is son of Mrs. Lelia (sic) Bradley, 431 Mosby. He attended Grant and Manassas schools.

After making his professional debut in London last July, Bradley gave a series of concerts in the Scandinavian countries. After a command performance before King Haakon of Norway he received a letter from the king inviting him to return. A Stockholm newspaper called him "the most gifted singer who has ever been in our city." He also gave a command performance for the Duchess of Kent.

THE MEMPHIS COMMERCIAL APPEAL
April 27, 1956

XXX.

A Return To Where It All Began

The Spring air of 1956 was charged with excitement at the return of J. Robert Bradley to the National Baptist Convention, USA, Inc. Obviously, he was in great demand everywhere. Everybody wanted to hear him sing. National Baptists had come to know him as "The little boy with the big voice." He had grown in stature to become "The **man** with the big voice." In spite of beginnings, whether he was born with a silver spoon in his mouth or in the sordid stench of depravity, none could boast of more lofty achievements than those enjoyed by J. Robert Bradley. One distinguishing factor was, however, he returned to be with his people.

The thrill and joy of J. Robert's return could not have been more strongly felt than that which was experienced in Memphis, Tennessee. Pastors and congregations all over the country were reaching for him, wanting him to come to them to demonstrate his versatile, vocal wares. His long-time friend and acquaintance, Dr. C. A. W. Clark, for example, led his people to begin to make arrangements to have him come to Dallas and the Good Street Baptist Church for a concert. The date of April 19, 1956 was set and an elaborate program was planned. But in Memphis, all over the city people were abuzz with pride-filled talk of their son, their co-worker, their friend coming back home. It did not take very much for the idea to be spawned and take on substance that he should be brought back to Memphis to where it all began. The people were simply ecstatic at the possibility that this might happen. Indeed, with Miss Lucy Campbell leading the effort, they began to work to make it happen.

Miss Campbell assumed the general chairmanship of the effort and was assisted by Mr. Early Gentry, Jr., who served as Promotional Chairman. The program was sponsored by the District Chorus of the Riverside Association. As the plans unfolded, the program was scheduled for Sunday, April 29, 1956 at 3:30 o'clock in the afternoon. The place, of course, was Ellis Auditorium. It was there in 1933 that as a young thirteen year old lad the National Baptist Convention, USA, Inc., was enthralled with his majestic voice. Then, it was a voice that was projected from the throat of one clothed in mud-spattered clothes, standing on feet bare and covered with hardened-mud. Twenty-three years later, however, the same youngster would stand on the same spot ennobled, fresh from a rendezvous in the stellar realm of musical virtuosos.

The people of Memphis worked hard. The committee was organized. The program was set. Advertisements and patrons were solicited for the printed program. When the printed program was completed, it was a masterpiece. Miss Lucy Campbell and the Reverend Dr. C. R. Williams both included panegyrical statements in the printed program. They were proud of J. Robert Bradley because they had been just as much a part of his discovery and success as anyone in the world. In the program, Dr. Williams opined:

> The pastor and members of the Bethesda Baptist Church take great pride in the part they have played in the life of J. Robert Bradley. It was ours to help start Robert off and is ours to welcome him home from a world's tour. Small world after all.
>
> WELCOME HOME ROBERT!!
>
> C. R. WILLIAMS, MINISTER

What Memphis Said About J. Robert Bradley In 1956

John Robert Bradley was born in Memphis, Tennessee in 1920 of the parents, John and Lelah Bradley. It was while he was watching the thousands of unfortunate children receive Christmas presents from the Goodfellows organization at Ellis Auditorium one Christmas eve, that he was discovered by Miss Lucie E. Campbell, who was directing a chorus for the occasion. Robert had no ticket, but was happy as could be, singing for other children. Miss Campbell immediately secured a ticket for Robert who too received gifts. His voice rang out so sweet and clear, that Miss Campbell gave him ballads of two songs, namely, "Is He Yours," and "Nobody Else But Jesus," which he sold between services at the National Baptist Convention which met at Ellis Auditorium in September 1933. This was his first money earned about $3.00 or $4.00.

Reverend C. R. Williams carried Robert to his first National S. S. and B. T. U. Congress in Kansas City, Kansas in 1936. His singing captivated the Congress. He is now on the road to success. Prof. E. W. D. Isaac took Robert as the official soloist for the B. Y. P. U. Board. No convention or Congress was considered complete without Bradley. He has charmed the thousands with such songs as, "Something Within," "Just To Behold His Face," "Touch Me Lord Jesus" and "Amazing Grace." His voice has been an inspiration to all of his listeners. For many years he knew only poverty, but this served to strengthen his will to win.

Dr. A. M. Townsend took Robert for the Sunday School Publishing Board in 1944 and sent him to New York to study under the great Wagnerian soprano, Edyth Walker. He was subsequently appointed Associate Music Director of National Sunday School and Baptist Training Union Congress of which Dr. W. H. Jernigan is president. In 1952, he went to London to study. After three years of hard work he made his debut recital in Royal Festival Hall, London, England, July 1955.

He has sung in Brazil, Mexico, Scandinavia, and other European countries, and recently made a successful television appearance.

oOo

In the printed program, Miss Lucy Campbell was styled as the "Discoveree." As such, she had these words to say,

> Twenty five years ago when I picked this lily out of the cesspool of poverty, my one prayer was that some day this child would be recognized as one of the world's greatest singers. Today my dream comes true and my prayer is answered.

Surely Miss Campbell was filled with humble pride when her discovery, "The Little Boy with The Big Voice" came back to Memphis to demonstrate the result of her investment. What a demonstration it was. On that Sunday evening, Ellis Auditorium was filled to capacity. His mother was there, dressed in her best and, of course, with her ever-present lace handkerchief. Of course, Miss Lucy Campbell and Dr. C. R. Williams were on the front row. His family and friends were all present. When J. Robert Bradley stepped to the microphone, he lived up to all expectations. He gave his audience a full evening of a musical menu replete with reflections of his comprehensive training that started so many years ago in Pinch.

J. ROBERT BRADLEY
(Bass - Baritone)
with LESS WILLIAMS at the Steinway

PROGRAMME

In Questa Tomba Oscura......................Beethoven (1770-1827)
This is a setting of a poem by Giuseppe Carpani.
"Leave me to rest in this dark tomb: when I was alive, you should have thought of me. At least let the bare shadows enjoy their peace and do not pour poison on my ashes. Leave me to rest in this dark tomb, ungrateful one."

Aria from "Elijah"..........................Mendelssohn (1809-1847)
                "Lord God of Abraham"
Draw nearer all ye people come to me
            Lord God of Abraham, Isaac and Israel
This day let it be known that thou are God!
            And that I am thy servant,
            Lord God of Abraham.

Aufenthalt..............................Schubert (1797-1828)
       I linger by the rushing stream, the rustling
wood, the precipitous rocks. As wave follows wave,
so my tears flow eternally, my heart beats unceasingly.
And like the age-old ore of the rocks, my grief remains
unchanging.

And die Musik (To Music).............................Schubert
       Gentle art, how many times, when Life's wild
whirl has overwhelmed me, has thou made my heart glow
with warm love, hast thou borne me away to a better
world! Oft a sigh from thine harp a sweet and holy
chord from thee, have opened the portals of better times.
Gentle art, for this I thank thee.

Gruppe aus dem Tartarus............................Schubert
       Hark how the angry sea murmurs, how a brook
sighs in a rocky hollow. A deep and tortured sigh is
heard. Grief distorts the face of the mountains, their
jaws gape in despair, their eyes are hollow. They ask
softly and anxiously, will there not be an ending?
Eternity throws circles above them and breaks the scythe
of Saturn in two.

Aria: Oh! Isis and Osiris (The Magic Flute)..Mozart (1756-1791)
Tu lo sai......................Torelli (1650-1708)
       Thou knowest how much I loved thee, I desire no
other favour than that thou remember me, though despising
me as unfaithful.

Vittòria, vittòria!.......................Carissimi (1605-1674)
       Victory, my heart! Weep no more, the vile
servitude of love has been banished. The meaning looks,
the deceitful tricks, the cheating, the sorrows are ended,
the ardour of its crude fire is spent.
       No arrow strikes my breast to wound me mortally.
All ties are broken, all my fears have fled.

Aria: Il lacerato spirito (Simon Boccanegra)..Verdi (1813-1901)

Feisco hears the wailing cry of "Miserere" from his palace and realizes that his daughter, Maria, is dead. This aria is the lament of an anguished heart. The proud palace is now the sepulchre of his beloved angel; her father's spirit is now weary and broken. Heaven has given her a martyr's garland, and he implores her to pray for him in Paradise.

Hear me, Ye Winds and Waves....................Handel (1685-1759)

INTERMISSION

COME AWAY DEATH   Roger Quilter

Come away, Come away, Death and in each cypress let me be laid,
Fly away, fly away, breath, I am slain by a fair cruel maid.
My shroud of white, stuck all with yew.
O prepare it: my part of death no one so true did share it.
Not a flower, not a flower sweet, on my black coffin let there be
                    strewn,
Not a friend, not a friend greet my poor corpse,
        where my bones shall be thrown.
A thousand signs to save.
Lay me where sad, true lover never find my grave,
To weep there, to weep, to weep there.

DRINK TO ME ONLY WITH THINE EYES   Roger Quilter

Drink to me only with thine eyes
And I will pledge with mine,
Or leave a kiss within the cup,
And I'll not ask for wine.
The thirst that from the soul doth rise
Doth ask a drink divine,
But might I of Love's nectar sup,
I would not change for thine.

I sent thee late a rosy wreath,
Not so much honouring thee,
As giving it a hope there
It could not withered be.
But thou thereon didst only breathe,
And sent'st it back to me.
Since when it grows and smells, I swear,
Not of itself but thee.

O MISTRESS MINE   Roger Quilter
O mistress mine, where are you roaming,
O stay and hear your true love's coming,
That can sing both high and low,
Trip no further, pretty sweeting,
Journey's end in love's meeting,
Ev'ry wise man's son doth know.

What is love? tis not hereafter
Present mirth hath present laughter,
What's to come is still unsure,
In delay there lies no plenty
Then come kiss me, sweet and twenty,
Youth's a stuff will not endure, Not endure,
Mistress mine, where are you roaming?

CLOSE THINE EYES   (King Charles I)

Oh, no John, no John   English Folk Song
This well-known song was collected in Somerset and arranged by
Cecil J. Sharp

(a) **TRADITIONAL NEGRO SPIRITUALS**
  Dere's a man goin' roun' takin' names
                                    Lawrence Brown
  Didn't my Lord deliver Daniel
                                    Lawrence Brown
  Sometimes I feel like a motherless child
                                    Lawrence Brown
  Witness
                                    Hall Johnson

(b) **TWENTIETH CENTURY SPIRITUALS**
  Touch Me Lord Jesus   L. E. Campbell
  Something Within   L. E. Campbell
  He'll Understand and Say Well Done   L. E. Campbell
  God's Amazing Grace   Roberta Martin
(Programme subject to change if necessary)

  The thrill and euphoria which accompanied his presence on the stage of Ellis Auditorium were indescribable. With mud from the Mississippi River oozing through his toes and traces of it about his face and hair, it was here on this stage that for him his public career began in 1933. Miss Lucy had stood him in a chair to sing one of her songs to the National Baptist Convention, USA, Inc. Dr. L. K. Williams had looked over his shoulder to ask, "Miss Lucy, where did you get him?" "Out of the river," was her response. He said to her, "You'd better keep him, he will be a blessing to us."

Emotions ran high in his bosom, as he reflected on those days. The rushing tremulous forces of the human spirit swept over him as he sang before people who knew him from boyhood. To think of what that Sunday concert meant to him was almost more than he could stand. He wanted to shout.

As the years rolled on following his return to the United States, the popularity of J. Robert Bradley soared with meteoric speed. But there was none more proud of their son and who did much to keep track of his movement than Memphians. Ever since his discovery, the columnist, Eldon Roark, cited his progress in his column, **STROLLING** in the **Memphis Press Scimitar** Newspaper:

> It seemed to me then that such a boy song director, who could move an audience as he had, was destined for fame.
>
> Robert was poor, but with the help of God and human friends he managed to study voice both in this country and abroad. He keeps climbing toward the stars. Memphis and the Mid-South can be proud of him.

THE MEMPHIS PRESS SCIMITAR
October 11, 1960

Soar toward the stars he did. After his Memphis concert, his travels took him to the West Hunter Street Baptist Church in Atlanta, Georgia where the Reverend Dr. Samuel Pettigrew was pastor. There he shared with Dr. L. G. Jordan in his last meeting before he died. Dr. Jordan was the Executive Secretary of the Foreign Mission Board of the National Baptist Convention, USA, Inc. From all over the country and the world, invitations came pouring in. From Europe came an invitation from friends in Germany and the Scandinavian countries to come again and give a concert. He wrote Mr. Roark to tell of his invitation to return to Europe to render a concert:

> "The Baptist Youth of Germany have asked for my services from Aug. 28 through Sept. 8," he writes. "And on Sept. 10 I will open up in Oslo, Norway.
>
> "On this tour I will sing in every principal city in most of the countries of Europe.
>
> "This is a very special trip for me. The 300 people in each town are working to pay my expenses and provide me with a little pocket money. The money they will raise (from the concerts) will go for their great mass meeting to be held in **1965, when Baptists from all over Europe** will celebrate **evangelical year.**
>
> "What a privilege this is for me as an American to be called by these people to serve my God, my country. I have never had any money and am too old to try to make it now, but I am rich in friends and the love of God this world over. What more can a person from my humble beginning ask for?

"I believe many of the new world's problems will be solved through art, and especially through music. Its language is international. People will listen to music, or **listen to you speak. I believe this is** the key **to bring** brotherly love to all mankind."

When you hear Robert sing, you think that perhaps he has found the answer.

THE MEMPHIS PRESS SCIMITAR
July 10, 1964

XXXI.

Flirting Momentarily With Disaster

J. Robert had never indulged in anything that might threaten his career as a singer. He was cautious to protect his voice. After all, it was the only thing he had to carry him through life. He had people who helped him. Teachers all along the way disciplined him in how to take care of himself. It was his friend John Adkins who really drove the point home of the need to protect his major asset, his voice.

It all began while he was in New York City training in voice. He met many people with whom he became friends. But one with whom he became exceptionally close was John Sharpe. He was a musician and taught in the city school system. When the two met, they struck a strong mutual friendship. He called on J. Robert one morning and the two went to see the play, **Gas Light**. The play lasted more than three hours. They came out of that theater and went to the Metropolitan Opera House to see Wagner's **Parsifal.** When the day was ended, the toll of two very long and engaging plays was taken on the body and mind of J. Robert. He was confined to bed for a week. But the result of that experience was the development of a friendship between John Sharpe and J. Robert Bradley.

The relationship brought about an almost devastating effect when J. Robert Bradley sought to be just like John Sharpe in one particular way. John Sharpe smoked a pipe. He looked handsome and dignified with the pipe in his mouth. Something clicked in J. Robert's mind that he wanted to smoke a pipe.

The love for music blended the two souls together in such a way that each wanted to emulate many of the characteristics of the other. A good example of this was on one occasion when the two visited St. Mark's Church at 137th Street in New York. John Sharpe was assistant organist there. He went there to practice. J. Robert accompanied him; so, he sat there and listened.

While sitting there listening to John Sharpe practice, he saw him slowly retard his pace of playing and finally stop. John Sharpe turned to J. Robert and began to talk. He said, "Wicked One" [which was a term he used to address people, even his closest friends], "...my mother worked in the white folk's kitchen, right here in New York City, to put me through. We were poor people like you. I went on to Union Theological Seminary to study hymnology. I had to write a piece of music for my graduation. This is what I wrote. My mother died two weeks before my graduation." Having said that, he returned to the organ's keyboard and began to play his song. The name of the song was "When the Roll Is Called Again," "O I want You to Meet Me Away In Glory." J. Robert sat there and thought about his own mother and, with the largeness of soul for friends, he cried. This experience seemed to draw the two close together as though they had been life-long friends. Truly, John Robert Bradley wanted so very much to be like John Sharpe.

A long time after this incident, after J. Robert had returned from his victorious training experience in London and Europe, he bought himself a pipe. The mistake he made, which was for his own benefit, was to go visit his longtime friend John Adkins. The friendship that John Adkins had with J. Robert was that anything he had his friend J. Robert could get without a great deal of fanfare, no matter what it was. There were times when he gave him five hundred or a thousand dollars, knowing all the while he would never see it again. Oh, he would talk roughly to J. Robert, "When you gonna pay back my money?" knowing all the time he would not get an answer. On occasion, when J. Robert went calling to secure some much needed cash, John Adkins conveniently continued to do whatever he was doing. If he were trimming the hedges in the front yard, he would continue to do so. He knew what J. Robert had come for. Knowing this, he all the more would trim the hedges or whatever he was doing. Sometimes, he would literally take all day.

On this one occasion, J. Robert went to see John Adkins, strutting with his pipe in his mouth. As was a common occurrence for John Adkins in the summer, especially when the funeral home business was slow, he was found piddling about the yard. When J. Robert walked up with his pipe in his mouth, John Adkins did a double take. He saw what he had not wanted to see. He quickly snapped his head back toward what he had been doing. But, compulsion turned his head slowly back toward J. Robert. When he saw the pipe in his mouth, quicker than the eye could see, he hit J. Robert up side the head. Startled and frightened out of his wits, J. Robert saw ten trillion stars circulating in his shaken cranium. Just as quickly as he had hit him, John Adkins jerked the pipe from the mouth of J. Robert and broke it. As if it all were done in one furious finely choreographed motion, John Adkins broke the pipe into two or three pieces and hurled it farther than the eye can see. "If I ever catch you with a cigarette or pipe or cigar in your mouth, I will kill you. You hear me?" said John Adkins.

That was the last time J. Robert ever thought to have a pipe, cigarette, or cigar in his mouth.

XXXII.

Knighted: Sir. J. Robert Bradley

In the hands of God, J. Robert Bradley went higher and higher. In 1955, the National Baptist Convention, USA, Inc., met in Memphis, Tennessee. It was always the responsibility of J. Robert to be on the stage to provide music. Ms. Lucy Campbell had headed the music department for the convention during the administrations of Dr. L. K. Williams and Dr. D. V. Jemison. When Dr. J. H. Jackson became president of the convention, Ms. Lucy was adroitly moved from her position and Mrs. Johnnie Howard Franklin was brought on to lead the music for the convention. In spite of the change, J. Robert continued to have his place on stage to provide music.

During the Memphis session, Dr. William Tolbert, president of the nation of Liberia, West Africa, was in the audience. Dr. Tolbert was a Baptist preacher and pastor of the Providence Baptist Church in Monrovia, Liberia, West Africa. He was sitting right down front in the auditorium when J. Robert Bradley's time came to render a solo for the convention. J. Robert's offering for the occasion was "If I Can Help Somebody." The fervor of the song was so powerful that the Holy Spirit swept through the auditorium. Then an unusual thing happened. People were gathered about the front seats of the auditorium. Ushers were fanning someone who had become overcome by the Holy Spirit. At a closer look, it was noticed that it was the president of Liberia who was shouting and overcome by the Holy Ghost which was brought on by the singing of J. Robert Bradley. Notice was taken that the Liberian President had to have his personal assistant to restrain him in a chair while he was under the power of the Holy Spirit. All over the auditorium, there were demonstrations of emotional ecstasy by those caught in the power of the Holy Spirit. But this unusual expression by the president of Liberia caught the attention of all who were in the area. Indeed, after the session, everyone knew that the president of Liberia had gotten happy from the singing of J. Robert Bradley.

One of the persons close by at the time of the spiritual excitement of the president was the Reverend Charles Walker of the Foreign Mission Board. He had been in Liberia working with the Foreign Mission Board of the convention. He had developed an acquaintance with President Tolbert and knew him quite well. When the excitement was over and Dr. Tolbert had collected himself, he wanted to know who this young man was, J. Robert Bradley. Reverend Walker went to J. Robert and said to him, "Bob, you really made an impression on that man. He is one of the great men of this time, Dr. Tolbert. He followed Dr. Tubman as President of Liberia, West Africa. He wants you to come to West Africa. So, if he calls you to come to Liberia, you be sure to go, you hear?" J. Robert was elated at even the possibility.

Some time passed and J. Robert finally received a letter from Mansion House in Monrovia, Liberia, West Africa. It was from the Reverend Eric David, who was the brother-in-law of Dr. Tolbert. The content was that of an invitation asking J. Robert to come to Monrovia, Liberia. The time came for J. Robert to make the trip to Monrovia, Liberia. An airplane ticket was provided for the roundtrip. It was a long tedious journey by air, but one which was much more pleasant than the long arduous boat ride which took days on end from New York to London and return. The airliner was a giant four-engine propeller-driven airplane. Refueling stops were made in St. John's, Newfoundland, London, and Casablanca, Morocco before arriving at Monrovia. It was a tiresome, grueling trip, but well worth it because J. Robert had been invited by the President of the nation of Liberia.

Upon arriving at the airport, the Reverend Eric David and an entourage of officials from the Mansion House in Monrovia met J. Robert. They escorted him to a large limousine with large white official flags unfurled on the fender. As they moved out from the airport they fluttered in the hot sultry African tropic breeze.

He really was unaware of what awaited him in the hours and days to come, the honor that was to be bestowed upon him. But, since J. Robert was visiting Liberia, there were some things he especially wanted to see while there. He wanted to see the grave of the great National Baptist missionary, Sis. Frances Watson from Kansas City. She spent over forty years in Liberia on the mission field. He wanted to see Miss Davis who had spent over forty years in Liberia. She travelled by an ox-drawn cart to visit the babies delivered in the remote jungle areas of Liberia. She took care of them as babies and reared them so that they ultimately became doctors, lawyers, and other professional people. Some of the children she had raised had relocated in America to go on to success.

When J. Robert visited her house, he discovered that some of the people for whom she had been responsible for raising, had come back to build her a beautiful brick house in the jungle with hot and cold running water. It was there that she lived and died. J. Robert saw on her walls the pictures of all the children she had raised and sent on to become successful in life. From this lady, J. Robert came to know the strong sense of missions. He learned that missionaries such as Sis. Davis had lived through threats from the Witch Doctors who purported to throw spells at her to discourage her from doing her work. Dr. Tolbert provided him a chauffeur-driven limousine to make the trip to see these people. There were at least two concerts given by J. Robert while in Monrovia. One was at the Providence Baptist Church, where Dr. Tolbert served as pastor. The other was at the University of Monrovia. It was at the University of Monrovia that he was knighted. The knighting ceremony came as a great surprise. As far as J. Robert was concerned, his business in Monrovia in general and at the University was to sing.

On the night of the concert when the knighting ceremony took place, the auditorium on the campus of the University of Monrovia was packed to capacity. Dr. Tolbert and his wife were in their appropriate place as the head of state. In addition, there were other dignitaries from other parts of Liberia and of Africa present in the audience. There were two or three strong looking African women who spoke amicably to J. Robert. They shook his hand and congratulated him. He did not know it, but they were there to witness the upcoming ceremony.

At the conclusion of the concert, J. Robert sang especially for President Tolbert the song he had done in Memphis, Tennessee, which had made such an impression on Dr. Tolbert, "If I Can Help Somebody." When he sought to go to his seat, after singing the song, two large men came upon him and grabbed him rather roughly. It startled J. Robert. In his momentary anxiety, he excitedly said, "What's wrong?" They said, with stern authoritarian voices, "Nothing! Just do what we tell you!" All of a sudden, Dr. Tolbert came out from an ante-room and stood by the men. His demeanor was with a kind of spiritual sincerity and hallowed austerity. The men said to J. Robert, "Get on your knees!" Standing there in front of all the people packed in the auditorium, he could not imagine what was happening. Thoughts of tragedy raced through his head. Maybe they were planning to decapitate him for some reason. Had he committed some political mistake in his goings and comings? He momentarily thought the worst. To his surprise, the cadre of men who encircled him went religiously into the ceremony of knighting him as Sir J. Robert Bradley.

During the ceremony, Dr. Tolbert engaged in reading the litany. While he did so, certain persons stood about the auditorium. While J. Robert knelt with the hands of the men on his head, there came upon him a certain kind of spiritual ecstasy, the kind of fervor and fire he felt when Bro. Strawter placed his hand on his head at old Mt. Olive Baptist Church in Memphis.

REPUBLIC OF LIBERIA

To all whom these presents shall come greeting:

Know ye that I **William R. Tolbert, Jr.** President of the Republic of Liberia, taking into consideration the sentiments of humanity which are displayed by you **J. Robert Bradley** and being aware of your sincere wishes to be a useful helper in the Christian work of civilizing our brethren inhabiting the territory neighbouring to our Republic, desiring to give you a public testimony of our gratitude, using the faculties given us by the laws of our Republic, by these presents do ordain, constitute and appoint you Knight **Grand Commander** of the Liberian Humane Order of African Redemption, in virtue of which, from this day, you will be permitted to use and wear publicly the insignias of the Order in the class named, and may the Omnipotent God ever guide you in your efforts for the good of our brothers. In Testimony whereof I have caused the Seal of The Republic to be affixed.

Given under my hand at the city of Monrovia, The **Twenty-Sixth day of November** in the year of Our Lord, one thousand nine hundred and **Seventy-four** and of the Republic the **one hundred and twenty-eighth**.

William R. Tolbert
President

Mr. Eldon Roark of **The Memphis Press Scimitar** always kept up with the progress of J. Robert Bradley. He reported about the knighting ceremony in Monrovia, Liberia. Recently in a column about the distinguished career of Dr. J. Robert Bradley, Memphis singer, director of music promotion for the National Baptist Convention, I told you that he was leaving for a concert tour of Africa. Well, apparently it is a triumph.

As he prepared to leave, I asked that he let me know if anything unusual happened. Now I get this cablegram:

"Dr. J. Robert Bradley, visiting Liberia as special guest of the Liberia Baptist Missionary and Educational convention, in appreciation for his love for the arts and preservation of the hymns of the church, is awarded the distinction of Knight Grand Commander of the Humane Order of African Redemption by Dr. William R. Tolbert, Jr., president Liberia Baptist Missionary and Educational Convention and President of Liberia."

I say it came by "cablegram," but perhaps it came by radio over the Western Union system. Man, it took some addressing and coding to get that message to me! Here's the way it was addressed: "Press Smtr Mfs---W U Mfs---AB023---AAB)034(0535)(1-054149G 340)PD 12/0674 0534---ICS IPMIIHA IISS FM RCA 06 0534 PMS MFS TN---WUB5044 LYU757 125-349---URNX CO. LIMV 082---MONROVIA 83 5 246.

"Mr. Eldon Roark---485 UNION AVENUE---MEMPHIS TENNESSEE."

But, you know, despite all that confusion coding and stuff, the message came through! It reached me!

Congratulations, Dr. Bradley. I know those people in Africa will be sorry when you sing "I'll Fly Away"---that is, I mean they'll be sorry when you do fly away, not sorry because of the way you sing.

THE MEMPHIS PRESS SCIMITAR
December 9, 1974

XXXIII.

J. Robert Bradley And Race Relations

M r. Bradley's singing prowess did much to break down walls of segregation in Southern Baptist schools and churches. In Birmingham, Alabama, for example, Samford College, a Southern Baptist school had it said by one of its racist philanthropists that they would never have Jews, Negroes, or dogs on their campus. J. Robert Bradley went there and sang. He looked about the audience and saw nothing but white people. He commented humorously in the course of his concert that "I don't see anything in here but salt!" Everyone in the room laughed, but they got the message. It seemed that with his humor and yet deep sincerity in The Faith, he could get away with some things. He continued, "I don't see no pepper." Then he went on to continue his singing. He fittingly sang, "You've Got To Love Everybody If You Want To See God." The president called him into his office after the concert for a conference. From that time, he ordered that Blacks be admitted to the school.

Somehow, J. Robert perceived part of his mission in the world as that of ameliorating tension and harsh feelings among the Black and white races. Incredibly enough, he was able to bring Black and white people together with his singing. In 1966 in a letter to his friend, Clara Urguhart of London, England, he wrote:

> This has been a wonderful year for me. I have travelled from the West Coast to the East Coast, North and South. I have even been guest on the campus of the University of Alabama in Tuscaloosa, Alabama, where the racial trouble has been very, very bad. During my stay I was able to bring the Negro and the white together and things are very much at ease now.

It was quite a fete to accomplish in the '60's to bring black and white together in a volatile environment such as The South in the United States and do so with a minimum of friction. J. Robert became very effective at the use of music to accomplish this. He was cited publicly for doing so. Emmanuel L. McCall, a

Black minister of the Southern Baptist Convention, conveyed this honor to him. In a letter to Dr. D. C. Washington, he said,

> During the past year it has been my privilege to be with him (J. Robert Bradley) in several Southern Baptist meetings. In each instance, he has been the most effective witness for the brotherhood of man, the need for better race relations, and the ability of the Negro that we have ever had. He is able to do with music what the rest of us have difficulty in doing with lectures, sermons, and written materials.
>
> ....Wherever we have shared programming responsibilities Mr. Bradley has been an effective instrument for the Kingdom, and for the constructive building of better racial understanding.
>
> February 12, 1971

J. Robert's experience with white racism began when he moved to Nashville, Tennessee. Mr. Charles Bryan took him to sing in McMinnville, Tennessee and white people called Bryan a "Nigger lover." Mr. Bryan responded politely that he was and continued to play and J. Robert continued to sing. At Peabody College in Nashville, he experienced a quiet, cold treatment from whites on campus. His experiences with Southern Baptists in the early days of his career, after he went to Nashville, were very unpleasant. He went to Belmont Baptist Church in Nashville on one occasion to sing. They would not allow him to enter the church building through the front door. He had to go through the basement and meander through a series of narrow passageways before entering the sanctuary to sing for the white people. In Atlanta, at the First Baptist Church downtown, he was forced to enter through a back door before he was allowed to sing for the white people assembled there.

All of these dehumanizing experiences did not deter him from doing what brought joy to his life, singing and cultivating what God had given him. He was determined not to allow man to afflict him with jealousy and hatred, imprison his spirit so he could be of no service to man or God. He was determined to love everybody despite their race, color, creed, religious belief, or how they felt about him. Moreover, he was determined to do what he could to persuade mankind, regardless of race, color, creed, or religious belief, especially if he were a Christian, to accept him for who he was, a fellow Christian brother.

It is not ironic, then, that J. Robert Bradley opened up opportunities for his race to be equal to others. He was born a Black man, ensconced in poverty in the raunchy little section of Memphis, Tennessee called Pinch. He knew nothing but a world of segregation, discrimination and white racism. But, this did not prevent him from opening himself up to friendly relations with white people. He never really met a person, regardless of race, who was not his friend. In fact, white people had always been friendly to him and his family. Mr. Joe Brenner of the Memphis Power and Light Company was certainly a friend when he gave his mother an abundance of heating coal and food after hearing him sing at the city auditorium. At the age of seventeen, he met Mr. Eldon Roark of the **Memphis Press Scimitar** and **Commercial Appeal** Newspapers. He was fascinated with the voice of J. Robert and wrote of him in his column "Strolling" as the years rolled by. When he met Mr. Charles Bryan in McMinnville, Tennessee, it was as though he were meeting a Christian friend and brother. As his world widened and experiences broadened, his relations with white people became more frequent and, as a result, he drew closer to them.

His Christian love for all mankind and experiences in Memphis, McMinnville, and Cookeville, Tennessee were probably part and parcel the reason he was able to interact so easily with white people who came into his life, especially in New York and London. There never seemed to be any strain in relations with Edyth Walker in New York. Although a Black youth out of the ghetto of Memphis, Tennessee, without the luxury of education of any sort, he held his own in social intercourse with royalty and nobility in England and Europe. In contrast to what others may have experienced, J. Robert hardly experienced such. It was another manifestation of having been in the hands of God.

Opening the doors for better relations with Southern Baptists began with his frequent visits to Europe, the Scandinavian Countries and Germany. While living in London studying and preparing himself for his Royal Festival Hall debut, he often made trips to Norway, Finland, Denmark, Germany, and France at the invitation of Baptists in those countries. His music over the BBC, the British Broadcasting Corporation, reached into those countries. When they heard his magnificent voice, they sent for him to come sing for them. As his fame spread over Britain and Europe, so it did back home among Southern Baptists in America. Though they had never heard of him prior to his going to London, the name J. Robert Bradley became a household item in Southern Baptist circles in the United States.

Southern Baptists had heard J. Robert Bradley in Rio De Janeiro, Brazil. He had been sent there in 1953 by Dr. Jernigan, President of the National Baptist Congress of Christian Education, to represent the convention at the Baptist World Alliance Youth Congress. A corps of National Baptist musical luminaries joined J. Robert there. He sang before thousands and thousands of people. His name had begun to circulate all over the world as a result of these kinds of experiences.

After returning from London, J. Robert's popularity and prominence flourished over America and the world. He was invited to sing at the Baptist World Alliance in Miami, Florida. This was the first time he had heard the song "How Great Thou Art." It was sung by the bass soloist from Moscow in the Soviet Union. He introduced the song during that meeting. But the Baptist World Alliance was still smitten with racial prejudice, J. Robert Bradley was given charge of the "Black Choir" which was to sing at the Baptist World Alliance in Miami. Mr. Bradley's choir was larger than that of the larger culture. He did not complain about such prejudicial treatment, even after having been accepted as an equal in foreign countries. He knew the day would come when doors of opportunity would swing open.

While he was sitting with his "Black" choir in the Orange Bowl, Billy Graham stepped to the microphone and filled that cavernous stadium with his appeal, "J. Robert Bradley, will you come and bless our hearts?" Now the stadium platform was all the way across the field from where J. Robert was sitting with his choir. He jumped up and began to run across the field. He was unaware of the giant gopher holes which were all over the field. His leg went straight down into a hole. Fortunately, he was not injured. When he got to the platform, a place was waiting for him and he proceeded to sing, "Swing Low, Sweet Chariot, Coming For To Carry Me Home." It could be said that the progress in race relations in the Baptist World Alliance could be attributed to a considerable extent to J. Robert Bradley.

The amelioration of race relations for J. Robert Bradley did not come in some willy-nilly, effortless manner. There were confrontations. However, J. Robert had a way of dulling the edge of confrontation so that good came out of it. There was an occasion when Dr. R. G. Lee, pastor of the Bellevue Baptist Church in Memphis, Tennessee for more than fifty years, made the statement that "...there would be a 'Colored Folks' section in heaven." Dr. Lee would never allow Black people into his church. He would only allow them to look into the church on Mondays, this was when the custodian, who was Black, went about his chores of cleaning the church. Blacks were allowed to peek into the church while the custodian was cleaning it. Dr. Lee was a strict segregationist in the purest sense.

At a Pastor's Conference sponsored by Southern Baptists, and held at the Shriner's Auditorium in San Francisco, California, Dr. Lee was the preacher and J. Robert Bradley was the soloist. During one of Dr. Lee's sermons, he climaxed with an ending where he said "When I get to heaven, first I'm going to see Jesus. Then, I am going to see my mother and my father. I want to see Abraham, John, and Isaiah. And then, I'm going down on the street where 'the Colored Folks' live." J. Robert listened to what had been said with severe incredulity. If it were possible, he would have turned blue from anger at what had been said by this white preacher. When J. Robert stood up, he could not endure it any longer. He said, "Dr. Lee, you do not know me, but I know you. When I was a boy, I wanted to look inside your great church. You had it fixed so that I could not go into your church on Sunday morning. But, I will tell you this, Dr. Lee, I am a child of the King. I have the stamp in my forehead. When I get to heaven, Dr. Lee, I am going to live all over God's heaven. There will be no special street for me to live on." When he said that, the whole place erupted with emotion.

In 1970, J. Robert travelled with the great Dr. W. A. Criswell, pastor of the First Baptist Church in Dallas, Texas. He was another segregationist. He did not allow Blacks into his church building for some time. The 1970 trip was extensive, stretching from India, to Thailand, to Korea, to Japan, and to China. Dr. Criswell preached and J. Robert Bradley sang. Their relationship was great. It was so successful that upon returning to the United States, Dr. Criswell suspended the prohibition of Blacks from his church on Sunday morning.

At the Virginia Baptist State Evangelistic Conference in Roanoke, J. Robert styled himself as "... the Black missionary to the Southern Baptists. ...They've been sending missionaries to the Black Baptists all these years ...and (now) we have found a way to communicate with them." There was racial tension during those days of January 1970. Some thought race mixing at the church meetings would bring trouble. Bradley said, "The white people were scared...the black people were scared. They asked me if I was scared, and I said: 'No, let's go on and have the meeting.'" (**The Roanoke Times**, Wednesday, January 14, 1970., pg. 17.)

The amiable spirit, humble attitude, gregarious behavior, forebearing strength, and Christian life all have endeared J. Robert to white people of all walks of life. This certainly has been true of whites in the church community, Baptists included. It is little wonder that for many years now, invitations have abounded from white congregations, associations, state conventions and movements of all sort asking him to join them and provide music to speak to their soul. His music, as a result, has done what other non-violent and violent efforts could not do.

Although many giant strides are yet to be made toward freedom for Blacks and minorities in America, J. Robert Bradley has done more than his share through the medium of music to open doors of opportunity for his people.

XXXIV.

Showering The Earth With Blessings

Ever since his return to the United States in 1955, J. Robert Bradley has been about a schedule of activity which amounted to a constant shower of blessings upon the land by one of God's greatest gifts to humanity. His dizzying schedule has been one that has carried him from one end of the United States to the other. He has not left any stone of opportunity for service unturned. In the international community of Christians, the name J. Robert Bradley resonates with great familiarity. He visited Rio De Janeiro, Brazil on three occasions for meetings related to the Baptist World Alliance. His visits to South America carried him to Cali, Columbia, and Venezuela. In those countries, he made lasting friends of the people. His work with the Baptist World Alliance carried him to Toronto, Canada on two different occasions. He participated in its meeting in Miami, Florida; London, England; and attended the session in Stockholm, Sweden. In Seoul, Korea, in 1970, he was decorated with the Iron Ship, one of the highest distinctions given by the people of Korea. The Seoul, Korea experience was a part of a gigantic swing through the Middle and Far East. Travelling with an entourage of Southern Baptist evangelists, Christian educators, and musicians, he sang in Bombay and Calcutta, India. In India, he stopped at Mahatma Ghandi's grave and the Taj Mahal. He sang for the Maharajah, or the great king of India. From there, he accompanied the team as they went on into the Far East, even into Taipei, Red China.

His appearance in Philadelphia, Pennsylvania at the annual session of the National Baptist Convention, USA, Inc., began a flurry of activity which staggers the imagination. He began immediately to prepare for his homecoming performance in April of 1956 in Memphis, Tennessee. He scheduled a concert with the Good Street Baptist Church in Dallas, Texas as a tune-up for Memphis. Following those two engagements, it was off to the four corners of the country.

J. Robert's concerts were not limited to the high and the mighty, the sophisticates and socialites, he offered himself to the who-so-ever-wills. The

National Baptist church community in Mobile, Montgomery, Pittsburgh, Charlotte and Raleigh, North Carolina; Macon, and Atlanta, Georgia; Buffalo and Brooklyn, New York; Chicago, Illinois; St. Louis, Missouri and Kansas City, Kansas sought for and were recipients of his services—the large congregations and the small ones; the city churches and those located in the distant regions of the rural; those who had adequate finance for remuneration and those who only had a modest offering. These all joined the plethora of cities, large and small, which sought the sonorous sound and rich resonance of the voice of J. Robert Bradley.

The crowds flocked to hear his repertoire of classical music, Negro Spirituals and Negro Gospel songs. J. Robert was the one artist who could blend all these in a very fine mix and be appreciated by all. There were very few, if any in the field of music, who dared employ his skills to sing **Te Deum, Isis, Osiris,** or an **Aufenthalt,** followed by a **Drink To Me Only With Thine Eyes,** and climax with **A City Called Heaven, Sometimes I Feel Like A Motherless Child,** and then **He Knows How Much We Can Bear** and **He'll Understand And Say Well Done.** Hardly would you expect such an offering by Paul Robeson, Roland Hayes, or Marian Anderson. An artist would venture to offer either one or the other. To dare to offer both was indeed unusual.

It became a common occurrence for J. Robert to appear on college and university campuses. He opened the door at Samford University in Birmingham, Alabama and appeared there on two occasions. He rendered concerts at most of the following colleges and universities or appeared on significant programs; Trevecca College, Nashville, Tennessee; Morehead College, Kentucky; Kentucky State University, Frankfort, Kentucky; Bishop College, Dallas, Texas; Morehouse College, Atlanta, Georgia; Tennessee State University, Nashville, Tennessee; Tougalou College, Mississippi; University of Alabama, Tuscaloosa, Alabama; Fisk University, Nashville, Tennessee; Hampton Institute, Hampton, Virginia; Arkansas Baptist College, Little Rock, Arkansas; Florida A. & M. University, Tallahassee, Florida; New Orleans Theological Seminary; and, Tuskegee Institute, Tuskegee, Alabama. One great attraction which drew the masses to hear J. Robert Bradley was his identification with people from every strata of life. Especially was he attractive to those who, like him, had not trafficked in the orbital realm of the elite and musical greats. This man had come out of the putrid bowels and nauseating stench of "Pinch" in Memphis, Tennessee. But, he made it! They could appreciate that. When they read his vitae, they did not read of a string of degrees from Fisk University, Morehouse College or Howard University. There was no reference to graduate study at Harvard, Yale, or training at Juilliard's School of Music. Obvious to them was that his education in music had been hard earned by the sheer grit of his own determination to learn in every way all he could and from whomever he could. His story was a success story indeed. People by the hundreds wanted to see and hear such a man. When they heard him, their response was, "What manner of man is this?" He sang the sentiments of the people.

His identification with the lowly and maintenance of his acquaintance with friends was reflected in his frequent appearance at funerals. While those who considered themselves to be more on the professional order had gone on to the concert halls and appeared at the Metropolitan Opera, J. Robert felt it an obligation to share with his friends and acquaintances in the moment of their grief. As often as they called upon him to sing songs over their dead, he responded. The times are myriad when he sang at funerals, with little or no remuneration involved. He sang for the well-known and the not-so-well-known. He sang for the high and mighty and the low nobodies. He sang for his relatives and those who bore no kin. He sang for the rich as well as the poor. He sang for those who had distinguished themselves by noble accomplishments and those who had nothing of note to claim. He was an ever-present fixture at every meeting for the National Baptist Convention, USA, Inc. Wherever and whenever he was called upon to sing at funerals, he sang.

There were those who tested and tempted J. Robert to seek out money in abundance from the unusual talent he possessed. Mr. A. E. Johnson, owner of the Grundig Company in Europe, simply wanted to know what he wanted. It appeared that financing adequate enough to assure the creature comforts for the rest of his life was his just for the asking. But that was not in the context of God's divine will for his life. Some of his fellow artists chided him for not going after the megabucks of which they thought he was worthy. There was no question about his worthiness, there was a question about his willingness to do so. He was clear on the perception of his ministry and mission in the world.

Mahalia Jackson once ridiculed him for staying with the Baptists and not making the kind of money he was likely to make if he pursued the stage. The thought was tempting. There were moments when he even entertained the notion. He voiced such a thought to Clara Urquhart in one of his TransAtlantic correspondence.

January 7, 1965

Mrs. Clara Urquhart
46 Wimpole Street
London, W. 1.

Dear Clara:
Thank you for your letter. I too was indeed glad to hear from you, and to know that you and Enrico are well and in the best of health made my Christmas a happier one, and gave me a hope in the New Year for all of us.

Clara, I think I am still singing well. Sometimes I think I made a mistake by casting my lot and my whole life in the field of religion, for as I grow older I find jealousy hitting at me from every side. I would like to get one big break outside of the holy walls before I die. You know voices do not last always and I celebrate the signs of the old man now. Don't ask me my age, Ha, Ha.

I do hope we will have the privilege of meeting again in real life, the three of us, if it is God's will. If not, there is a place where we are sure to meet, in the house of our Father, God Almighty.

May love and peace abide with you always. My love and deepest respect you will always have.

Sincerely yours,

J. Robert Bradley

JRB/gl

But his thought to pursue the stage in quest for larger amounts of money for his services was only momentary. The thoughts, moreover, were more out of frustration of the moment than a real desire for great sums of money from his talent to sing. For just as quickly as those thoughts came, they left. As they fled the chambers of his mind, he was off to some appointment, some concert, some funeral or some grand affair where the people wanted to hear him sing.

There came a time when he conceded to the idea of appearing before the people through the medium of phonograph record. His first album was **God's Amazing Grace** on the Decca Record Label out of Memphis, Tennessee. It was composed of standard songs for which he had become noted. At the encouragement of Dr. Morgan Babb, a widely known recording artist with the Radio Four Quartet, in 1974 J. Robert set his voice to the phonograph album again. This time it was on the Nashboro label and entitled, **I'LL FLY AWAY**. There were other efforts to record. There were singles and albums pressed. But none of these generated a great deal of revenue. The genre of music which was characteristic of J. Robert Bradley simply was not the jazzy gospel type or the kind which was pitched to the market simply to make sales. His music was that which sought to preserve a very important tradition, the Negro Spiritual, hymns and anthems, and conventional Negro gospels.

To bless the people with the power of his voice and refreshing message of the Gospel in song is the single desire and delight of J. Robert Bradley as he now enjoys the senior years of his life. As life's fleeting moments pass, he is yet found pouring himself out upon the people every chance he gets. He is a fixture at all sessions of the National Baptist Convention, USA, Inc., and the

National Baptist Congress of Christian Education. In fact, at the inception of the presidency of the eminent Dr. Theodore Judson Jemison, the son of the venerable and late president, Dr. D. V. Jemison, he was appointed as Director of Music for both of these august bodies. At long last, the student of Miss Lucy Campbell was elevated to the place where the mentor once stood. When the Mid-Winter Board of the convention convenes, he is found leading the music for Dr. Jemison and the people. At the National Congress sessions, the voice of J. Robert Bradley is heard. When Dr. Jemison, the distinguished president of the National Baptist Convention, USA, Inc., sounds the gavel, opening the session of the convention, he does so only to give over to J. Robert Bradley to open the devotional services with music. During the Mid-Winter Board Meeting in January 1992, held at the New York Hilton, New York City, New York, Dr. T. J. Jemison celebrated Dr. J. Robert Bradley as "A legend in his own time." At the December Conference of Christian Educators, Dr. J. Robert Bradley and his cadre of music-makers stand forth in service. Joining him is the ever-present friend and National Baptist co-laborer, Grace Cobb, lyric soprano and long-time member of New Bethel Baptist Church, Detroit, Michigan. Giving them instrumental support is the incomparable pianist, Gwendolyn Lightner of the Bethany Baptist Church, Los Angeles, California. Ms. Lightner was long-time instrumentalist for the late-great Mahalia Jackson. They all, following the lead of J. Robert Bradley, bless the people of the National Baptist Convention, USA, Inc., with music fit for angels.

Loyalty to The Lord and to his chief benefactor, Dr. Arthur Melvin Townsend, has been the prevailing catalyst for J. Robert Bradley, driving him to be a blessing for the people, to remain with the church. "Robert, when you are completed with your training, come back to your people and teach them to sing the hymns of the church." This was the challenge of Dr. Townsend in New York City following J. Robert's student concert at Carnegie Hall. This challenge haunted his every waking moment. In London, Europe, South America, the Far East, in the bright lights of America's cities, or wherever he was, he heard the voice of "Doctor" calling him to return to his people and be a blessing to them.

XXXV.

A Man Of Sorrow And Acquainted With Grief

It was the sorrow songs which propelled J. Robert Bradley into the hearts of the people of the world. Negro Spirituals seemed to be especially tailored for him. They evolved from hearts terribly broken from some of life's harshest circumstances. Sickness, death and suffering; loneliness, rejection, and a feeling of abandonment; and, injustice, oppression and dehumanization drove Black people of American Slavery to cry tears which flowed from of a soul smitten with brokenness, pain, and anguish; a heart overwhelmed with grief, sickness and death. In his personal life, J. Robert experienced all of this, it enhanced his singing.

"I have never had anything, but I have always been able to sing." This statement became the trademark of J. Robert Bradley as he meteorically rose to musical prominence. Hardly another person in his field of endeavor could make this claim. Really, he never ever had anything but pain and suffering, poverty and need, grief and sorrow; but, he was always able to sing.

In the early days of his youth, poverty, pain, and need was a way of life for J. Robert Bradley. Hunger pangs tore at his belly daily. Often he went without shoes on his feet. He wore the same roughhewn, tattered and torn denim clothes each day, only taking them down in the mornings and then hanging them back in the evenings on the familiar nail by his makeshift bed. His one lingering trademark, his missing eye, was the result of his mother, Miss Cookie's, inability to pay for him to go to the doctor to treat the infection that resulted from cinders thrown by a playmate. But he emerged from all this saga of sadness as "The little boy with the big voice." He was always able to sing.

Sorrow and grief stalked the path of J. Robert. At times, it seemed that his career was threatened, but he always emerged with the ability to sing to overcome it. The death of Edyth Walker in 1949 (50), the instructor who shaped his musical career for the world stage, was so devastating that his world almost came to an end. When she died, he thought surely the only friend he had in the world of music was gone, and so was his career. Such a thought virtually paralyzed him so that he could not sing for a protracted period of time. But he emerged from that excruciating experience able to sing. God placed Lawrence Brown in his path. He took him to a higher orbit.

In 1955, J. Robert was smitten in the heart once again with grief and sorrow from the death of one who meant so much to the development of his career. It had only been a few precious months since Charles Faulkner Bryan and his wife, Edith, had made a special trip to England to see their pride and joy, Robert. During the time they spent together, thrill and delight captured each passing moment. There was an indescribable euphoria which seized the time they were together. J. Robert was fueled by this visit to go on to face the challenge of preparing for his Royal Festival Hall debut and then to go on to conquer that experience. He was wafted to the mountaintop of success on that July Sunday evening in 1955 when he successfully sang at his Royal Festival Hall debut. But following hard on the heels of that epochal experience was a plunge deep into the bowels of despair. The next morning, on his way to the Royal Albert and Queen Victoria Hall to open the Baptist World Alliance, he opened the letter from Edith Bryan informing him of the death of his mentor, Charles Faulkner Bryan. In the taxi in which he was riding, he lost all control of himself. One of the major influences in his life, probably the reason he was in London at that very moment, enjoying such prominence and success, had left him alone in the world. But by the grace of God, after pulling himself together somehow, he went on to the Royal Albert and Queen Victoria Hall and sang before the Baptist World Alliance as he had never sung before.

The valley and the shadows of death came to be a very familiar experience in life for J. Robert. Upon his return to the United States from London, National Baptists swept him to the pinnacle of popularity and prominence. The name of J. Robert Bradley was on the lips of everyone. He had penetrated the hearts of all the people. But the lingering shadows of death and the nagging nemesis of sadness and sorrow continued to be ever-present with him. Like a tidal wave, friends and loved ones who had meant so much to his development slipped away from him, carried away in the clutching, merciless, relentless jowls of death.

In April of 1959, the death of Dr. Arthur Melvin Townsend was tantamount to the world coming to an end for J. Robert Bradley. Dr. Townsend had not been sick, only that the ravages of old age dogged his steps as it does all sons of men. But, death had not been expected. He was a strong man, often musing that the only vacation he would take would be the one he'd take in heaven. He was not expected to go soon, even though he had experienced eighty-five years in the world, and well over half of those in service to National Baptists. Life was unthinkable without Dr. Townsend. But, ready or not, death came. Preparing to go to the Sunday School Publishing Board that April Spring morning 1959, as was his custom for so many years, he could not negotiate the task of putting on his shoes. He conceded to the powers of death and slumped over while making the effort. When his trusted assistant arrived to transport him to his post of duty at the Board, as was his custom, he discovered that "Doctor" had taken another journey. He finally had taken the trip for his vacation in heaven.

The news was completely devastating to J. Robert Bradley. The one person who had financed his training, from Chicago, to New York City, to London and all over the world was now gone. The one person who took serious interest in the entire family situation of J. Robert was no longer available to do so. The death of Dr. Townsend plunged J. Robert deep into the valley of despair. Still, he emerged singing, offering that service at the funeral of his major benefactor when he sang "Amazing Grace."

\\

FUNERAL SERVICES
Dr. Arthur Melvin Townsend

1875 - 1959
Physician-Educator-Financier-Minister-Builder

SPRUCE STREET BAPTIST CHURCH
Rev. L. H. Woolfolk, Pastor
Nashville, Tennessee

Friday, April 24, 1959
Eleven O'clock A. M.

o0o
OBITUARY
DR. ARTHUR MELVIN TOWNSEND

On Monday, April 20, 1959, as he was preparing to go to his office, death came to Dr. A. M. Townsend, and forced him to take a merited vacation---one which he had denied himself during his lifetime. For with A. M. Townsend there was no time for a vacation, and he compressed into his years a record of distinguished service in many careers---any one of which would have brought merit and distinction to the ordinary man. But A. M. Townsend was no ordinary man.

Born in Winchester, Tennessee, October 26, 1875, into the family of Rev. and Mrs. Doc Anderson Townsend, he was surrounded with the inspiration which came from the homes of pioneer teachers and religious leaders. His father was the Principal of the Elementary School at Winchester and Director of the Colored Public Schools of Winchester for a period of fifty years.

In 1891, Dr. Townsend came to Nashville and enrolled in Roger Williams University. In 1898 he was graduated with the A. B. Degree, with honors as valedictorian of his class. He then entered Meharry Medical College, from which he was graduated with honors in 1902. He began the practice of medicine in Nashville, and served on the faculty of Meharry Medical College as instructor until 1913.

But already another career was beginning to emerge. During his student days he was organist in Nashville churches, conducted Sunday School class and missions to the hospitals and jails. He became associated officially with the Spruce Street Baptist Church of Nashville, and there found Miss Willa Hadley, who later became his bride.

Although blessed with a successful medical practice, Dr. Townsend's interest in religion and religious causes did not lessen. He became active in the Tennessee Baptist Missionary and Educational Convention, and became its Secretary, directing its financial campaigns, and putting the Convention on a solid financial footing.

In the meantime, still another career was also developing. Successful in his medical practice, Dr. Townsend was also successful in his handling of business. He became active in fraternal organizations in Nashville, and Tennessee, and served for many years as Endowment Treasurer of the Masonic Grand Lodge of Tennessee. A 33rd Degree Mason, he was instrumental in the building of the Masonic Home for the Aged, and later in reclaiming this property for use by Negroes. He was elected cashier of the People's Bank and Trust Company, and saved that institution in a time of crisis, "touching the dead corpse of the Bank's credit and bringing it to its feet." His contacts with people led to the understanding of people, and built up a reservoir of good will which was later to prove useful in his efforts to build and pay for the Publishing House.

In 1913, Dr. Townsend answered the call of the Baptists of Tennessee to stand at the helm of Roger Williams University as its president. Urged on by his spirit of loyalty and devotion to his Alma Mater, he gave up his lucrative medical practice to devote himself to this task. As a member of the Board of Directors of the new "Roger Williams," and Financial Secretary of the Tennessee Baptist M. and E. Convention, he led in the purchase of the new site of the School, and the erection of the Administration Building on the campus.

In the meantime he had accepted the call to the Gospel ministry, and was serving as interim pastor at his beloved Spruce Street. With Mrs. Townsend as head of music, and Director of the Roger Williams Singers, tours were made through Tennessee and other states to raise funds for the school and to erect "Townsend Hall"----a dormitory and class room building and a President's Home for the campus.

After five years as President, Dr. Townsend accepted the pastorate of the Metropolitan Baptist Church in Memphis, Tennessee. In 1920, in Indianapolis, Indiana, Dr. Townsend embarked on a new career. For in that session of the National Baptist Convention he was elected Secretary of the Sunday School Publishing Board. On his return to Nashville he found a small labor force working in small and rented quarters to produce literature and materials for the Sunday School of the constituency of the National Baptist Convention, U.S.A., Inc. He immediately set in motion plans both to improve the quality of the materials and publication and service of the Board, and to build a plant to house these activities.

Among the first publications of the Board were the **Baptist Standard Hymnal,** Spirituals Triumphant and the Gospel Pearls. These, along with other inspirational books, helped get the Baptists of America singing and hailed as Standard in every respect, and their demand has remained undiminished throughout the years. Dr. Townsend also undertook the recruitment of a staff of writers, to be located in Nashville, at the Publishing House, to produce the lessons for printing. He also instituted work in Christian Education, which meant that teachers could be trained to use the new materials published by the Board.

In the meantime the Publishing House had to be built. In 1920 the convention gave to a Committee of three, headed by Dr. Townsend, the authority to "buy or build a Publishing House," but gave no money with which to do the job. Land was secured in a spot where Negroes were once sold as slaves. In 1926 the building was dedicated. From this building literature still goes forth. The Board, under his leadership, increased its services to the denomination, forged ahead in Christian education, in publication. But this was not enough to exhaust the seemingly inexhaustible energies of Dr. Townsend.

Erecting the building was only part of the job. It had to be paid for.

Dr. Townsend became head of the campaign to pay the debt on the Publishing House. He recruited workers who traveled to conventions, associations, churches and individuals, in the effort to raise funds.

But even this was not enough. Dr. Townsend was a charter member representing the National Baptist Convention in the establishment of the American Baptist Theological Seminary, and served as Chairman of the Board of Directors of the Seminary for 16 years. He was a Charter member of the National Baptist Missionary Training School, and served as the only Chairman of the School's Board of Directors.

As Executive Secretary of the Finance Commission of the National Baptist Convention, U.S.A., Inc., Dr. Townsend assumed the oversight of Convention properties, as to insurance, basic property improvements, minor repairs. In the meantime, his work as Secretary of the Sunday School Publishing Board brought him to leadership in the National Sunday School and B.T.U. Congress for a period of twenty years, first as Associate Director General, then as Director General.

Dr. Townsend spread beyond the borders of his own denomination. He was a leader in the International Sunday School Association, and later in the International Council of Religious Education, and a member of the North American Committee of the World Council of Christian Education and Sunday School Association. Under his guidance interest in Christian Education grew, and the program of the Board expanded into areas of rural work, field programs, Missionary Education, Vacation Bible Schools and leadership training.

When the National Baptist Convention voted to purchase the Woodmen of Union properties in Hot Springs, Arkansas, Dr. Townsend was placed at the head of the committee to renovate the properties, supervise the purchase, execute the business and begin the operations. The National Baptist Bath House today is a monument of his achievements.

In the meantime Dr. Townsend was active in service in another career---interim pastor, leader and financier in the Spruce Street Baptist Church. Twice in "dark days," following disaster he rebuilt the old church. And just a few years ago he led in the task of relocating and rebuilding a modern Spruce Street. Always looking to the future, Dr. Townsend two years ago, led in the purchase of a plot of ground to build a new printing plant, and embarked on a $200,000 renovation program that the Morris Memorial Building could remain in the Capitol Hill Redevelopment Area, a credit not only to the Baptists throughout the nation but to our race. He was in the midst of this project when his vacation came.

Because of Dr. Townsend's many official interests and connections, many people view him through official eyes. But he was also a warm personality, full of wit, with a quick story for every situation. Many knew him for his sternness, but he was also a gentle family man---giving credit for his success to the woman by his side. Many knew him as a factual business man with a flair for figures, statistics and records, but he was also a friend of the aged, and one deeply concerned about the preservation of traditions and history of "other days." Many marveled at his power and influence in the Baptist circles, but he also was a man appreciative of life's little things. Many saw in him rugged individualism and dogged determinism, but there was also the struggle of soul and the planning and careful thought which went into his decisions, turning them into fires of conviction.

But then death came, relieving him of the responsibilities he carried so well for so long, and closed the career for the man who never had a vacation on earth, but "is taking his vacation in heaven."

He leaves to mourn their loss his son, Dr. A. M. Townsend, Jr., St. Louis, Mo.; grandchildren, Arthur M. Townsend, III, Washington, D. C.; William Madison Townsend, London, England, and Miss Beverly Banks, Chicago; sister, Mrs. Laura M. Moore; nephew and niece, Mr. and Mrs. Leroy Bone, Nashville; foster children, Dr. and Mrs. L. A. Johnson, Memphis, and Mrs. Sadie Banks, Chicago; cousins and other relatives and many friends.

o0o

FUNERAL SERVICE

Rev. Charles L. Dinkins, Master of Ceremonies

Preludes.. Wm. J. Cawthon, Organist

> *Sleep On In Visions of Rest*—Schumann
> *Elegie*—Massenet
> *Andante Cantabile*—Tschaikewsky
> *Farewell Will I Give Thee*—Teachner—Bach

Processional, *"Come Sweet Death"*—Bach .... Rev. L. H. Woolfolk, Leading
Selection---*"Servant of God, Well Done"* .... Choir
Reading of The Scripture: Psalm 90................................. Rev. F. P. Phillips
Prayer .... Rev. C. R. Williams
Selection--*"Come Ye Disconsolate"* .... Choir
Acknowledgements .... Rev. C. L. Dinkins

Three Minute Remarks:
  Dr. A. M. Townsend, Citizen..................................... Mayor Ben West
  Dr. A. M. Townsend, Physician and Educator .... Dr. Harold D. West
  Dr. A. M. Townsend, Businessman and Builder .... Mr. Calvin L. McKissack
  Dr. A. M. Townsend, Friend....................................... Dr. L. A. Bowman
  Dr. A. M. Townsend, His Religious Influence .... Rev. L. H. Woolfolk

Solo---*"I've Done My Work"*...................................... Mrs. R. C. Barbour

Three Minute Remarks:
    Federation of Women's Clubs . . . . T. W. Deaderick
    Citizens' Trust Company . . . . Atty. A. T. Walden
    Spruce Street Baptist Church . . . . Mr. H. E. Clark
    Employees, Sunday School Publishing Board . . . . Miss F. A. Owen
    Tenn. B. M. and E. Convention . . . . Dr. C. M. Lee

Selection---"*It is Well With My Soul*" . . . . Choir

Three Minute Remarks:
    Southern Baptist Convention . . . . Rev. John D. Freeman
    National S.S. and B.T.U. Congress . . . . Dr. O. Clay Maxwell
    National Baptist Convention, Woman's Aux. . . . . Dr. Nannie H. Burroughs
    National Baptist Convention, U.S.A., Inc. . . . . Dr. A. E. Campbell

SELECTION-----"*Amazing Grace*" . . . . **Mr. J. Robert Bradley**

Eulogy . . . . Rev. M. H. Ribbins
                Chairman, Sunday School Publishing Board

Selection--"*It Pays To Serve Jesus*" . . . . Choir

Recessional . . . . "*Going Home*" . . . . Rev. L. H. Woolfolk, Leading

Interment---Mausoleum---Family Plot, Greenwood Cemetery

oOo

HONORARY PALLBEARERS

Members, Sunday School Publishing Board
Employees, Sunday School Publishing Board
Ministers
Officers, National Baptist Convention, U.S.A., Inc.
National Medical Association
Volunteer State Medical Association
R. F. Boyd Medical Society
Trustees, Meharry Medical College
Tennessee Regular B. M. and E. Convention
Tennessee B. M. and E. Convention
Agora Assembly
Alpha Phi Alpha Fraternity
Business Associates

ACTIVE PALLBEARERS
Official Board, Spruce Street Baptist Church

FLOWER LADIES
Deaconesses, Spruce Street Baptist Church

ACKNOWLEDGEMENT

The family gratefully acknowledges with sincere appreciation your expressions of sympathy rendered through cards, telegrams, messages of sympathy, and every act of kindness, during this their hour of bereavement will be individually acknowledged at a later date.

oOo

Interment---Mausoleum---Family Plot---Greenwood Cemetery
John W. Adkins, Licensed Mortician, Director
Sam Magee, Licensed Mortician, Assistant Director
Mrs. J. W. Adkins, Notary, Lady Attendant
Associates

E. T. Carothers   C. W. Lee   N. L. Brayboy   F. W. Adkins
1223 Pine Street   Nashville, Tennessee

///

In the same year of 1959, sadness and sorrow knocked at the door once again. J. Robert received a letter from a friend of his, Dorethea Ashdown, of London. The letter was dated November 27, 1959 and bore the text of the following:

J. Robert Bradley Esq.,
330 Cedar Street,
Morris Memorial Building,
Nashville,
Tennessee, U.S.A.

Dear Mr. Bradley

I do not like having to write sad news, but I feel you would like to know that Mr. Johnson passed away on Wednesday evening last, the 25th November.
As I told you in my letter of the 9th October, he had started to recover to the extent that he could come to the office for an hour two or three times a week, but at the end of that month he did have a serious relapse and had to be taken straight to Hospital.
As you can appreciate, we here are all most upset at what has happened as he was such a friend to everybody and, although we feel he was too young to leave us, God does know best.
With all kind regards,

Yours sincerely,

Dorethea Ashdown.

Mr. Johnson referred to in the letter from Dorethea Ashdown is Mr. A. E. Johnson, owner of the Grundig Company in Europe. Mr. Johnson was the London businessman who financed J. Robert's debut at the Royal Festival Hall in July of 1955. He had heard him on a train in Europe while J. Robert was singing on board. Without the support of Mr. Johnson, J. Robert's possibility of performing at the Royal Festival Hall would have been nil. The news of Mr. Johnson's death was the conductor's signal to begin the orchestral dirge of the soul.

In 1963, "The Man Goin' 'Round Takin' Names" called the name of Mrs. Lucy Eddy Campbell-Williams. Miss Lucy Campbell was "The One" who discovered J. Robert Bradley in 1933 by presenting him as a muddy, barefoot boy to the National Baptist Convention, USA, Inc. With the death of Miss Lucy, a part of J. Robert died. The two of them became one in mind, heart, and soul. Her departure tore a part of his mind, heart, and soul away from him. When J. Robert said farewell to Miss Lucy, he vowed to spend the remainder of his life singing her songs and encouraging vocalists all over the country and the world to do the same.

<<<<<<<<<<<<<<<<<<<<<<<<<<<<<<<<<<<<<<<<<<>>>>>>>>>>>>>>>>>>>>>>>>>>>>>>>>>>>

OBSEQUIES
OF
MRS. LUCIE EDDIE CAMPBELL WILLIAMS
COMPOSER---TEACHER---CHRISTIAN WOMAN
From
Mt. Nebo Baptist Church
Dr. Roy Love, Minister
Memphis, Tennessee

Dr. J. H. Jackson, President, National Baptist Convention,
U.S.A, INC., OFFICIATING
MONDAY, JANUARY 7, 1963
ONE O'clock P. M.

o0o

OBITUARY

MRS. LUCY EDDIE CAMPBELL WILLIAMS
If when you give the best of your service
Telling the world that the Savior is come;
Be not dismayed when men don't believe you;
He understands; He'll say "Well, done."
Misunderstood, the Savior of sinners
Hung on the Cross; He was God's only son
Oh! hear Him calling His Father in Heav'n,
"Not my will, but Thine be done."

Miss Lucie Eddie Campbell was born to the late Mr. Burrell and Mrs. Isabella Wilkerson Campbell, being one of nine children, at Duck Hill, Mississippi.

Miss Campbell moved with the family to Memphis, Tennessee, while still very young. She entered the public schools of Memphis, finishing from Carthage School (Booker T. Washington High School) as valedictorian of her class. She furthered her education at Rust College, Holly Springs, Mississippi, where she earned the A. B. degree. She did graduate study at the University of Chicago and Columbia University; and was awarded the Master of Arts Degree by Tennessee A. and I. University, Nashville, Tennessee.

Miss Campbell began her public career as a teacher at the age of fourteen years. She taught at Carnes Grammar School in Memphis and later joined the faculty of Booker T. Washington High School, Memphis, Tennessee, where she served for a period of forty years.

The activities of Miss Campbell were wide and varied. She was known in many circles. At an early age, she joined the Metropolitan Baptist Church, under the pastorate of the late Reverend Jackson. Her activities as a Christian caused her to cast her lot with the Central Baptist Church and the Bethesda Baptist Church of Memphis. Recently, she joined the Abyssinia Baptist Church, Reverend J. H. Hardin, Jr., Pastor, Nashville, Tennessee.

Miss Campbell was the first woman to serve as President of Tennessee State Teachers' Association, Director of Music for the National Sunday School and Baptist Training Union Congress and was one of the original members of the committee called by Dr. E. W. D. Isaac, Sr., in 1915 for the organization of the Congress.

As a teacher she has earned sectional and national recognition over and beyond her ability as a writer of religious songs, and over and beyond her attainments in the national organization of her church. In the field of education she has achieved honors with the same skill that she scaled the heights in music and religious work. She had served as president of the Bluff City Teachers' League, city-wide organization of more than five hundred Memphis Negro public school teachers. She has been president of the West Tennessee Educational Congress, comprising the Negro teaching personnel of some seventeen counties in West Tennessee. Then for five years she was president of the Tennessee Negro Educational Association (the TNEA). In the national realm of teaching, Miss Campbell has served as Vice President-at-large of the American Teachers' Association (ATA). In 1956, her commission as a consultant on the National Policies Planning Commission of the NEA (National Education Association) expired. She served as associate director of the A. and I. State College Extension School, whose branch in Memphis is offering graduate work and on-the-job training to Negro teachers coming from three states.

Miss Campbell is best remembered as a composer of religious music. Although her compositions are too numerous to list in their entirety, many of them have become hallmarks in the churches of the nation. Her first published composition, "Something Within" was written in 1919; followed by "He'll Understand and Say Well Done" and "Heavenly Sunshine."

The more than forty-five published compositions written by "Miss Lucie" have retained their popularity across a span of more than forty years, because they were "God inspired." Her deep Christian conviction, humility of spirit and desire to be of service were expressed in the words of her unforgettable music.

When asked her philosophy of life, the famed woman answered in words which constitute the following paragraph:

> "I have the habit of planning my work not only for tomorrow, but for the future, and then I work my plan. I decide trifles quickly. I prime my head with ideas, facts and inspiration. I work more and worry less. I respect the rights of others, and try to use each minute before it disappears forever. I have naught in my heart against no one. And above all, I have a deep and abiding faith in God, the Creator of the universe."

It may not be an accident that Miss Campbell's ability as a composer received such wide acclaim. Perhaps her position and activity as a national officer of her church enabled her to understand and interpret the feelings of her fellow church members so well through the medium of music. She was the music director of the National Sunday School and Baptist Training Union Congress of America; vice president-at-large of the National Baptist Music Convention, an auxiliary of the National Baptist Convention, Incorporated. She was also president of the National Baptist Choral Society of the National Baptist Women's Convention of America. Miss Campbell was a charter member of the National Song Leader's Convention.

January 14, 1960, she climaxed a life-long friendship in her marriage to the Reverend Dr. C. R. Williams, Secretary of the National Baptist Training Union Board, who survives.

Had Miss Lucie loved gala and splendor, she would be a member of the "Golden Record Club of American Artists." If she had worked to enjoy the fruits of Hollywood, the "Oscars" would fill the trophy case. Were she a television spectacular, "Emmy Awards" would shower upon her. If she sought world fame, she would have won the "Nobel Prize." But all Miss Lucie wanted was to help the world see Jesus---and she has done this with remarkable distinction. And without reservation, we take pride in joining with thousands of Baptists in nominating a Grand Lady of the National Baptist Convention and the world for the most coveted prize of all---a crown of life.

Other relatives in addition to the widower are: A niece, Mrs. Mae Willie Wilson and her husband, Mr. Al Wilson, Waterloo, Iowa; two nephews, Mr. T. J. Robinson, Memphis, Tennessee, and Mr. Robert Robinson, Waterloo, Iowa; and many other relatives and friends who loved.

> *If when this life of labor is ended,*
> *And the reward of the race you have run;*
> *Oh! the sweet rest prepared for the faithful;*
> *Will be His blest and final "Well Done."*
> *But if you try and fail in your trying*
> *Hands sore and scarred from the work you've begun'*
> *Take up your cross and run quickly to meet Him;*
> *He'll understand and say "Well Done."*
> *Oh, when I come to the end of my journey,*
> *Weary of life and the battle is won;*
> *Carr'ing the staff and the cross of Redemption,*
> *He'll understand, and say "Well Done."*
>
> Lucie E. Campbell

o0o

PROGRAM

Dr. Roy Love, Leader, Pastor's Division
National Sunday School and B. T. U. Congress, Presiding

Processional. . . . . Organist
Selection - *"Footprints of Jesus"*. . . . . Chorus
   Assistant Dean, National Sunday School and B. T. U. Congress
The Prayer. . . . . Dr. J. Lewis Powell
     Dean, American Baptist Theological Seminary,
     Nashville, Tennessee
Selection - *"Something Within"* . . . . Chorus

Expressions: (Two Minutes Each)
>   Representative of Baptist Pastors Alliance Memphis, Tennessee
>   Dr. A. E. Campbell, President, Tennessee Regular Baptist Convention
>   Dr. S. A. Owen, President Tennessee Baptist M. and E. Convention
>   Dr. Mary O. Ross, President, Woman's Auxiliary,
>   National Baptist Convention, U.S.A., Inc.

Solo - *"Twenty-third Psalm"* .... **Mr. J. Robert Bradley**
>   Director of Church Music, Sunday School Publishing Board
>   Dr. Blair R. Hunt, Retired Principal, Booker T. Washington
>   High School, Memphis, Tennessee
>   Dr. D. E. King, Pastor, Zion Baptist Church, Louisville, Kentucky
>   Dr. C. A. W. Clark, Editor, National Baptist Voice
>   Dr. E. C. Estell, ,Vice President, National Sunday School and B. T. U. Congress
>   Dr. O. Clay Maxwell, President, National Sunday School and B. T. U. Congress
>   Dr. D. C. Washington, Executive Director,, Sunday School Publishing Board,
>   National Baptist Convention, U.S.A., Inc.

Solo - *"Touch Me, Lord Jesus"* .... Dr. O. M. Hoover
>   Pastor, Olivet Institutional Baptist Church, Cleveland, Ohio

EULOGY .... **DR JOSEPH H. JACKSON, PRESIDENT**
>   National Baptist Convention, U.S.A., Inc.

Selection - *"In The Upper Room"* .... Chorus
>   Under the direction of Mrs. Bessie McKenzie, Memphis, Tennessee

View of Remains

Recessional .... Organist

National Baptist Voice: January, 1963; Volume XXXVII, Number 1.

———

<<<<<<<<<<<<<<<<<<<<<<<<<<<<<<<<<<<<<<<<<<<<<<<<

The following years were a veritable parade to the grave by J. Robert Bradley. In 1972, he bade farewell to Lawrence Brown, his teacher of the early 1950's who prepared him for The London Experience in a most unusual way. The next year, he bade farewell to Dr. O. Clay Maxwell, president of the National Baptist Congress of Christian Education. It was Dr. Maxwell who took the responsibility of sending J. Robert to his first Baptist World Alliance Youth Congress in Rio De Janeiro, Brazil in 1953. In 1977, Dr. Countee Robert Williams was called to the Silent City Of The Dead. It was Dr. Williams, along with Miss Lucy, who interceded with Dr. A. M. Townsend to employ J. Robert at the Sunday School Publishing Board in Nashville. Dr. Williams, along with Miss Lucy, could be credited with saving the career of the convention's superstar of the future by making this intercession. Although it was not to be the end of the line for J. Robert's somber sojourn to the funeral bier, the saddest of them all was in January 1985 when he said goodby to his Momma, Lela Ellis Bradley. The pain of losing his Momma was indescribable. He had brought her to Nashville to live with him so he could take care of her in the last days of life. He had the pleasure of providing for her some of the creature comforts she was unable to provide for him in his youth. For whatever consolation that brought, it did not assuage the deep-seated hurt which came to the heart when his mother closed her eyes in death.

These journeys through the valley and shadows of death produced a J. Robert Bradley who really came to know what it meant to sing the Negro Spiritual, "Sometimes I Feel Like A Motherless Child." To hear him sing the songs of his people, whether it be the Negro Spiritual, the Negro Gospel song of the genre of Lucy Campbell, or of a more modern sort such as Andre Crouch's "Through It All," one heard a man who had identified with sorrow and had become acquainted with grief.

A most moving experience is to witness J. Robert as he sings one of his peoples' songs of sorrow and be so moved that his entire lower chin violently trembles while a steady stream of tears flows down his cheek. The tears speak loudly and proclaim that he has seen sorrow and has been acquainted with grief.

XXXVI.

His Living Shall Not Be In Vain

If I can help somebody, as I pass along,
If I can cheer somebody with a word or a song;
If I can show somebody he is going wrong,
Then my living shall not be in vain.

If I can do my duty, as a Christian ought,
If I can bring back beauty, to a world up-wrought;
If I can spread love's message, as the Master taught,
Then my living shall not be in vain.

This song was among the repertoire that J. Robert sang in 1955 in Memphis, Tennessee at the National Baptist Convention, USA, Inc., annual session. He sang with such pathos, passion, and meaningful soul that the Holy Spirit used him mightily to the benefit of many people. Spiritual ecstasy seized many of the saints. Therapeutic expurgation of the soul demonstrated itself all over the auditorium where the meeting was held.

Among the thousands in attendance was the president of the West African Country of Liberia, Dr. William R. Tolbert. Dr. Tolbert, a Baptist preacher and pastor of the Providence Baptist Church in Monrovia, was so moved by The Holy Spirit as he listened to the singing of J. Robert Bradley that he was completely overcome and required attention from a corps of ushers to be contained. J. Robert was a very special blessing for the President of Liberia. He was so effective in lifting the spirit of this noble head of state that Dr. Tolbert invited him to visit his country where he was knighted.

J. Robert's singing has moved mayors of cities the same as presidents of nations. The passionate engagement of music, mind, and spirit has caused those involved in the arduous and sometimes suspect world of politics to praise God. Such was reflected in the following correspondence from an educator in Nashville.

3122 Richmond Hill Drive
Nashville, Tennessee 37207
May 17, 1976

Dr. J. Robert Bradley
Capitol Towers Apartments
Nashville, Tennessee

Dear Dr. Bradley:

Mayor Richard Fulton paid you the highest compliments Thursday night when he stated his thoughts, wondering why it should be he [had] to follow a performance such as yours on the program. It would have been difficult for him to have chosen more laudable terms to express his sincere feelings of your magnificent performance.

As you sang I sat in my chair completely mesmerized, as you projected your words with perfect enunciation. Your choice of songs for the Adult Education Gala Banquet could not have been more appropriately chosen. Certainly adult educators do strive to be a light and to let that light shine. Teachers of adults do endeavor to "help somebody." The words of your songs probably evoked different thoughts in different people, but one thing was certain: the effect on your audience was overwhelming.

The stillness which permeated the room as you rendered your superb performance was the result of the undivided attention given you by students and teachers alike. Had I been in the Mayor's place, I too would have wondered why it should be I of all people, to follow such a captivating performance.

Sincerely,

L. C. Batson
Teacher, Adult Basic Education

CC: Mrs. Florence Weiland
Adult Basic Education

J. Robert Bradley's blend of scholarship and soul captured the intellect, the scholar, and the college student, all. Especially has it been impressive how he has helped members of the white race appreciate the fervor of the Christian religion and finesse and acceptability of Black musical intellect. Such was forcefully demonstrated on the campus of Samford University in Birmingham, Alabama after a performance by J. Robert. Dr. Wayne Flynt, Associate Professor of History and Chairman of Convocation Subcommittee on Programs described it on this wise:

> Student reaction to Dr. J. Robert Bradley was the most remarkable of any reaction to a weekly all campus convocation program this year. A student body which does not care for compulsory chapel sat in rapt attention as the first Negro speaker ever to appear at convocation sang selections ranging from classical to Negro Spirituals. In capturing the deep religious heritage of the Negro in America, Dr. Bradley not only added a dimension to the spiritual experience of our students, but he also bridged a barrier of race which separated black and white men. His program was a highlight of the school year in bringing a religious meaning to the Christmas season. I have never heard so much favorable response from our students to any speaker at convocation. But perhaps the best testimony was the absolute quiet that prevailed as 2,800 people silently left our gymnasium after Dr. Bradley concluded his program

It could be said that J. Robert Bradley has done as much as any person living or dead to advance the cause of ameliorating the differences between white and Blacks, breaking down racial barriers, and improving race relations. He has helped whites and Blacks to know that

"...*We've got to love all men as brothers,*
You've got to love everybody if you want to see God."

Through the medium and marvel of singing, J. Robert has effectively made breakthroughs to white youth as well as adults. Overriding the difficulties of language and culture, J. Robert utilized music to speak to young whites and win their souls to God and command their respect for the intellect of Blacks. A young white boy from Clarksville, Tennessee attests to this reality:

> Dear Dr. Bradley,
>
> Remember me the kid you met at the Crusade in Clarksville named Robert? Well I just wanted to say that I love your singing. Also I will always keep that little song book. But again I love your singing. Never refuse such a God-given talent.
>
> Love,
>
> Robert White

The high and low have benefitted from the ministry of music of J. Robert Bradley. The young and not so young have been inspired. The rejected and dejected have all been lifted to orbital levels high above the miry bog of their misery. Souls weighted down and burdened by the tyranny of death have been encouraged to see it through. The latter is typified in the following correspondence:

> Hi Bradley, I am enjoying and feasting each night---this reminds me of Memphis and the good old days. I shall always remember the first time that I heard you sing---"Collins Chapel C. M. E. Church"---You were just a boy, but what an ever lasting impression you made upon me. . . .Sing beautifully for me---and if you can arrange please do the song you sang at papa's funeral 28 years ago "Touch Me Lord Jesus."
>
> Forestine Lewis Barnett
> Nee Forestine

The uniqueness of J. Robert Bradley is a combination of many things. It is the pain of having grown up in the raunchiest ghetto any city could have, **Pinch**, in Memphis, Tennessee. Memphis, Tennessee and the Mississippi Delta produced some of the most unique musical virtuosos the world has ever known. Certainly, J. Robert Bradley is one of these, standing at the top of the list. Born Black in a section such as **Pinch** surely had its adverse affect on him. That condition certainly made itself manifest in the state of depravation in which the Black person found himself. The exigencies of living in such a socially-deprived condition bore a certain sadness into the soul that only such an one who experienced it would know. Growing up with a father who was only seen once in awhile, and then not at all, brought him into an affinity with hundreds and thousands of other souls of kindred experiences. On and on the saga goes which caused him to shed tears that flowed from a pained and bleeding soul.

In the Christian Faith, **a la** National Baptists, J. Robert discovered in Jesus Christ that force and support needed to overcome every adversity. So when he sang, the passion, fire, fervor, conviction, and convinced spirit was all poured out upon his listener. The youthful and comical J. Robert shared this helpful spirit with the distraught lady on the steps of old Mt. Olive Baptist Church. Her husband had died and grief had overcome her. J. Robert, accompanied by Leonard Mitchell, used his singing prowess and power of witnessing to allay the fears and frustrations of the dear lady.

As time has progressed, he has continued to blend his acquired intellect with tears, pathos, spiritual fervor, and passionate witness for Jesus to reach those in distress. Such was the case with Ms. Valarie Gibson of Tampa, Florida who wrote to express gratitude for his powerful witness,

Sun. July 22, 1990

Dearest Mr. Bradley:

 It is always so good to call and hear your voice. I am thrilled to know that you are well in spirit, soul and body. I am sure that you will recover fine with our Lord's help.

 As I mentioned over the phone, I am in Tampa, Florida and am working as a Branch Manager for NCNB Bank of Florida. It is a financially sound banking institution. At this time, we are the Southeast's leading institution. Although only No. 5 in Florida, we are stable. I said all of that so you would know that I made a good career choice.

 Although I only speak with you once a year or so, you have made a **lasting** impression in my mind and heart. There is no one in this world, before or to come, that could sing "Yes, Jesus Loves Me" the way you do. If memory serves we well, you also sang, "He's Got the Whole World in His Hands" in Cocoa, Florida at Rev. Wells' church.

 Just to catch you up a little, I **did** graduate (Hallelujah!!!) from the University of Florida on May 5, 1990.

 I am now in Tampa working. No matter where I go or what I do, I will always be grateful for God allowing us to meet.

 You have done nothing spectacular, but 10 years ago you allowed yourself to be used by God to touch a little girl from Miami. **I will never forget how you kneeled, and sang, and wept as though you were weeping for me. You sang, "Yes, Jesus Loves You," and said, "Yes, he surely does love you" as if you knew how difficult it was living with an alcoholic father. I watched you and began to believe your words** (Emphasis added.) Mr. Bradley, you have planted a seed that will forever blossom **for God** in me. **Thank** you so much for being you. If I can touch one life the way you have touched mine, my singing and writing will not be in vain. I love you!

            Sincerely,

            Valarie

In the rich and fruitful life of John Robert Lee Bradley, God has given the world one whose living shall not be in vain.

APPENDIX

I

Fourth and Poplar street sign which marks the neighborhood in which Pinch was located, where J. Robert Bradley was born and raised.

The approximate site at which J. Robert Bradley was born.

The alley near Poplar and Fourth where J. Robert Bradley lived, grew up, and played.

LEONARD MITCHELL
Boyhood playmate of J. Robert Bradley

MISS LUCY EDDIE CAMPBELL-WILLIAMS
Discovered J. Robert Bradley in 1933 at the National Baptist Convention in Memphis, Tennessee.

THOMAS H. SHELBY
Big brother, first trainer, and accompanist of J. Robert Bradley.

DR. E. W. D. ISAAC, JR.
He gave J. Robert Bradley his first job with the National B.Y.P.U.

THE REVEREND B.J. PERKINS
The Reverend Perkins was a pastor in Clarksdale, Mississippi and official of the National Baptist Convention, USA, Inc. As a young singer, J. Robert Bradley accompanied him on revivals throughout Mississippi.

ORIGINAL GOODWILL SINGERS
Left to Right: James E. Gayle, Cleavon Derrick, J. Robert Bradley, Thomas Shelby, Dr. W. S. Ellington, Jr., Dr. E. W. D. Isaac, Jr.

DR. ARTHUR MELVIN TOWNSEND
Executive Secretary of the Sunday School Publishing Board, 1922-1959 and the major sponsor of the training of J. Robert Bradley.

PROFESSOR CHARLES FAULKNER BRYAN
Professor Bryan discovered J. Robert Bradley at a revival concert at the St. Mary Baptist church, McMinnville, Tennessee. He took upon himself the responsibility of teaching J. Robert music for two years or so after they met.

DR. W. T. CRUTCHER
J. Robert Bradley served at Mt. Olive Baptist church, Knoxville, Tennessee in its early days when it was pastored by Dr. Crutcher. The two developed a working relationship and friendship which lasted for more than fifty years.

DR. CECELIA NABRIT ADKINS
Cecelia Nabrit Adkins was the youngest daughter of Dr. James Madison Nabrit, General Secretary for the National Baptist Convention, USA, Inc. She now is Executive Director of the SSPB, NBC, USA, Inc.

DR. LACY KIRK WILLIAMS
President of the National Baptist Convention, USA, Inc., 1924-1940, he led the formation of The Goodwill Singers of which J. Robert Bradley was a member. Just before his tragic death, Dr. Williams invited J. Robert to join the music department at Olivet Baptist Church, Chicago, Illinois.

DR. D. V. JEMISON
President of the National Baptist Convention, USA, Inc., 1941—1952. Dr. Jemison led the convention while J. Robert Bradley was in Chicago, Illinois. It was under his leadership that the Morris Memorial Building of the Sunday School Publishing Board was paid off and rendered free of debt.

EDWARD BOATNER
Mr. Boatner was soloist and director for one of the choirs at the Olivet Baptist Church, Chicago, Illinois when J. Robert Bradley was invited to join its music department. He was responsible for coordinating the musical program for the annual session of the National Baptist Convention, USA, Inc.

J. ROBERT BRADLEY AND THOMAS A. DORSEY
While in Chicago, Illinois, J. Robert Bradley met and became a friend to Mr. Dorsey. Mr. Dorsey was an outstanding gospel songwriter.

MS. EDYTH WALKER
Ms. Walker was a world renowned musical virtuoso. Late in life, she agreed to take on J. Robert Bradley as a student. Her training technique produced a student who ultimately sang on the stage of the Royal Festival Hall in London, England.

MS. MAHALIA JACKSON
The world renowned Mahalia Jackson became a personal friend of J. Robert Bradley.

DR. ALBERT SCHWEITZER
J. Robert Bradley was privileged to meet Dr. Schweitzer while training in London, England.

MS. MARIAN ANDERSON WITH J. ROBERT BRADLEY
Fascinated and encouraged by Ms. Anderson, J. Robert Bradley came to know her and share with her in the world of music.

DR. THEODORE JUDSON JEMISON
President of the National Baptist Convention, USA, Inc.
Upon assumption of the position of president of the convention, Dr. Jemison elevated J. Robert Bradley to the directorship of music for both the Convention and Congress of Christian Education.

DR. C. A. W. CLARK
Dr. Clark teamed up with J. Robert Bradley and worked with him for many years in revival and evangelistic campaigns.

APPENDIX II

Letters and Documents

As sung by PAUL ROBESON

LAWRENCE BROWN

NEGRO FOLK SONGS

No. 1. DIDN'T MY LORD DELIVER DANIEL?
2. WHO'S BEEN HERE?
3. HEAR DE LAM'S A-CRYIN'
4. GOIN' TO RIDE UP IN DE CHARIOT
5. DERE'S A MAN GOIN' ROUN' TAKIN NAMES

Price 4/- Net

SCHOTT & Co. Ltd.
48 GREAT MARLBOROUGH STREET,
LONDON, W.1

This is the cover of an anthology of music arranged by Lawrence Brown. After the death of Edyth Walker, J. Robert Bradley began to study under him. It was Lawrence Brown who prepared J. Robert for the London music society.

New York 23. VII. '48

Dear Bradley!

Thank you most sincerely for your fine letter and the noble sentiments which you express. I am sure that you will attain what you deeply desire – to glorify God with your beautiful voice. What about coming with S Z E, or alone, Tuesday afternoon? that I may hear the progress you are making. Call me up Tuesday!

Most cordially

Edyth Walker

Many thanks for the lovely card from Mr. Smith.

Letter from Edyth Walker.

LIST OF PASSENGERS

Mrs. Leila Adamowicz
Mr. Alexander Adams
Mr. H. L. Africa
Mrs. Africa
Miss Cele Alin
Mrs. Florence Andrew
Mrs. Marilyn Andrew
Miss Amalie Ansorge
Mr. A. G. Arbous
Mrs. Elizabeth N. Arguelles
Mrs. Joanne Armstrong
Miss Paula J. Armstrong
Mr. Frank Arnold
Mrs. Arnold
Rev. Paul Arthur
Mrs. Margaret Ault
Mrs. Nan D. Ayers
Mr. Abdur M. Aziz

Dr. Adams Bailey
Mrs. Bailey
Mr. Herbert Baldwin
Mrs. Baldwin
Miss M. O. Bardon
Mrs. O. E. Barlow
Mr. M. Barnett
Mrs. Barnett
Mrs. E. W. Bartlett
Dr. M. L. Beach
Mrs. Frieda Beck
Mr. J. M. Beck
Mr. M. Benjamin
Mrs. Erna Berlin
Mr. Ignacio Bernal
Mrs. Bernal
Mr. Walter Bertz
Rev. E. L. Best
Mrs. Best
Mrs. N. B. Betts
Miss J. Beverly

Mrs. I. W. Beverly
Mr. Alex Bing
Major M. J. D'A. Blackman
Mrs. M. J. Blackman
Miss J. L. Blackman
Miss D. K. Blackman
Mr. N. Blankstein
Mr. Alberto Boada
Mrs. Boada
Mr. George Bona
Mrs. Bona
<u>Mr. J. Robert Bradley</u>
Miss Mary Branch
Mr. Richard H. Brehm, III
Bro. Theodore Brenner
Mr. David Bresler
Mrs. Bresler
Mrs. William Bresler
Mr. Stanley Bresler
Mstr. Roger Bresler
Mr. G. Carl Bristow
Mrs. Bristow
Miss Marcia Bristow
Mr. Stephen Brooks
Mr. G. Carl Bristow, Jr.
Mrs. Anna M. Brix
Miss W. Brunkoetter
Miss Dorothy Buehler
Mrs. J. H. Bufkin
Miss Frances Burnett
Mr. Karl Butter
Mr. Carmelo Buttigieg
Mrs. Buttigieg
Miss Ethel Buzzard

Mrs. Catherine Campbell
Mr. Robert F. Cancio
Mrs. Cancio
Mr. Henry Carmichael
Mrs. A. A. Casey
Mr. Antonio Cecere

This is the list of passengers who sailed for England on the steamship, **The Queen Elizabeth**, on August 6, 1952. J. Robert Bradley was listed among the passengers.

> 23 Acacia Road
> N.W.8
> (tel. Primrose 0089)
>
> Friday
> Sep 12th
>
> Dear Mr Bradley
> Could you telephone me tomorrow (Saturday) morning between 10 o'clock and 10.30? I have been trying to telephone you at the Regent Palace this morning, but you were probably out. I want to hear you *sing*, before anything else!
> In haste
> Yours very sincerely
> Roger Quilter

A letter from Roger Quilter. Notice the date, Friday, September 12. According to subsequent letters, the year was 1952. This is indictive of the rapid movement of J. Robert Bradley in establishing himself in London's music community as a serious student.

Letter from Roger Quilter.

> 23 Acacia Rd
> N.W.8
> (tel. Primrose 0089)
>
> Sep 19th
>
> Dear Robert
> My brother died last night — & I may have to go very soon to Suffolk for the funeral.
> Mr Heaton will know my movements — so would you mind telephoning tomorrow morning here.
> ever yours
> Roger Quilter
> forgive this haste.

23 Acacia Road
N.W.8
Sep 22ⁿᵈ   (tel. Primrose 0089)

Dear Robert
    Thank you so much
for your kind letter, and
understanding sympathy.
I go tomorrow to Woodbridge, Suffolk —
but I shall be back again on
Thursday —
Please let me know your new
address, and we can arrange
a meeting —
Gratefully and very sincerely
    Roger Quilter

Letter from Roger Quilter.

Greetings

MAY CHRISTMAS AND THE NEW YEAR BRING YOU HAPPINESS

from Roger Quilter

P.T.O

23 Acacia Road
N.W.8.

Dear Robert
    I hope you do not
think I have forgotten you.
I have had a horrid complaint
of the nerves, which has had
the effect of a dreadful
irritation of the skin —
So it has been very difficult
to arrange anything.
I shall be better soon.
I hope, meanwhile, that you
are getting on with your
singing teacher.
    ever yours Roger Quilter

A Christmas Card from Roger Quilter.

Oct 1st 1952

23 Acacia Road
N.W.8
(Tel. Primrose 0089)

Dear Robert

How very kind and thoughtful of you to send me the ration-tickets! Very many thanks!

I am so terribly busy this week, would you mind if we put off our meeting till next Monday? Would 3.30 suit you?

If you have not got a seat for Marian Anderson on Sunday, would you come with me, if I can get tickets?

ever yours
Roger Quilter

Letter from Roger Quilter.

23 Acacia Rd
N.W.8
(Tel PRI 0089)

Friday.

Dear Robert

Would you telephone me tomorrow, Saturday, when you receive this note, to say if you would like to come for a lesson on Sunday — I am away tomorrow afternoon —

But please telephone about 10 a.m. or before you leave the house

ever yours
Roger Quilter

Letter from Roger Quilter.

This is the music workbook used by J. Robert Bradley while studying at Trinity College of Music, London. Obvious to the observer is J. Robert's ability to traffick in the intricacies and technicalities of the written form of music.

TRINITY COLLEGE OF MUSIC, LONDON

MANUSCRIPT MUSIC

PUBLISHED BY TRINITY COLLEGE OF MUSIC
MANDEVILLE PLACE, LONDON, W. I.

This is a copy of the program rendered by the Fisk Jubilee Singers at the Royal Festival hall on September 26, 1952, shortly after J. Robert Bradley's arrival in London.

THE
JUBILEE SINGERS

THE JUBILEE SINGERS

ROBERT BRADFORD   STARLING HATCHETT

GEORGE GOODMAN   DANIEL ANDREWS

Pianist and Accompanist: MATTHEW KENNEDY

Director:

MRS. JAMES A. MYERS

Presented by arrangement with MARCEL DE VALMALETE (Paris)
(European Representative)

General Manager: IRWIN PARNES (Hollywood)

21st September	...	B.B.C. Broadcast
22nd ,,	...	Colston Hall, Bristol
23rd ,,	...	Free Trade Hall, Manchester
25th ,,	...	Sophia Gardens Pavilion, Cardiff
26th ,,	...	Royal Festival Hall, London

Royal Festival Hall

General Manager - T. E. BEAN

IN ACCORDANCE WITH THE REQUIREMENTS OF THE LONDON COUNTY COUNCIL

(i) The public may leave at the end of the performance or exhibition by all exit doors and such doors must at that time be open.
(ii) All gangways, corridors, staircases and external passageways intended for exit shall be kept entirely free from obstruction, whether permanent or temporary.
(iii) Persons shall not be permitted to stand or sit in any of the gangways intersecting the seating, or to sit in any of the other gangways. If standing be permitted in the gangways at the sides and rear of the seating, it shall be limited to the numbers indicated in the notices exhibited in those positions.

September 26th, 1952

LONDON COUNTY COUNCIL

in association with

S. A. GORLINSKY

presents

The Jubilee Singers

Under the Direction of

MRS. JAMES A. MYERS

Programme

I

SPIRITUALS

Live a-Humble

Chorus Live a-humble, humble, humble yourself
         The bell done rung.

Verse   You see God, you see God in the morning
         He'll come riding down the line of Time
         Fire'll be falling, He'll be calling,
         Come to Judgment, Come——

Verse   Did ever you see such a man as God
         Give up his Son for to come and die
         Just to save my soul from a burning fire.

Climbing up the Mountain

Chorus Good Lord, I'm climbing up the mountain, children
    I ain't got long for the stay,
    If I never more see you again
    I'll meet you at the Judgment Day——

Verse Daniel in the lion's den, he began to pray
    The angel of the Lord locked the lion's jaws
    And Daniel went his way——

Verse Baptist go by water, Methodist go by land
    But before they get to heaven, Lord,
    They must go hand in hand——

Hold On

Chorus Hold on, Hold on, Keep your hand on the plough and Hold on——

Verse 1 Noah, Noah let me come in; Doors are fastened and the windows pinned——
    Keep your hands on the plough and *Hold on.*

  2 Noah said you done lost your track
    You can't plough straight and keep a-looking back—*Hold on.*

  3 If that plough stays in your hand
    It will lead you straight to the promised land—*Hold on.*

  4 If you want to go to heaven, I'll tell you how——
    Just keep your hands on the Gospel Plough—*Hold on.*

Good News

Chorus Good News! The Chariot's coming and I don't want it to leave me behind——

Verse There's silver slippers in the Heaven I know
    And I don't want it to leave me behind——

Verse There's a starry crown in the Heaven I know
    And I don't want it to leave me behind——

King Jesus is a-listening

Chorus King Jesus is a-listening all night long
    To hear a sinner pray

Verse The Gospel Train is a-coming, 'tis rumbling through the land
    I hear the car wheels rolling, get ready for the Gospel Train——

Verse I know, I've been converted, I ain't goin' make no 'larm
    My soul's been anchored in my Jesus, and the devil can't do me no harm.

II

Star   *Rogers*

Gue, Gue, Solingaie   *Creole Folk Song*
                               arr. Camile Mickerson

The Lost Chord   *Sullivan*

III

Wade in the Water (Spiritual)   *arr. for piano by Margaret Bonds*

Soloist: MATTHEW KENNEDY

IV

SPIRITUALS

Deep River

Deep River, my home is over Jordan
Deep River, Lord, I want to cross over into camp ground——
Oh, don't you want to go to that Gospel feast
That promised land where all is peace——
Deep River, I want to cross over into camp ground.

Swing Low, Sweet Chariot

Chorus Swing low, sweet chariot, coming for to carry me home
Swing low, sweet chariot, coming for to carry me home:
If you get there before I do— Tell all my friends I'm a-coming too——

Verse   Swing low, sweet chariot, coming for to carry me home.

I Want to be Ready

Chorus I want to be ready to walk in Jerusalem just like John

Verse   Oh John, Oh John, what do you say—That'll be there at the coming day——
John said that City was just four square—And he declared he'd meet me there——
Oh, I want to be ready to walk in Jerusalem like John——

Shout all over God's Heaven

INTERVAL

V

Arise ! Subterranean Winds ("Tempest")	*Purcell*
Zueignung	*Strauss*

Soloist: GEORGE GOODMAN

In this Solemn Hour ("The Force of Destiny")	*Verdi*
The Sleigh	*Kountz*

Duettists: STARLING HATCHETT *and* GEORGE GOODMAN

VI

SPIRITUALS

Walking on the Green Grass

(*This song came into being in 1825 and was handed down to Addison Foster through his great-grandmother. Its charm and simple faith appeals to the hearts of men everywhere*).

       Walking on the green grass—Fal-dal-di-del-lum !
       Through the window, Julie, through the window, Julie—Fal-dal-di-del-lum !
       A-walking on the green grass, Julie——

Verse 1 Miss Julie's gone a run a-round, walking on the green grass
       Fal-dal-di-del-lum—Through the window, Julie——
       Gonna walk and talk with the angel in that army by and by
       Goin' and tell God " Howdy !" in that army by and by——

    2 Can't you hear the lambs a-crying over on that other shore ?
       Oh, good shepherd, feed me sheep !
       Walking on the green grass, Fal-dal-di-del-lum !
       Through the window, Julie.

Lawd, How come we Here—arr. Fred Hall

(*This song is 90 years old, and was handed down to Fred Hall through his great-grandfather.*)

Chorus Lawd, how come we here ? Wish I never been born——
       Work in the field at sunrise, work in the field till sunset——
       Work until my head is aching—Work until my hands is bleeding——
       Work until my back is breaking——
       Lawd, how come we here ? Wish I never been born.

There's a Plenty Good Room

There's a Meeting here Tonight

Chorus Get you ready ! There's a meeting here tonight
       Come along, there's a meeting here tonight
       I know you by your daily walk—there's a meeting here tonight——

Verse My father says it is the best —To live and die a Methodist——
       There's a meeting here tonight
       I'm a Baptist bred and a Baptist born—Lord, when I'm dead,
       There's a Baptist gone—There's a meeting here tonight.

Hail Mary—arr. Dawson

       Mary had a lit'l baby born in Bethlehem
       Every time the lit'l baby cried, she rock'd Him in a-weary lan'.
       He was born in a lowly manger, 'cause there was no room in the inn
       Every time the lit'l baby cried, she rock'd him in a weary lan'.
       There were shepherds abiding in the field
       Keeping watch o'er their flock by night
       " Unto you a babe is born tonight " said the Angel of the Lord to the shepherds in the field.
       Hail Mary, Virgin Mary—Hail ! " Child of God "——
       Every time the little baby cried, she rock'd him in a weary lan'
       Oh, she rocked and rocked,
       She rock'd Him in a weary lan' all night long——

The Jubilee Singers

The first group of Jubilee Singers, born in slavery, originated in 1865 at Fisk University, the famous Negro educational institution in Tennessee, and toured the United States in a desperate effort to raise funds for the extension of their University. After overcoming many obstacles, they won admirers in all parts of North America and set out in 1873 on a triumphant tour of Europe. Here they sang before Queen Victoria, the King and Queen of Holland, Gladstone, and other notabilities, and this led the way to further successful European tours.

The present group represents the third generation of Jubilee Singers and they are carrying on the tradition of their predecessors. In America they have sung with the Symphony Orchestras of Boston and Los Angeles, and have been heard weekly over the N.B.C. network as well as on television. In Europe before the war they had the honour of singing before King George V and Queen Mary, and since the war they have sung before enthusiastic audiences in the major cities of France, Italy and Switzerland.

For more than 40 years, their Director, Mrs. James A. Myers, has dedicated her life to keeping the beloved old Negro Spirituals pure and intact in their original settings handed down from the days of slavery. Her late husband was one of the tenors of the Jubilee Singers and now his widow continues the direction and training of the ensemble.

The Jubilee Singers' concert tour of Britain will mark over 70 years of continuous musical " missionary work " in the spreading of the words of faith and brotherhood, as expressed in their immortal spirituals.

Presenting the World's Greatest Artists

S. A. Gorlinsky

announces

1952-53 Season
(*London and Provincial Concerts*)

ARTURO TOSCANINI
(*Conducting the Philharmonia Orchestra*)

SIR THOMAS BEECHAM, Bart.
(*Conducting the Royal Philharmonic Orchestra*)

SIR JOHN BARBIROLLI
(*Conducting the Hallé Orchestra*)

EILEEN JOYCE	LUIGI INFANTINO
(*Recital Tour 1953*)	(*Recital Tour Feb.-March 1953*)
LILY PONS	ANDRÉ KOSTELANETZ
TAGLIAVINI	EFREM KURTZ
EDMUND KURTZ	CARMEL HAKENDORF
DON COSSACK CHORUS	THE JUBILEE SINGERS

LEADING SINGERS FROM LA SCALA, MILAN

including

MARIA CALLAS	EBE STIGNANI	RENATA TEBALDI
FEDORA BARBIERI	GIANNI POGGI	MIRTO PICCHI
GIULIO NERI	ELENA NICOLAI	CESARE SIEPI

and the

SCALA OPERA QUARTET
(*London and Provincial Tour, October 1952*)

S. A. GORLINSKY Ltd.
123 PALL MALL . LONDON S.W.1
Tel. WHItehall 9676/7   Telegrams: Gorlinsky, London

MRS. BESSIE ESTELL, SECRETARY
BIRMINGHAM, ALA.

J. C. OLIVER, TREASURER
CHICAGO, ILL.

National Sunday School and B. T. U. Congress
U. S. A.

DR. W. H. JERNAGIN, PRESIDENT
1728 WEBSTER STREET, N. W.
WASHINGTON 11, D. C.

14 April 1953

Mr. J. R. Bradley
24 Devonshire Terrace
London W. 2, England

My dear brother Bradley:

    Your recent letter was brought to my attention by Mrs. Jernigan on my return from Korea. I was indeed glad to hear from you and to know that God is still blessing you and that you are continuing toward higher heights. He who put his trust in God will never have to regret it.

    In regard to the Rio conference of the young Baptist, nothing would please me better than to see you in Rio at the Fourth Baptist Youth Conference of the Baptist World Alliance on July 15. Under conditions I can not see at this moment how we may assist you in getting there. Find out what the round trip fare is from London ti Rio is and let me know.

    I did not understand you when you said you did not know Dr. Lord. It may be that the secretary spelled his name Lloyd but I meant Dr. Lord, President of the Baptist World Alliance. I did not want you to talk to him in terms of a paying position, but simply let him know that you would be glad to sing for him at any time a selection that you can be used in public worship without cost to him. I want you to let my friends there to know that I asked you to contact them because they can open many doors for you. If you will go to the Baptist House there, you will meet Dr. O. W. Lewis and Dr. T. G. Dunning. Let them know that I was anxious for you to meet them and that you are assistant musicaldirector for my Congress. Tell them what you are doing there and that you would be glad to render service to any church that desires it. The Baptist House is located at 4 Hampton Row.

    Hoping to hear from you by return mail, I am,

Yours truly,

W. H. Jernagin

Letter from Dr. W. H. Jernagin, President of the National Baptist Congress of Christian Education. This correspondence sets forth the approval for J. Robert Bradley to journey to Rio de Janeiro to represent in the Baptist world Alliance.

MRS. BESSIE ESTELL, SECRETARY
BIRMINGHAM, ALA.

J. C. OLIVER, TREASURER
CHICAGO, ILL.

National Sunday School and B. T. U. Congress
U. S. A.

DR. W. H. JERNAGIN, PRESIDENT
1728 WEBSTER STREET, N. W.
WASHINGTON 11, D. C.

2 June 1953

Mr. J. Robert Bradley
24 Devonshire Terrace
London, W.2, England

My dear brother Bradley:

You will find enclosed your fare to Rio from the Foreign Mission Board of the National Baptist Convention, Incorporated, Dr. C. C. Adams, Secretary. Please write him a letter of thanks at: 701 South 19th Street, Philadelphia, Pennsylvania.

I shall be looking forward to seeing you in Rio not later than July 14th.

Everything is shaping up fine for a great meeting in Brooklyn. I am sure we are going to miss you this year when the Congress meets.

Yours truly,

W. H. Jernagin

WHJ:gp
Enc

Letter from Dr. W. H. Jernagin indicating that the fare for the trip to Rio de Janeiro is enclosed.

TRINITY COLLEGE OF MUSIC

TELEGRAMS
MUSICATIIS, WESDO, LONDON

TELEPHONE
WELBECK 5773

Instituted 1872

MANDEVILLE PLACE
LONDON · W·1

F/W   4th June 1953.

To whom it may concern.

      This is to certify that Mr. J. Robert Bradley has been a part-time student of this College since September 1952 during which time he has made regular attendance, good progress and proved himself a most diligent and worthwhile student

                                        Secretary.

ALL COMMUNICATIONS SHOULD BE ADDRESSED TO THE SECRETARY.

A letter from the officials of the Trinity College of Music in London confirming that J. Robert Bradley is a student in good and regular standing with the school.

ATESTADO DE SAÚDE PARA TEMPORÁRIOS
CERTIFICATE OF HEALTH FOR TEMPORARY VISITORS.

Atesto que examinei o Sr./a Sra. *J. Robert Bradley*
I certify that I have examined Mr., Mrs. or Miss

idade *33* nacionalidade *American* profissão *Singer*
age / nationality / profession

e que o mesmo/a mesma não apresenta sintomas ou manifestações de
and that he or she does not present symptoms or manifestations of

lepra, tuberculose, tracoma, elefantíase, doença venérea em período contagiante,
leprosy, tuberculosis, tracoma, elephantiasis, venereal disease in contagious period,

cancer, afecção mental, e não é alcolista ou toxicômano/toxicômana.
cancer, mental affection, and that he or she is not an alcoholic or drug addict.

26. CHESTER ST. , *1* de *June* de 19 *53*
London. S.W.1. (place) (date)

(visto consular)   (ASSINATURA DO MÉDICO)
(consular visa)   Signature of Doctor

REGULAMENTO DE IMIGRAÇÃO—DEC. N. 3.010 de 1938.

A certificate of health for J. Robert Bradley's temporary visit to Rio de Janeiro.

CONSULADO DO BRASIL EM LONDRES

DECLARO, COMPROMETENDO-ME A DIZER A VERDADE, E
I hereby declare, binding myself to speak the truth, and
SOB AS PENAS DA LEI BRASILEIRA, QUE NUNCA PRATIQUEI
under the penalties of the Brazilian Law, that I have never practised
QUAISQUER ATOS PELOS QUAIS PUDESSE SER OU TENHA SIDO
any of those acts by which I might be, or be
CONSIDERADO NOCIVO À ORDEM PÚBLICA, À SEGURANÇA
considered to be, harmful to Public Order, National
NACIONAL, OU À ESTRUTURA DAS INSTITUIÇÕES POLÍTICAS
Security or the structure of Political Institutions
DO MEU PAÍS DE ORIGEM OU DAQUELES EM QUE TENHO
of my country of origin or of those in which I have
RESIDIDO.
resided.

DECLARO, MAIS, QUE NUNCA FUI EXPULSO DO BRASIL,
I further declare that I have never been expelled from Brazil
NEM ME FOI RECUSADO VISTO DE ENTRADA NO TERRITÓRIO
nor have I ever been refused a visa to enter Brazilian
BRASILEIRO; E FINALMENTE, QUE NUNCA FUI CONDENADO, EM
territory and finally, that I have never been condemned in
PAÍS ALGUM, POR CRIME QUE, SEGUNDO AS LEIS BRASILEIRAS,
any country for a crime for which I could be extradited under the
PERMITA A EXTRADIÇÃO.

Londres, _____ 19 ____
London

J. Robert Bradley

H & S 7528/52

This is a document where J. Robert Bradley affirms that he is morally, ethically, and politically fit to make the trip to Rio de Janeiro.

8,266 Baptists from 60 countries attended the 1955 Baptist World Congress in London

This is a picture of Royal Albert and Queen Victoria Hall in London where the Baptist World Alliance was held in 1955 and J. Robert Bradley sang at the opening session and throughout the following week.

THE WHITE HOUSE

WASHINGTON

February 15, 1966

Dear Mr. Bradley:

I wrote you on January 19 that I had submitted your name to the Department of State with the request that you be considered for an "entertainment tour." I now have some further information about these tours.

Normally, the Cultural Presentations Program does not sponsor tours of individual artists. For some years, however, the office has found it possible on occasion to arrange additional concerts for individual artists who have gone abroad on their own. This would mean arranging your own transportation to and from the United States on a private or commercial tour, with the Department perhaps financing travel and concerts in adjacent areas.

To qualify for such support the individual artist must be approved by one of their artistic advisory panels--in your case the Music Panel.

I enclose a General Information Circular which describes (on page three) the procedure for making application for sponsorship. As the circular indicates, you may send the material directly to Mr. Charles M. Ellison, Director of the Office of Cultural Presentations, Department of State.

I hope this information will be helpful to you, and I wish you continued success in your musical career. You have a very fine voice.

Sincerely yours,

Brooks Hays
Consultant to the President

Mr. J. Robert Bradley
Director of Music
Sunday School Publishing Board
National Baptist Convention
330 Charlotte Avenue
Nashville, Tennessee 37201

Enclosure

In this correspondence, Brooks Hays, Consultant to the President of the United States of America, invites J. Robert Bradley to be a part of an "entertainment tour" for the Department of State.

May 31, 1966

Mrs. Clara Urquhart
46 Wimpole St.
London, W. L1.

Dear Clara:

Thank you again for your encouraging letter, truly your words have come true as if you brought about a miracle with me looking at you. This has been a wonderful year for me. I have travelled from the West Coast to the East Coast, North and South. I have even been guest on the campus of the University of Alabama in Tuscaloosa, Alabama, where the racial trouble has been very, very bad. During my stay I was able to bring the Negro and the white together and things are very much at ease now. I visited Tuskegee Institute at Tuskegee, Alabama; Selma University in Selma, Alabama and New Orleans Theological Seminary. I do not preach them a sermon, I just sing love songs to them and you would be surprise how powerful it has been.

Continue to pray for me that I will be an instrument that can be used in this way, music does have a universal language and our brothers and sisters who are at odds with us will listen to music when they will not talk with us nor read any of our writings, so I am happy to tell you that your good thoughts on the wave links is bringing me much happiness.

Give my best regards to Enrico and tell him I would like to come to Africa and sing before I die.

Your friend who will always love and have great respect for you.

J. Robert Bradley

JRB/gl

A letter to Clara Urquhart from J. Robert Bradley.

**LIBERIA BAPTIST MISSIONARY AND
EDUCATIONAL CONVENTION, INC.
P.O. BOX 390
MONROVIA, LIBERIA**

August 3, 1974

Dear Dr. Washington:

    For sometimes we have worked together in the interest of Mission work. We have always welcomed missionaries from Foreign Mission Board as they gave themselves for service to Suehn and Bendu. It is our sincere wish that such cordial relations will always continue.

In an effort to strengthen our scholarship program to aid unfortunate boys, and girls, our convention sponsors an annual dinner. This year our annual dinner will be on Tuesday, November 19, 1974.

    We are extending an invitation through you to Mr. J. Robert Bradley to be our guest soloist for the occasion also to tour Liberia singing to our people in an effort to inspire us to give our talents in useful service for Kingdom Building.

    I have heard Mr. Bradley on numerous occasions and am proud that he can use his gift to the glory of God. A Convention tour of Liberia will be one good way to bring us closer together.

I would be more than grateful were you to grant Mr. Bradley leave for this special occasion.

    We anxiously await your kind reply as we are in process of arranging our program for publication.

Best regards,

In Christ,

Eric L. David

Eric L. David
GENERAL SECRETARY, LBMEC

Dr. D. C. Washington
Executive Director
Sunday School Publishing Board
330 Charlotte Avenue
Nashville, Tenn. 37201

This communication from Eric L. David, General Secretary of the Liberia Baptist Missionary and Educational Convention, Inc., appeals to Dr. D. C. Washington to permit Mr. J. Robert Bradley to journey to the African nation of Liberia.

Samford University

Birmingham, Alabama 35209

August 26, 1970

Dr. J. Robert Bradley
Sunday School Publishing Board
330 Charlotte Avenue
Nashville, Tennessee

Dear friend Robert:

I am overwhelmed with your generous gift of the moonstone tie-tack. I certainly did not expect to get it, for I felt that this was too valuable a gift for you to give me. Needless to say, I am grateful to you for it, but even more so for the friendship which prompted your gift to me.

I can never begin to say thank you for the wonderful work you did at the Baptist World Congress. It warmed my heart to know that you were the only soloist in the entire Congress who received an encore. It was indeed well deserved.

I hope that our paths may cross again in the very near future. I still hope someday to write your biography, for indeed it is a story which needs to be told.

Abidingly your friend,

CLAUDE RHEA, Dean
School of Music

CR:mc

In this letter from Claude Rhea, Dean of Music at Samford University in Birmingham, Alabama, he indicates that there was an interest in 1970 on the part of Southern Baptists to write the biography of J. Robert Bradley. In 1993 that interest became reality, but through the efforts of the Sunday School Publishing Board of the National Baptist Convention, USA, Inc.

APPENDIX III

Honors, Citations, and Medals

Certificate honoring J. Robert Bradley as knight.

The Iron Ship, one of the highest honors granted by the nation of Korea.

Memorial medals honoring Dr. Albert Schweitzer.
These are in the possession of J. Robert Bradley.

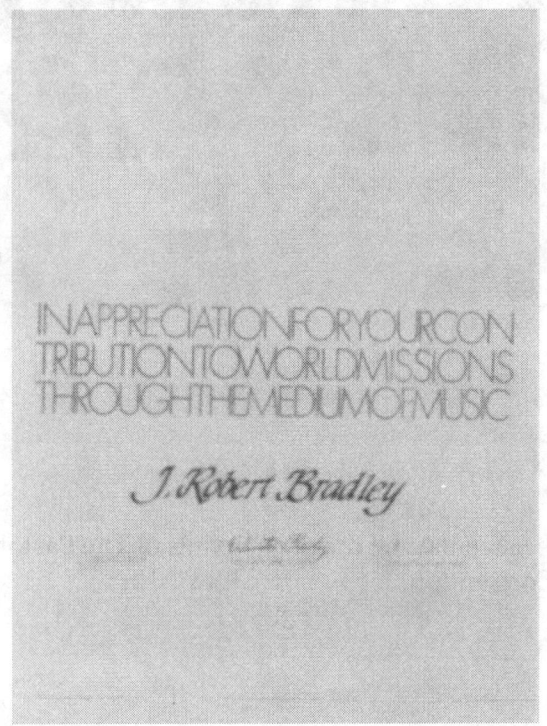

Appreciation citation from the Foreign Mission Board
of the Southern Baptist Convention.

J. Robert Bradley is listed among the participants of The Pastor's Conference of the Southern Baptist Convention.